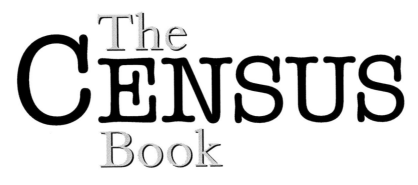

The CENSUS Book

A Genealogist's Guide
to Federal Census Facts, Schedules and Indexes

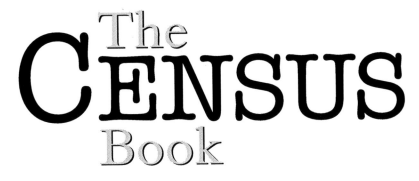

The CENSUS Book

A Genealogist's Guide
to Federal Census Facts, Schedules and Indexes

With Master Extraction Forms for
Federal Census Schedules, 1790–1930

by William Dollarhide

Cover photo by James A. Derheim, European Focus
Cover design by Kyle Follett and Brian O'Conner

Heritage Quest
North Salt Lake, Utah
2000

ON THE COVER
Actors, in period clothing, depict census taking in the mid 1800s. Photographed on location at Old Deseret Village—
a living historic village displaying life as it was lived in early pioneer Utah.

Cover photo by James A. Derheim, European Focus
Cover design by Kyle Follett and Brian O'Conner

Heritage Quest, a division of AGLL, Inc., PO Box 329, Bountiful, UT 84011-0329

© 2000 by William Dollarhide and Heritage Quest, a division of AGLL, Inc.
All rights reserved. Published 1999 by Heritage Quest
Printed in the United States of America
03 02 01   5 4 3

Library of Congress Catalog Card Number 99-073068

Hardbound: ISBN #1-877677-99-X
Softbound: ISBN #1-877677-98-1

Contents

Illustrations

Forms

Maps

Tables

Preface

This book presents a comprehensive review of U.S. Federal Census facts, schedules, and indexes. The five sections include the following information:

1. An essay on the historic U.S. Federal censuses, detailing census copies, census losses, and some little-known facts about censuses in general.

2. A review of the contents of all U.S. Federal Censuses, 1790-1920, tabulated to show their availability for each state; maps for each census year; and an identification of all known census indexes ever published, whether book, microform, or CD-ROM.

3. A list of countywide census extractions and indexes compiled for each state; those published separately from statewide census indexes.

4. A descriptive review of non-population census schedules, their value to genealogists, and the location of original and microfilmed copies in American repositories.

5. A set of twenty-nine U.S. census extraction forms, covering the period 1790-1930, including Population, Slave, and Mortality Schedules; plus Union Veterans, Soundex, and census comparison sheets.

The Census Book is aimed at an audience of amateur genealogists, who represent the largest number of census researchers in America. Census records can provide genealogical data, but they can more frequently provide critical information about a person living in the past, information that may lead a researcher to a precise location in America where even more genealogical sources can be searched. So, in a broader sense, census records are really finding tools for genealogists. They help a family historian find the place where an ancestor lived.

In this personal computer era, census indexes on CD-ROM disks have revolutionized the speed, cost, and availability of these databases. The leading vendor of census indexes on CD-ROM, however, has very little history in genealogy; and this review spends considerable space correcting errors found in descriptions of censuses and indexes found on CD-ROM publications.

Included with this book is a CD-ROM diskette containing the complete text of the book in the same format and page layout, including all tabulated charts, U.S. maps, and census extraction forms. For computer users, the CD-ROM version will allow for printing pages of text, tables, and full-size maps or census extraction forms directly to a printer with no loss of printing quality.

Historical U.S. Censuses

Genealogists are avid users of the U.S. federal censuses available to the public. Most libraries or archives in the U.S. with large collections of census records on microfilm can confirm that fact. For example, in all of the regional branches of the National Archives, amateur genealogists represent 90 percent of the patrons using those facilities. Most of the regional archives provide a complete set of microfilmed censuses, 1790-1920, all in one room, an attraction most genealogists cannot resist.

Though most genealogists are familiar with the use of U.S. census records to help identify their American ancestors, some facts about the censuses overall may not be obvious. Some hidden aspects to the various censuses may be missed by even experienced genealogists.

Perhaps a review of some of these obscurities may help a genealogist understand why certain census records exist while others do not, or why an ancestor does not appear when he should appear in a census. Hopefully, this information will encourage a genealogist to go back to the census records and look again for information that may have been missed the first time.

Why a Census?

Ask someone on the street why a census is taken in the United States every ten years. A common answer might be, "for taxes." Several people might answer, "for reapportioning the seats of the U.S. House of Representatives." Both answers would be correct.

In Article I, Section 2, the Constitution of the United States says:

> Representatives and direct taxes shall be apportioned among the several states which may be included within this Union according to their respective numbers, which shall be determined by adding to the whole number of free persons, including those bound to service for a term of years, and excluding Indians not taxed, three-fifths of all other persons. The actual enumeration shall be made within three years after the first meeting of the Congress of the United States, and within every subsequent ten years, in such manner as they shall by law direct.

Beginning in 1790, the United States of America became the first country in the world to call for regularly held censuses. Note that the Constitution did not treat everyone as equal. "Free persons" excluded Indians living on treaty land and who were exempt from paying taxes (or voting). However, any male Indian who had joined the white population was taxed like whites and was considered a "free person" and had the right to vote. "All other persons" meant slaves, who were counted as 3/5ths of a person for determining

1

representation in Congress. This latter provision was to offset the large slave populations of states like Virginia and South Carolina, where, in 1790, slaves represented 39 and 43 percent of their population, respectively. In comparison, Connecticut and New Jersey had slave populations of 1.1 and 6.2 percent, respectively.

It may come as a surprise to some that "direct taxes" were authorized in the Constitution of the United States. But, except for one national direct tax levied in 1797 to defray debts left over from the Revolutionary War, Congress took more than 120 years to do it for real, when personal income taxes were first levied directly on individuals.

The primary action of Article I, Section 2, was to carry out a national census to be taken every ten years. As in so many other areas of the U.S. Constitution, the wisdom of the document is revealed in how it simply states what must be done and leaves the details of carrying out a census to Congress "in such manner as they shall by law direct." For every ten years since 1790, Congress has enacted a law specific to and authorizing a census to be taken. None of the laws is the same, and each specifies more information to be gathered than in the preceding census.

After every census taken in the U.S., Congress first decides how many total seats there will be in the U.S. House of Representatives, then divides that number into the figure for the total U.S. population. This determines how many persons one congressman will represent. By dividing that number into each state's population, it can be determined how many U.S. representatives can come from each state. After each decennial census, it is the responsibility of the state legislatures to decide the new congressional boundaries within their state, and to ensure that each area is equal to that portion of population for one U.S. representative. The exception to this rule applies to states whose entire population is less than one congressional allotment—all states must have at least one U.S. representative.

The phrase in the Constitution, "the actual enumeration shall be made," was debated early in Congress, because one could say that it meant an "actual count" and nothing else. From the first census of 1790 forward, however, more information has been included than just the tally of persons; and each subsequent census has included more information than the previous one. For this, genealogists are very grateful. However, the language of the Constitution also stated that Congress should carry out the censuses "in such manner as they shall by law direct." That provision established that Congress could broadly determine the content and manner of taking censuses, and that provision has never been challenged judicially.

Ironically, in 1997, the Census Bureau announced that the census in the year 2000 would be the first census ever taken that would not attempt an "actual enumeration" of every citizen. They wanted to collect an actual count of 90 percent of the population, based on the return of census forms. This time, the Census Bureau wanted to "sample" (estimate) the remaining 10 percent rather than continually go back time and again to find the remaining persons who did not return the forms. But Congress challenged this "sampling" proposal because of the constitutional provision for an "actual enumeration."

Census accuracy has always been a matter of contention. Over the years, several major cities have sued Uncle Sam because the cities thought they were unfairly deprived of numbers, therefore, a loss of federal block grants based on population. Usually, the courts have held that under-counting in a census is an inherent part of taking a census, and no compensation or recounts were due. Exceptions to this were in 1870, when the northern cities of Indianapolis, Philadelphia, and New York City were each granted a second enumeration. A few southern cities had also asked for a recount in 1870, without success. This may have been in keeping with the times; because after the Civil War, northern carpetbaggers were used as census takers in the South. They were known to under-count their enumeration districts on purpose in an attempt to keep the political influence of the South less important in Congress. In 1880, the city of St. Louis was granted a second enumeration.

The Early Census Takers

Since the first census of 1790, the states have not been involved in taking a national census except to review and act on the reports generated. The national census has always been a federal responsibility. Congress did not get around to creating a "Census Office" until just before the 1850 census. If it were not a responsibility of a state, who was the agency responsible for taking the censuses?

The first nine censuses (1790-1870) were conducted by assistant federal marshals of the United States Federal Court system. One U.S. marshal was assigned to each federal court district, and it was his job to hire and manage the assistant marshals to take the census in his district. In each territory, the territorial governor was responsible for the census enumeration.

The federal court districts did not always match up with state boundaries. For example, at the time of the 1790 census, there were 16 federal court districts, but only 14 states. Vermont entered the Union as the 14th state in early 1791. Soon after, Congress passed a special law to include Vermont in the first census, with a census day designated as the first Monday in April, 1791, and with five months allowed to take the census there. In 1790, Virginia had two federal court districts, each with their own United States Court House. One Virginia district had the same boundaries as what was to become the state of Kentucky in 1792. Massachusetts also had two federal court districts, one of which had the same boundaries as the future state of Maine. The rest of the states had federal court district boundaries that were the same as their state boundaries in 1790. In subsequent censuses, several states had more than one federal court district. Today, some larger states have as many as four or five federal court districts.

The 1790 census was taken for determining seats in the U.S. House of Representatives. Since people living in territories did not have representation in Congress, no perceived need existed for a census to be taken in the old Northwest Territory or the Southwest Territory. Soon after the law providing for the 1790 census was enacted, Secretary of State Thomas Jefferson, perhaps as an afterthought, wrote a letter to the governor of the Southwest Territory (the territory that became the state of Tennessee in 1796). Jefferson asked Governor Blount if he wouldn't mind taking a census, even though it was not required under the law; and he had neither money allocated, nor a federal marshal to do it. But, since he knew that Blount had "sheriffs who will be traversing their Districts for other purposes," Jefferson wondered if the Governor could ask them to take a census "arranged under the same classes prescribed . . . for the general census." Blount complied, in a way, by providing the secretary with a count of the territory's inhabitants but without listing their names. His report was dated 19 September 1791. Presumably, Jefferson would have asked the same for Governor St. Clair of the Northwest Territory in 1790, but St. Clair was up to his neck fighting off Indian attacks and not available for much else that year. No enumeration of the Northwest Territory was taken until 1800, which in that year had been reduced in size with the creation of Indiana Territory.

Before the 1790 census, there was much debate in Congress about the various aspects of the first census, including the compensation for an assistant marshal. Several members of Congress were worried that the amount was not high enough to attract people to the job. One member of Congress reminded his colleagues of the Bible story about King David, who was blamed for a terrible plague in Israel immediately after a census was taken. The representative from New York remembered that back in the 1770s most of the residents of a New York town had fallen sick right after they had been visited by a British census taker. The representatives wondered if taking a census would ever be possible, given the prevailing superstitions about censuses overall. Nevertheless, in the end, a sum of about $44,000 was spent in taking the 1790 census which was reported to the President in a pamphlet of fifty-six pages. In comparison, the 1990 census was reported in over 1,200 volumes.

Compensation paid to the assistant marshals who were taking the 1790 census was set by law to be $1.00 for every 300 persons in cities and towns containing more than 5,000 people, and $1.00 for every 150 persons in rural areas. However, the law allowed the U.S. marshal to pay $1.00 for every 50 persons in areas determined to be sparsely populated or difficult to reach, subject to a ruling by the federal judge in his district. Each assistant marshal was given a sample copy of the 1790 census form; and he was expected to make all his own copies, ruling the lines of the forms himself. He was also required to pay for his pens, ink, paper, and all other expenses incurred in taking the census.

Samuel Bradford, the assistant marshal for the city of Boston, began his work door-to-door on 2 August 1790, and by 21 August had completed his enumeration. His notebook shows that the work required seventeen working days. He enumerated an average of more than one thousand persons per day. As his compensation was $1.00 for every 300 persons, his earnings amounted to about $3.30 per day, a figure much higher than his rural counterparts and not a bad wage for 1790.

Mr. Bradford could have learned how to increase his pay even more by the example of Clement Biddle, the U.S. marshal for the state of Pennsylvania. Biddle was in charge of the 1790 census taken in that state. Coincidentally, in 1791, Biddle published a directory of the city of Philadelphia, which, apparently, was a profitable success. Comparing the names in the 1791 directory with the 1790 census returns for Philadelphia reveals that Mr. Biddle added very little to his directory. Publishing the city directory may have been a plan of Mr. Biddle's all along—the Philadelphia census list included occupations for heads of household, which, of course, was information repeated in the Biddle directory.

Still, most census takers were not having much job satisfaction. For example, after taking the Morgan County, North Carolina, census in 1790, the assistant marshal there wrote a few words of complaint at the end of his list of names:

I have been Closely Employd Since the 25 of December Last. One Other man has been closely Employd Since the 6th of January; one other has been Employd Since the 12 of January; a third one Since the 1st of March and Two others A Week Each and all had Since to fall behind. After riding horses almost to Death. This is a True State of Facts. No one Man Can Number the People in the District of Morgan Going from House to House in 18 Months I Aver, and if there is no Provision to Collect the people in the Next Law, no man that understands will have anything to do with it.

At the end of the 1820 Hall County, Georgia, schedules, the assistant marshal wrote the following:

The difficulties were very considerable that attended taking the census, in the first place, the inhabitants are very dispersed, in the second place the country being but lately settled, there are but few roads, in the third place great part of the Country are very Mountainous, and in the fourth place it was, except in the oldest settled parts, difficult to get nourishment for either myself or horse, and often when got, had to pay very high, in the 5th place had often to travel a considerable distance through fields to get to the dwelling cabins, often, and generally, drenchd in dew, particularly in August and September; and often had to walk many miles where it was so steep that I could not ride, or even set on my horse.

The Census Day

In each enabling law authorizing a census to be taken, Congress specified a "census day" for gathering the census information from each household in America. From 1790 to 1820, the census day was the first Monday in August. The census day was not the day the enumerator arrived at a household; it was the day for which all the statistics of the census was collected. The actual instructions given to all the U.S. marshals before the 1820 census explains:

. . . all the questions refer to the day when the enumeration is to commence; the first Monday in August next. Your assistants will thereby understand that they are to insert in their returns all the persons belonging to the family on the first Monday in August, even those who may be deceased at the time when they take the account; and, on the other hand, that they will not include in it, infants born after that day.

Similar instructions have been given for every census, 1790-1990, but with different census days. Table 1 shows the census day for each census, 1790-1920, and the time allowed to take the census.

Table 1		
Census Year	Census Day	Time Allowed
1790	2 August	9 months
1800	4 August	9 months
1810	6 August	10 months
1820	7 August	13 months
1830	1 June	12 months
1840	1 June	18 months
1850	1 June	5 months
1860	1 June	5 months
1870	1 June	5 months
1880	1 June	1 month
1890	1 June	1 month
1900	1 June	1 month
1910	15 April	1 month
1920	1 January	1 month
1930	1 April	1 month

South Carolina could not complete its 1790 enumeration in nine months. The U.S. marshal complained that he was having great difficulty finding people to take the job because of the resistance to the census being taken. A Charleston jury met to decide the fate of six persons who had "refused to render an account of persons in their households as required by the census act." A South Carolina census taker was brought on trial for neglect of duty. He did not complete the census in his district. These and other problems led to South Carolina being granted an extension; and the census returns were dated 5 February 1792, a full eighteen months after the census day.

Genealogists should record two dates when copying information from the censuses, the census day and the enumeration date. No matter how many months it took for an enumerator to reach a house, he was supposed to gather the information as if time had stopped on the census day. However, we will never know for sure if the enumerator always followed his instructions. Every person whose regular abode was in a particular household on the census day was to be enumerated, even if a person were away at the time of the enumeration.

From Table 1, which shows the census days, 1790-1920, note that the census day changed from the first Monday in August in 1820 to the first day of June in 1830. If one is researching families appearing in the 1820 and 1830 censuses, looking at these censuses again may be important. Since the census days for 1820 and 1830 are not exactly ten years apart, the two-month difference may reveal some surprising results. For example, if a person were born between 1 June 1820 and 7 August 1820, that child would appear in the 1820 census in the "under 5" category. But in 1830, that same person would appear in the "under ten" rather than the "of 10 and under 16" category, since the person had not turned 10 yet. Comparing the other age categories for a person appearing ten years later and not in the correct age category may give a clue to a person's date of birth within a two-month period.

The Census Counting Machine

Table 1 also shows the time allowed in the legislative act for taking each census, 1790-1920. Note the change from 1840 when eighteen months was deemed necessary to take the census; while in 1850, only five months were allowed. The reason for this change has an interesting history:

Soon after the Census Office was created in early 1850, two young men from Poughkeepsie, New York, approached the director with a proposal. They had invented a "counting machine" they thought could help in tabulating the census returns. They demonstrated a prototype machine that used flat metal cards with slots and holes punched in them in a precise pattern so that a metal rod could be passed through the holes and slots

and lift out certain cards with holes in the same location. By a process of elimination, cards with a particular pattern of holes could be removed; and in the process, they could be counted.

The director of the new Census Office was impressed. The two men opened a business and with the Census Office's good recommendation, borrowed a small sum. The new company developed a working model of the machine; and within a few weeks, the machine proved so reliable that the Census Office decided to use it in the tabulation of the 1850 census. They estimated that it would cut the time to take the census from eighteen months to five months, and that is the time they recommended to Congress in their budget request. Since the 1850 census, the Census Office has used the counting machine in every census taken. In fact, every year after that, the machine was improved in speed and accuracy. That little two-man company that presented their invention to the Census Office back in 1850 goes by a different name today. It is called the IBM Corporation.

Early Census Losses

The 1790 law required the U.S. marshals to deposit the original returns from their assistants with the clerks of the U.S. District Courts. These name lists remained in the clerks' offices, while the marshals' summaries from the various districts were sent to the president of the United States. The law required that the president receive "the aggregate amount of each description of persons within their respective district." The marshals were to "file the original returns of their assistants with the clerks of their respective district courts, who are hereby directed to receive and carefully preserve the same."

This requirement was repeated in the enabling laws for the 1800, 1810, and 1820 censuses. The president was to receive not the name lists, but summaries of the census tallies. This fact contradicts what several well-known publications use as the reason for many early census losses. For example, several genealogical reference books say that when the British burned Washington in 1814, the earliest census returns were destroyed. This incorrect statement can be found in National Archives guides, Family History Library guides, and repeated in many other publications. The only census schedules that could have been in Washington, D.C., in 1814 were the 1810 schedules for the District of Columbia which had its own U.S. District Courthouse. Since the 1810 D.C. schedules are lost, they may have been the only censuses destroyed when the British burned Washington in 1814.

In 1830, Congress passed a law calling for the return of the original censuses for the years 1790-1820. The original census returns were to be sent to Washington by the various clerks of the district courts—the same clerks who had been admonished in earlier laws to "receive and carefully preserve" the original census returns. Obviously, some clerks failed in their duties. According to the provisions of the 1830 law, the census schedules of 1790-1820 for the two districts of Massachusetts (Massachusetts and Maine) were transferred to Washington. Also transferred were the 1790-1820 original censuses for the states of New Hampshire, Vermont, Rhode Island, Connecticut, New York, Maryland, Pennsylvania, North Carolina, and South Carolina.

Certain original census returns were lost before enactment of the 1830 law, or the law was ignored by clerks of the district courts. Georgia's 1790, 1800, and 1810 census returns never reached Washington; and what happened to them is not known. Even worse, the first four New Jersey censuses, 1790-1820, were never received at Washington. Also lost were the 1790 returns for Delaware and Virginia's two federal court districts (old Virginia, including present-day West Virginia and the district which later became the state of Kentucky) and the states of Virginia, Kentucky, and Tennessee for 1800. In addition, the census returns for the Northwest Territory and Indiana Territory, which both had complete censuses taken in 1800, never reached Washington. The 1810 census schedules for Tennessee and the territories of Michigan, Missouri, and Mississippi were also not received at Washington and are presumed lost. See Table 2 for a complete summary of census losses, 1790-1820.

All of the statewide census losses occurred in the first four censuses taken, 1790-1820, with the exception of the 1890 census. More than 99 percent of the original 1890 schedules were destroyed in a fire in the Commerce Building in Washington in January 1921. Most of the early losses occurred before 1830. The failure of some clerks of the district courts to comply with the 1830 law asking for the return of the original censuses may account for most of the losses. For example, the 1820 Michigan census returns were found where they had been all along—in the office of the clerk of the district court in Michigan, but discovered many years after the 1830 law had demanded their transfer to Washington.

There is a slight possibility that some early 1790-1820 lost censuses still exist. If any of the old censuses have survived, they are probably buried in some sub-basement or attic of a federal courthouse district—because that is where they were first deposited.

Table 2 shows the status of censuses from 1790 to 1820. A dash in a column means a census

was not taken for that state in that year. "Lost" means the census returns never reached Washington in 1830 and were probably lost. "Extant" means the manuscripts of the census returns survive, and microfilmed copies of them are available.

Table 2
Summary of Statewide Census Losses, 1790-1820

State/Territory	1790	1800	1810	1820
Alabama	—	—	—	lost
Arkansas	—	—	—	lost
Connecticut	extant	extant	extant	extant
District of Columbia	—	—	lost	extant
Delaware	lost	extant	extant	extant
Georgia (1)	lost	lost	lost	extant
Illinois	—	lost	(2)	extant
Indiana (3)	—	lost	lost	extant
Kentucky	lost	lost	extant	extant
Louisiana	—	—	extant	extant
Maine	extant	extant	extant	extant
Maryland (4)	extant	extant	extant	extant
Massachusetts	extant	extant	extant	extant
Michigan	—	—	lost	extant
Mississippi	—	lost	lost	extant
Missouri	—	—	lost	lost
New Hampshire (5)	extant	extant	extant	extant
New York	extant	extant	extant	extant
New Jersey	lost	lost	lost	lost
North Carolina (6)	extant	extant	extant	extant
Northwest Territory	—	(7)	—	—
Ohio	—	—	lost	extant
Pennsylvania	extant	extant	extant	extant
Rhode Island	extant	extant	extant	extant
South Carolina	extant	extant	extant	extant
Tennessee	—	lost	lost	(8)
Vermont	extant	extant	extant	extant
Virginia (9)	lost	lost	extant	extant

Notes:

1. Three counties are missing from the 1820 Georgia schedules.

2. Of Illinois Territory's two counties in 1810, Randolph is extant and St. Clair is lost.

3. Missing from the Indiana 1820 schedules is Daviess County.

4. Three counties are missing from the Maryland 1790 schedules.

5. Missing from the 1790 New Hampshire schedules are thirteen towns in Rockingham County and eleven towns in Strafford County.

6. Missing from the North Carolina schedules are three counties in 1790, four counties in 1810, and six counties in 1820.

7. In 1800, about a fourth of the population of the Northwest Territory was in Washington County, whose census was discovered among the papers of the Ohio Company in Marietta, Ohio. All other counties were lost.

8. In 1820, two federal court districts were in place in Tennessee, one with a U.S. Courthouse in Nashville, the other in Knoxville. The original censuses returned to Washington according to the 1830 law were from the Nashville district only, representing the western two-thirds of the state. The twenty eastern counties enumerated within the 1820 Knoxville district were not received in Washington and are presumed lost.

9. The "Heads of Families" index to the 1790 census includes Virginia. However, these names were extracted and compiled from county tax lists of Virginia, 1785-1787.

Census Copies, 1790-1820

In the first four censuses, the assistant marshals were only required to make one set of the name lists they had collected. Sometimes, however, census takers made copies of their work. This can be seen in certain states of the 1790-1820 censuses where all the names are listed for a county in alphabetical order, obviously compiled from an earlier draft. With no requirement that a copy be made of the name lists, any such earlier drafts were probably discarded.

The format of the schedules for the first six censuses (1790-1840) was a listing with only the names of the heads of household, but with age brackets for males and females included in each household.

A special consideration unique to the 1820 form asks for all males "16-18" years of age and in another column, all "males 16-26" years of age. The purpose of these two categories was to determine the number of young men in the U.S. of military age. If a male was shown in the 16-18 column, he would also be in the 16-26 column.

To confirm this, add all the marks for males and females, then go to the far right-hand side of the form and find the "total number in the household" figure. If a male were in the 16-18 category, and at least one male was in the 16-26 category, the number in the "total number" column should confirm that a person was not counted twice. Further confirmation of this can be found in the 1820 instructions to the U.S. marshals which read as follows:

> It will be necessary to remember, that the numbers in the columns of free white males between 16 and 18 . . . must not be added to the general aggregates, (they) will all be repeated in the column of those between 16 and 26.

Genealogists who have recorded the number of persons and age categories from the 1820 census need to understand the significance of the added male "16-18" category. One should go back to the same census sheets to confirm that the correct number of persons in the household were noted. It may be enlightening to learn about that "extra" young man in a family in 1820 found no where else.

Census Copies, 1830-1840

In a change of policy, the laws authorizing the 1830 and 1840 censuses required that two copies of the census schedules be prepared. One would be retained by the clerk of the district court, the other sent to Washington. Congress had decided that one copy of the name lists was not enough; and after the experience of several earlier census returns disappearing, they asked that the clerks prepare a name-by-name copy. Several examples show that the copy, not the original, was the census schedule sent to Washington. Only the Washington copies of the censuses were transferred to the National Archives and microfilmed many years later. What happened to the various copies retained by the clerks for 1830 and 1840 censuses is a mystery.

Scanning any microfilmed census schedules and looking at the handwriting is one way of learning if it is the clerk's copy or the original. If the handwriting changed from one assistant marshal's district to the next, then the records are probably the originals, not the copies. If page after page of the handwriting is by the same person, crossing over various town, district, or county boundaries, then it is probably the clerk's copy, not the original.

It is known that various clerks of the District Courts complained loudly about having to make extra copies of the census schedules— they did not think that Congress had provided enough funds for the extra work. As it turned out, the clerks' involvement with census taking ended with the 1840 census.

Census Copies, 1850-1870

The first Census Office began operations in 1850, and a new set of procedures for taking the census was put in place. Although the door-to-door census takers were still the assistant marshals of the Federal District Court system, the clerks of the District Courts were taken out of the census business. For the 1850 through 1870 censuses, they were replaced by the secretary of state in each state or territory.

The job of the new Census Office was to collect the census schedules and prepare the reports after the various U.S. marshals and secretaries of state had completed their work. The Census Office did not have complete control of the job, nor did it even hire its own census enumerators. After each enumeration from 1850 through 1890, the Census Office was disbanded, then recreated again ten years later. The Census Office did not become a permanent federal agency until 1902, when it was named the Bureau of the Census. Since about the time of World War I, the agency has been more often referred to as the "Census Bureau."

Enabling laws for the 1850, 1860, and 1870 censuses asked for an original and two additional copies of the census schedules to be prepared. This was a result of a new procedure for handling the census schedules that began in 1850. Upon completion of an enumeration, the original schedules for an entire county were placed in public view at a county courthouse. Copies of the census schedules were made with the following procedure:

- A complete set of the original census schedule for one county was displayed at each county courthouse after the censuses for 1850, 1860, and 1870.

- The supervising assistant federal marshal made a complete copy of the name lists for the county or counties under his jurisdiction. A "clean copy" of the countywide schedules was to be sent to the state or territorial secretary of state, and the original schedules were to remain in the courthouse for the applicable county. The new copy was to become the "state copy."

- The state or territorial secretary of state received all of the copies of county schedules for his state, then made a "federal copy." The state copy was to be retained at the secretary of state's office. The federal copy was to be sent to the Census Office in Washington.

The original copy of the census schedules made by an assistant marshal in each county was supposed to remain in that county, but it is not known if the marshals always followed their instructions. It is disappointing that so few of the original censuses for 1850-1870 have ever been found in county courthouses. A few years ago, a genealogist looking through case files in a county probate court noticed that many packets of files were wrapped with strips of paper. Unwrapping these packets revealed that the strips of paper were torn off that county's original 1850 census pages. One county's officials obviously had little regard for their old censuses. They used them for scrap paper.

The same is true for the census schedules retained in the offices of the various secretaries of state. It is not known what happened to most of the state copies of the 1850-1870 censuses. One explanation is that they may have been given to various state representatives and senators as "mailing lists" for their counties and districts.

Genealogists should remember that when reading the microfilmed censuses for 1850-1870, they are handwritten copies of the original, or even copies of copies of the originals. If a genealogist is reading a copy (perhaps one that is twice removed from the original), does that explain why an ancestor's name is misspelled, or not there at all?

In a few cases, we have evidence that the originals and state copies of the 1850-1870 censuses were better versions than the microfilmed federal copies. A few county originals and a few state copies, such as those that exist for Minnesota and Wisconsin, have been found. The Wisconsin State Historical Society has the original state copies of Wisconsin 1850-1870 federal censuses. By visiting the Society's library in Madison and comparing the original state copy with the microfilmed federal copy, one will see some dramatic differences.

Harry Hollingsworth reported some of these differences in his article, "Little Known Facts About the U.S. Census," *The American Genealogist* 53 (1977):11.

> I have personally found many discrepancies between the Federal and State copies themselves, and vast differences between them and the originals (i.e., the county copies)! Whole names have either been changed or omitted. Ages have been copied wrong. Whereas, in the originals, the surnames of each family are generally written over and over again, in the copies the word "ditto" or its abbreviation "do" appears instead. When written over and over, a surname has much less chance of being written incorrectly! In one Federal entry, I find Rebecca Gey but "Grey" in the original. In another Federal entry, Amanda Vandyke appears, but she is Amanda A. Vanslyke in the original. Esther Hollinsworth of the original—the correct name—appears as Esther Hollenback in the Federal copy!

When Leland Meitzler was looking for his great grandparents in the 1860 Wisconsin census, he compared the state copy and federal copy. He found the name was spelled "Metzern" in the microfilmed federal copy, but correctly spelled "Meitzler" in the state copy. There are many other examples of the federal copy being in error; and specifically, common human errors were made while transcribing handwritten names and information from one document to another. Unfortunately, the federal copies of the 1850-1870 censuses—the copies with the most errors—are the ones available from the National Archives today, and the ones microfilmed for the public.

Census Copies, 1880

The last census conducted under the jurisdiction of the federal courts and the U.S. marshals was the 1870 census. In the enabling act for the 1880 census, the reconstituted Census Office was expanded and given a substantial boost in budget. However, the big change was that the Census Office, for the first time, was given full power to hire its own census takers and take full control of the job of taking the census completely. The federal court system was no longer involved, and the secretaries of state were bypassed as well.

The new, improved Census Office did a marvelous job of it; and the dramatic results compared with any earlier census were obvious. Five times the number of enumerators were used in conducting the 1880 census compared with the 1870 census. For the first time, the schedules listed relationships for every member of a household to the head. Not only was a birthplace given for each member of a family, but the birthplace of the parents was given. Also, the 1880 census tracts were organized into "Enumeration Districts." Each

district had a supervisor who managed the enumerators under him and managed the work of making copies of the census schedules that would go to Washington. In 1880, an original and one additional copy of the census schedules were made.

As with the 1850-1870 censuses, the 1880 original schedules were to remain in each county of the U.S. The original schedules were bound into books for each county, and this was the copy that stayed at the county courthouse. Meanwhile, copies of the original schedules were made under the supervision of a district supervisor, whose area of responsibility may have been part of a county, one whole county, or more than one county. The supervisor collected the schedules by Enumeration District and county and sent them off to the Census Office in Washington. So, the originals stayed in a county, the copies went directly to Washington—no district court was involved, and no secretary of state office made copies.

Census Copies, 1890-1920

Due to a fire, the only federal census schedules taken for the year 1890 were lost. What is not readily known is why only one copy was made, when earlier censuses had as many as three sets, and even the previous census for 1880 had two sets prepared.

In 1890, the Census Office created a completely different method of recording the census enumeration, one that was unique to the 1890 census and was never repeated. One family was enumerated on one sheet of paper, making the 1890 census schedules much

greater in volume than the 1880 schedules, where as many as ten families were shown on one page. With the increased volume of paper, Congress decided to finance just one copy and make any additional copies an option to any county in the U.S. that wanted their own set. The counties were required to pay for the cost of making their own copy of the census schedules.

It is not known if any of the 2,813 counties in the U.S. in 1890 paid to have an official copy made. Only two counties are known to have surviving population census schedules for 1890—Washington County, Georgia, whose officials copied their census name lists into their county records; and Ascension Parish, Louisiana, where the original work copies of the 1890 census were found. Fragments of the schedules that survived the 1921 fire in Washington, D.C., are together on one roll of microfilm, all indexed, listing 6,160 persons out of the entire 1890 population of 62,979,766 people. Genealogists have learned to use substitutes for the lost 1890 census, in particular, the many city directories printed around 1890.

After 1890, the next three censuses revealed a population increase in the United States that rose from 62 million in 1890 to 106 million in 1920. The censuses of 1900, 1910, and 1920 again were enumerated in one set of schedules; and very few copies were made, if any. For each of these censuses, Congress required any county wanting their census schedules to pay for the cost of making the copy—but it is not known if any counties ever asked for their own copies.

During World War II, the problem of storage space became acute for the original census schedules held by the Census Office, part of the Commerce Department, in Washington, D.C. By 1940, the early census schedules from 1790 through 1880 had already been transferred to the National Archives; but the original schedules from 1900 through 1940 were still stored on several floors of the Commerce Building. To save space, the Census Office undertook a major project to microfilm the census schedules of 1900 through 1940; and when the microfilming was complete, the original census schedules were burned. Since then, genealogists have discovered that poor microfilming for various census schedules will never be corrected completely. The copies we read for 1900 and later censuses are now only available on microfilm. (It is hoped that the future technology of electronic image enhancement may be the answer to restoring the quality of the microfilmed census records into Compact Discs and other media.)

Changes to the Census Statistics, 1790-1920

As genealogists, we have been the beneficiaries of our federal government that took on more than the Constitution asked of them. From 1790 through 1840, the censuses have given us the names of heads of household, age categories of members of a household, and other facts about people.

From the 1850 census and on, the names of all members of the households in America are listed. With that kind of information available, census records have become essential genealogical sources.

The dramatic change in the number and type of questions asked on the 1850 census form came about because of the influence of a group of men in America concerned with the collection of vital statistics. In 1834, a special organization was formed in Washington called the American Scientific Society. This is the same organization that currently has the longest consecutively published magazine in America, *The Scientific American.*

From its very beginning, members of this organization began lobbying Congress to add more statistical information in the decennial census schedules. There was no national standard for the collection of vital statistics in the U.S., and yet the country was experiencing continual epidemics of various diseases that seemed to be localized in certain parts of the country. Gathering statistics about the number of deaths, causes of death, and so on was a growing concern expressed eloquently by prominent men of the American Scientific Society.

As a result, the law enacted for the preparation of the 1850 census included a new concept in which much more information was gathered. Also in 1850 a special schedule was added, called a "Mortality Schedule," in which every person who had died during the previous 12 months was named, along with the cause of the person's death.

From 1850 to 1900, it was believed that the federal censuses could provide the means of collecting national vital statistics. However, since the information came in ten year intervals, the statistics about births and deaths was not very meaningful for the period between census years. In 1901, Congress passed a resolution asking each state to gather information about births and deaths on a statewide basis. But, because Congress gave no money to the states to do it, it took several more years before it happened in every state. By 1925, all 48

states had laws requiring registration of all births and deaths.

Coinciding with these events, more vital records statistical questions were added to each census from 1850 to 1900 with the 1900 census having the most of these, e.g., age, plus month and year of birth; number of children born to a mother, and number still living, etc. But since 1900, census schedules have asked less of these types of questions, mainly because the matter of national vital statistics information had been handed over to the states.

There have been unique questions added for each subsequent census since 1920. For example, in the 1930 census, one of the questions was whether the household had a radio set. In 1940, there were some extra schedules that were not microfilmed, such as the "housing schedules" which asked several questions about construction materials, running water, and whether the house was served by an indoor flush toilet or an outhouse. Another 1940 statistic was each person's address five years earlier: "In what place did this person live on April 1, 1935?", to which a full address was to be given if different from the 1940 address.

The 1880-1920 Soundex Indexes

When Social Security began in 1935, the first old-age pension system was established for every citizen of the United States of the age of 65 or over. An immediate concern was how to prove an age for a person applying for social security, since not very many people could produce a birth certificate in 1935. Many people who were qualified could not prove their age.

To counter this problem, a special branch of

the Census Office was created, called the Age Search group. This group would take a person's application for social security and attempt to find that same person in a census record where a name and age would be given. It was soon determined that indexes would be needed to speed up the work of finding a particular person's name and age listing.

The Census Office hired the Rand Corporation to design an indexing system based on phonetic sounds for a name, which become known as "Soundex." Under the supervision of the Age Search Group, the Works Progress Administration (WPA) employed several hundred clerical workers to create the indexes to the 1880, 1900, and 1920 censuses. For several months, the WPA workers prepared index cards for heads of household from the 1880 census with children 10 years or younger, as well as the index cards for all heads of household from the 1900 and 1920 censuses. The Soundex code was given at the top of the index card, followed by the name of the head of the household. The names and ages of each member of the family were listed below, showing a citation to the census schedules on which they appeared. The cards were then arranged by the Soundex codes for each census index.

For the Age Search Group's purposes, it was decided that the 1880 census did not need to be completely indexed. People in 1935 who were 55-65 years old would have been 10 years or younger in 1880. The 1880 Soundex, therefore, was to be used to provide another check to confirm a person's age. Since the only copy of the 1890 census had been destroyed by fire, the Age Search Group decided they needed to have a complete heads of household Soundex for the 1900 and 1920 censuses.

In the early 1960s, the Age Search Group, on their own, undertook a census index of the 1910 census but limited the index to twenty-one states. The 1910 index was the first to employ the use of computers. Two systems for coding the names in the 1910 census were used. The coding used was either the Soundex or Miracode system, but both systems were exactly the same for coding a surname. (The index cards for

Miracode or Soundex differ only in the citation to a visitation [house] or page number on the full schedules.) Today, all the 1880-1920 Soundex cards prepared by the WPA for the Age Search Group have been microfilmed and made available to genealogists. The computer-generated 1910 Soundex/Miracode indexes were also microfilmed.

All of the Soundex cards have been heavily used. But clearly, the 1920 Soundex cards were the most heavily used by the census office's Age Search Group. Evidence of this was seen at the top of the 1920 cards which were nearly black from thousands of thumbs and fingers passing over them. After the 1920 cards were microfilmed, it was nearly impossible to read the top of many of the cards because of this darkness. Since the Soundex code itself was at the very top of the card, it created a serious problem. However, genealogists may be pleased to learn that one company has been correcting this problem. Heritage Quest of North Salt Lake, Utah, maintains a complete microfilm set of the 1790-1920 censuses as well as all Soundex indexes. Since the 1920 Soundex index was first released in 1992, Heritage Quest (HQ) has been enhancing the images of the micro-filmed Soundex cards, many of which are very difficult to read. Hundreds of master rolls of microfilm have been completely refilmed, photographically changing the light exposure to make the images more readable on subsequent copies. As a result, HQ's set of microfilm for the 1920 Soundex is now more readable in many cases than are the microfilm masters at the National Archives. All of HQ's microforms are available for sale; they now have made them available for sale on CD-ROM and for loan to its members.

Personal Census Search

The Age Search Group of the Census Office is still in operation. The services of this group can be used for a personal census search to locate one person in a census 1930-1990. The request must be for yourself, a deceased ancestor, or for any person alive today who provides written permission. The fee for the search is $40.00 plus $10.00 for a "genealogy" search (which adds the full details for one person on a particular census schedule). The application for a search must be on a Bureau of Census form BC-600, "Application For Search of Census Records," which can obtained by writing to Age Search Group, Bureau of the Census, PO Box 1545, Jeffersonville, IN 47131, or by stopping by any local office of the Social Security Administration and asking for a copy of form BC-600.

County Boundary Changes

When using census records for genealogical research, it is important to understand how the old county boundaries changed over the years. Since the basic census enumeration unit in all censuses, 1790-1920, was a county, understanding the genealogy of counties is part of locating the place where an ancestor lived.

For example, if a genealogist knows that an ancestor lived in Allegheny County, Pennsylvania, in 1790, the county courthouse there is a resource for old deeds, marriages, and other court records, and a place where an ancestor's name may be mentioned. In 1800, due to the formation of counties taken from Allegheny, there were nine counties covering the same area: Allegheny, Beaver, Butler, Mercer, Crawford, Erie, and parts of Armstrong, Venango, and Warren Counties.

Take the example of county boundary changes in Oregon. Any marriage for a couple in the little town of Linkville in Linn County in 1850 would have been recorded in Albany, the county seat; but in 1860, due to the formation of new counties in Oregon, all marriages performed in Linkville, now in Wasco County, were recorded in The Dalles.

In 1870, a marriage performed in Linkville was recorded in Jacksonville, the county seat of Jackson County (but later the county seat was moved to Medford). In 1880, a marriage performed in Linkville was recorded in Lakeview, the county seat of Lake County; and in 1890, for the first time, a marriage performed in Linkville was recorded in the same town since Linkville became the county seat of Klamath County—but then the name Linkville was changed to Klamath Falls. The boundaries of Klamath County have not changed since 1890.

Of course, the town of Linkville never moved. As the settlement of Oregon took place, new counties were created; and earlier county boundaries were changed, placing the town of Linkville-Klamath Falls in five different counties from 1850 through 1890. Therefore, all county records such as deeds, probates, marriages, etc., for a family that lived in Linkville, Oregon, are spread across the state and stored today in five different county courthouses.

These examples can be repeated in virtually every state. Table 3 shows that the number of counties in the United States increased from

292 in 1790 to 3,076 by 1920. It is common that genealogists attempting to identify the places their ancestors lived must first face the reality of changing county boundaries over the years.

A source that can be used to visualize the county boundaries for every county of the United States and for each census year is a book by William Thorndale and William Dollarhide, *Map Guide to the U.S. Federal Census, 1790-1920* (Baltimore: GPC, 1987). This book has 393 maps showing each applicable census year and all county boundary changes, 1790-1920. Each map shows both the old boundaries and the modern boundaries for each state and census year, so a comparison can be made.

Table 3
Statistics of U.S. Censuses, 1790-1990

Year	U.S. Population	No. of States	No. of Counties	Territories included in Census
1790	3,929,214	14	292	Southwest (tally only)
1800	5,308,483	16	419	Northwest, IN, & MI
1810	7,239,881	17	574	IL, IN, MI, MS, LA (MO), & Orleans
1820	9,638,453	22	759	AR, MI, & MO
1830	12,860,702	24	988	AR, FL, & MI
1840	17,063,353	26	1,279	IA, FL, & WI
1850	23,191,876	30	1,623	MN, NM, OR, & UT/1851
1860	31,443,321	33	2,080	KS, NM, NE, UT, WA, Indian, & Unorganized Dakota
1870	38,558,371	37	2,295	AZ, CO, ID, NM, MT, UT, WA, WY, Dakota, & Indian
1880	50,189,209	38	2,570	AK, AZ, ID, NM, MT, UT, WA, WY, Dakota, & Indian
1890	62,979,766	44	2,813	AK, AZ, NM, OK, UT, & Indian
1900	76,212,168	45	2,862	AK, AZ, HI, NM, OK, & Indian
1910	92,228,496	46	2,962	AK, AZ, NM, HI, Puerto Rico
1920	106,021,537	48	3,076	[AK, HI, Guam, Midway,
1930	123,202,624	48	3,110	Canal Zone, Puerto Rico,
1940	132,164,569	48	3,108	American Samoa, Virgin
1950	151,325,798	48	3,111	Islands, & Wake Island]
1960	179,323,175	50	3,133	[Guam, Midway, Canal Zone,
1970	203,211,926	50	3,142	Puerto Rico, American
1980	226,545,805	50	3,137	Samoa, Virgin Islands, &
1990	248,709,873	50	3,141	Wake Island]

Notes:

1. Alaska is the only state without counties. The numbers above include the census subdivisions of Alaska.

2. In Louisiana, a parish has the same function as a county in other states.

3. Since 1790, there have been 138 counties reported in the censuses that have since been renamed or abolished and subsequently absorbed into other counties.

4. Through 1920, there were 44 cities in Virginia independent of any county.

References

Alterman, Hyman. *Counting People: The Census in History.* New York: Harcourt, Brace & World, 1969.

Barrows, Robert C. "The Ninth Federal Census of Indianapolis: A Case in Civic Chauvinism." *Indiana Magazine of History* 73 (1977).

Bureau of the Census. *200 Years of U.S. Census Taking: Population and Housing Questions, 1790-1990.* Washington: GPO, 1989. Reprint, Bountiful, UT: AGLL, 1996.

Davidson, Katherine H. and Charlotte M. Ashby. *Preliminary Inventory of the Records of the Bureau of the Census, National Archives Preliminary Inventory No. 161.* Washington: NARS, 1964. Reprint, 1997.

Eckler, A. Ross. *The Bureau of the Census.* New York: Praeger, 1972.

Forstall, Richard L. *Population of States and Counties of the United States: 1790-1990.* Washington: U.S. Bureau of the Census, 1996.

Holt, W. Stull. *The Bureau of the Census: Its History, Activities and Organization.* Washington: Brookings Institution, 1929.

Lauer, Jeanette and Robert H. Lauer. "St. Louis and the 1880 Census: The Shock of Collective Failure." *Missouri Historical Review* 76 (1981).

Rossiter, W. S. *A Century of Population Growth: From the First Census of the U.S. to the Twelfth, 1790-1920.* Washington: GPO, 1909. Reprint, Orting, WA: Heritage Quest Press, 1989.

Russell, Donna Valley, ed. *Michigan Censuses. 1710-1830 Under the French, British, and Americans.* Detroit: Detroit Society for Genealogical Research, 1982.

Thorndale, William and William Dollarhide. *Map Guide to the U.S. Federal Census, 1790-1920.* Baltimore: Genealogical Publishing Co., Inc., 1987.

Scott, Ann Herbert. *Census U.S.A.: A Fact Finding for the American People, 1790-1970.* New York: Seabury Press, 1968.

Wright, Carol D. and William C. Hunt. *The History and Growth of the United States Censuses.* Prepared for the Senate Committee on the Census. Washington: GPO, 1900.

Section 2

Published Statewide Censuses and Indexes, 1790-1930

Genealogists know the value of the U.S. federal censuses for finding their ancestors. From 1790-1840, federal censuses were taken which list the names of heads of household for each state and most territories. From 1850 and on, the censuses list the names of every member of a household. With a privacy law prohibiting the Census Office or National Archives from releasing to the public any census name list for 72 years, the latest census schedules available to the public are the 1920 census name lists. (72 years was the average life-span of a person in the U.S. when the law was enacted in the early 1950s.) Accordingly, the 1930 census schedules are expected to be released by the National Archives in the year 2002.

The 1790 through 1870 censuses were all conducted by assistant federal marshals of the United States Federal Court system. Their court districts were used as census divisions. The area served by a district court has never crossed state lines, and each state has always had at least one federal court district. But even in the early years of census taking, the most populated states had more than one federal court district within their state boundaries. The first nine censuses taken were organized by state and federal court districts within a state, and then by the counties within a district.

Within a state or territory, no federal census division encompassed an area greater than one county, the county being the basic unit of enumeration for every state except Alaska. Alaska is the only state without counties. The census divisions for Alaska have been the judicial districts and municipalities, the latter having many of the same functions as counties in other states. In Louisiana, a parish has the same function as a county in other states.

In the New England states of Maine, Massachusetts, New Hampshire, Vermont, Rhode Island, and Connecticut, a town may have more importance as a genealogical record repository than a county. However, even in these states, the counties have always been the basic unit of enumeration for each federal census taken there. In 1960, the state of Connecticut abolished all county govern-ment functions except for census enumera-tions and other statistical purposes.

The federal government did not have genealogists in mind when they created the census name lists. Census lists are not alphabetical by the surnames of the residents (except in rare early censuses where an enumerator chose to make a copy of his list in alphabetical order). With very few exceptions, the names of persons are strictly organized by the geographic unit of enumeration, i.e., a rural district; an area served by a particular Post Office; a village, township, town, or city; or some other subdivision of a county. Today, the Census Bureau has formalized these divisions as Minor Civil Divisions (MCD) for which detailed maps are readily available.

Because of this geographic orientation and before the advent of published census indexes, genealogists searching for their ancestors in the census name lists had to know the exact geographic area where a person lived. Many old-time researchers are familiar with the tedium and eye-straining task of searching page after page of the microfilmed census lists. Today, the task has been made much easier because of the many computer-generated surname indexes to the censuses that have been produced. In this section, all known census indexes produced for 1790 through 1920 are identified.

A Brief History of Computer-generated Census Indexes

For censuses before 1880, any name indexes produced have been mostly a private undertaking, employing the use of computers to enter and then rearrange the names in alphabetical order. Before personal computers, a few genealogical groups prepared typed or handwritten indexes to censuses. For example, the Ohio Library Foundation prepared indexes to the 1820 through 1860 censuses of Ohio. They began their work in the early 1960s, well before the coming of personal computers. A few other statewide indexes were done in the same manner by other groups, such as the index for the Indiana 1820 and 1850 censuses prepared for the Indiana State Library.

The first computer-generated, printed census indexes began appearing in the late 1960s from Accelerated Indexing Systems (AIS), a company founded by Ronald V. Jackson of Bountiful, Utah. Jackson pioneered the use of main frame computers for indexing censuses several years before personal computers existed. Over a period of some twenty-five years, AIS head-of-household indexes were prepared for all states, 1790 through 1860, and several for 1870. A few 1880 and later censuses were also prepared. The AIS indexes are now available as printed books in many libraries and archives across the U.S. Accelerated Indexing has gone by different names, i.e., A.I.S.I. and A.G.E.S.; but genealogists generally refer to all of this company's publications as "AIS indexes."

In the late 1980s, Mr. Jackson provided his entire database of census indexes to the LDS Family History Library (in the form of microfiche). Soon after, all of the AIS computer-generated indexes were licensed for use by Automated Archives, a company in Orem, Utah, which began reformatting and publishing CD-ROM versions of the AIS census indexes. In 1994, Automated Archives was taken over by Banner Blue, the publisher of Family Tree Maker software; and within a few months their huge sales of CD-ROM disks caught the attention of Brøderbund, a major software development company. Brøderbund took over Banner Blue; and today, Brøderbund is the undisputed leader in the distribution of CD-ROM census indexes and other CD-ROM database publications for genealogical research. Brøderbund, a part of the Mattel company for a time, is now owned by Genealogy.com, an A&E company.

A few years after AIS began indexing censuses, other companies began indexing projects as well. A small company called Index Publishing produced several statewide indexes in the mid 1980s using its Apple II computers. Soon after, Precision Indexing, a division of AGLL (dba Heritage Quest), began producing census indexes using IBM-PCs, concentrating on the 1870 census. In addition, a few other individuals and groups have prepared indexes to various statewide censuses. All of these modern census indexes have become powerful tools for genealogists. It is to a researcher's advantage to know that more than one version of a statewide census index exists, if only to compare the data for completeness and accuracy.

It is unfortunate that during the process of converting census indexes to CD-ROM, certain facts concerning the surviving censuses have not been maintained very well. Several Brøderbund titles show that a CD-ROM contains a "census" for a state for which no census exists. For example, references exist for censuses for 1790 Virginia, 1790 Georgia, 1790 and 1800 Kentucky, etc., which are not censuses at all, but reconstructed lists of names from surviving tax lists. Inexperienced genealogists using the Brøderbund titles may not be aware of these inaccuracies.

In addition, if a genealogist relies on the currently popular CD-ROM publications of census indexes, he or she may miss the many alternative census indexes published. Not all census indexes have been converted into electronic media, and a genealogist may miss finding an individual indexed in a publication that is only available in print or microfilm media. Because human errors in census indexes are notoriously high, it is just good, common sense to check any alternative census index available for the same state and year.

Consequently, this review is a description of any known, published index to the federal censuses. It is a guide to help genealogists gain a better understanding of what alternate census indexes may exist for certain years and states.

A table for each census year follows with facts about each, including the states or territories enumerated in a particular census year, the population of the state or territory, whether the census survives, any printed book index (by AIS or other company), and a list of CD-ROM census indexes for a particular census year.

Most of the census indexes were produced by AIS and subsequently licensed to Brøderbund; and if so, a CD-ROM number is indicated for each one. Alternate published indexes are identified in the notes section for each table.

1790 Federal Census

General Information: In 1908, the Census Office in Washington, D.C., undertook a project to extract and index the 1790 census name lists, a publication now commonly known as the "1790 Heads of Families." It includes the name lists for twelve of the sixteen federal court districts that were originally enumerated in the 1790 census. Vermont entered the Union as the 14th state in early 1791, its census taken as of 1 April

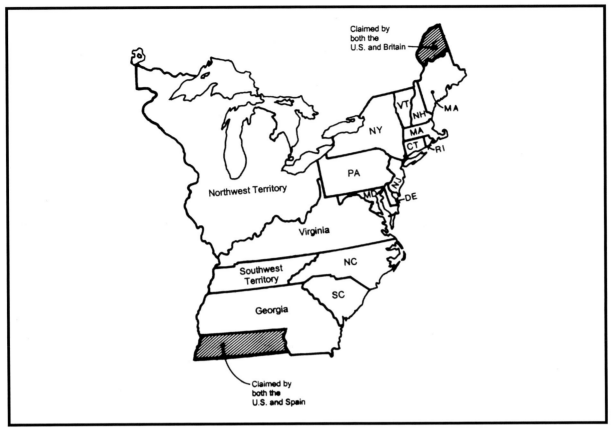

The United States in 1790

1791. Also, in 1790, Maine was still part of Massachusetts, but had its own census because it was a separate federal court district. The same was true of Kentucky, which was still part of Virginia but was a separate federal court district.

Content: The 1790 census format included the name of a head of household, the number of free white males under 16, and 16 or older, the number of free white females of any age, the name of a slave owner, and number of slaves owned by that person.

Census losses: 1790 districtwide census losses include those for Kentucky, Delaware, Georgia, New Jersey, and Virginia. Since Virginia had extant tax lists covering all of its counties for the years immediately preceding 1790, the Census Office used these tax lists to reconstruct the 1790 name lists for the entire state of Virginia. A few 1790 counties of other states were also reconstructed from tax lists, including certain counties in North Carolina and Maryland. The Census Office's 1790 volumes, therefore, are limited to the federal court districts of Connecticut, Maine, Maryland, Massachusetts, New Hampshire, New York, North Carolina, Pennsylvania, Rhode Island, South Carolina, and Vermont, and the reconstructed Virginia lists.

1790 U.S. Census Indexes

1790 State or Territory	State Population	Census exists?	AIS Index?	Other Index	Brøderbund CD #	Heritage Quest CD#	Comments
Connecticut	237,946	yes	yes (1)	(2)	CD#311 (3)	ACD-0032	HQ book A0301
Delaware	59,096	no *	no	(4)	—	—	* reconstructed from tax lists
Georgia	82,548	no	yes *	(5)	CD#311 (3)	—	* reconstructed from tax lists
Kentucky	73,677	no	yes *	(6)	CD#311 (3)	—	* district of VA reconstructed
Maine *	96,540	yes	yes (1)	(2)	CD#311 (3)	ACD-0032	* district of MA HQ book A0299
Maryland	319,728	yes	yes (1)	(2)	CD#311 (3)	ACD-0032	HQ book A0303
Massachusetts	378,787	yes	yes (1)	(2)	CD#311 (3)	ACD-0032	HQ book A0304
New Hampshire	141,885	yes	yes (1)	(2)	CD#311 (3)	ACD-0032	HQ book A0309
New Jersey	184,139	no	no	—	—	—	
New York	340,120	yes	yes (1)	(2)	CD#311 (3)	ACD-0032	HQ book A0302
North Carolina	393,751	yes	yes (1)	(2)	CD#311 (3)	ACD-0032	HQ book A0300
Northwest Territory	None taken	no	yes *	(7)	CD#311 (3)	—	* from early Ohio tax lists
Pennsylvania	434,373	yes	yes (1)	(2)	CD#311 (3)	ACD-0032	HQ book A0305
Rhode Island	68,825	yes	yes (1)	(2)	CD#311 (3)	ACD-0032	HQ book A0298
South Carolina	249,073	yes	yes (1)	(2)	CD#311 (3)	ACD-0032	HQ book A0307
Southwest Territory	35,691 *	no	—	—	—	—	* no name list, tally only
Vermont	85,425	yes	yes (1)	(2)	CD#311 (3)	ACD-0032	HQ book A0306
Virginia	747,610	no	yes *	(2)	CD#311 (3)	—	* reconstructed from tax lists

U.S. Total: 3,929,214

Other 1790 published censuses:

1. Computerized, printed indexes to the surviving 1790 statewide censuses were produced by Accelerated Indexing Systems (AIS), using the original microfilmed manuscripts. The complete AIS database (1790-1870) is available on microfiche at all LDS Family History Centers and at the Family History Library (FHL) in Salt Lake City, Utah. Printed versions for each state are available at the FHL, at the main and regional branches of the National Archives, and at many larger libraries throughout the country.

2. The 1908 Census Office's 12 volume extraction and index to the 1790 census was reprinted by American Genealogical Lending Library (AGLL) of North Salt Lake, Utah, and others. (AGLL now does business as Heritage Quest.) In addition, the 150-plus volume set of the American Genealogical and Biographical Index (AGBI) includes every name from the 1790 Heads of

Families index. The AGBI is published by the Godfrey Memorial Library of Middletown, Connecticut, and can be found in larger libraries in the U.S.

3. CD-ROM versions of all AIS indexes are available from Brøderbund. The 1790 censuses for the 12 extant districts are all on one CD (CD #311). The Heritage Quest version of the 1790 census was published as ACD-0032.

4. The lost 1790 Delaware census was reconstructed from local real estate tax lists and published as *Reconstructed 1790 Census of Delaware* (Washington, D.C.: National Genealogical Society, 1954).

5. The 1790 Georgia census name list was reconstructed from various tax lists, deeds, wills, voter's lists, and other sources by Marie Delamar and Elizabeth Rothstein (Baltimore: GPC, 1985). This list was then used by AIS

and is now incorrectly called the "Georgia 1790 Census Index." See also, *Some Early Tax Digests of Georgia*, edited by Ruth Blair, 2 vols. (Atlanta: Georgia Department of Archives and History, 1926).

6. The 1790 Kentucky census name list was reconstructed from voters' lists, tax lists, and other sources and published as the *First Census of Kentucky* by Charles Heinemann (Baltimore: GPC, 1965). This index was then used by AIS and is now incorrectly called the "Kentucky 1790 Census Index."

7. A partial substitute for the Northwest Territory index was compiled from tax lists and other sources and included in *Early Ohio Censuses* by AIS. See also *Michigan Censuses, 1710-1830, Under the French, British, and Americans*, by Donna Valley Russell (Detroit: Detroit Society for Genealogical Research, 1982).

1800 Federal Census

General Information: The 1800 federal census included two new states admitted to the Union since

1790: Kentucky, admitted in 1792; and Tennessee, previously the "Southwest Territory," admitted in

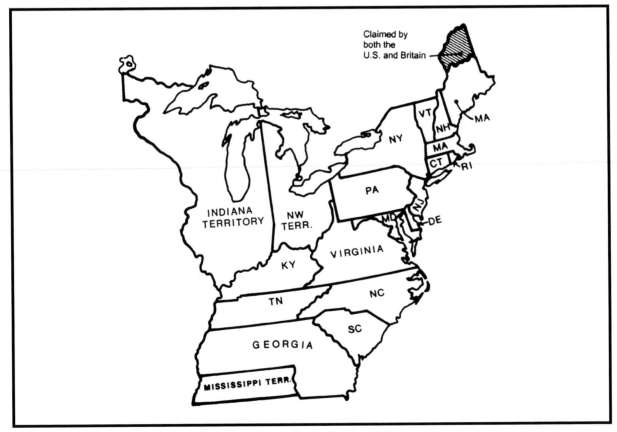

The United States in 1800

1796 for a total of 16 states in the Union. In addition, three territories were enumerated for the first time in 1800: Mississippi Territory, created in 1798 from lands obtained in a treaty with Spain; the Northwest Territory, created in 1787 (but not enumerated in 1790); and Indiana Territory, divided from the old Northwest Territory in early 1800. Maine was still a federal court district within the state of Massachusetts; and therefore, Maine had a separate census taken. The District of Columbia was created in 1791 from land ceded by Maryland and Virginia, but its first census of 1800 was taken with Maryland and Virginia.

Content: The 1800 census format included the name of a head of household, the number of free white males and free white females in specific age categories, the name of a slave owner, and number of slaves owned by that person.

Census losses: 1800 districtwide census losses include those for Georgia, Indiana Territory, Kentucky, Mississippi Territory, New Jersey, Northwest Territory, and Tennessee. These have no known substitutes except for some isolated tax lists. The 1800 census for Washington County, Northwest Territory (later Ohio), was found among the papers of the New Ohio Company. The papers are now at the Special Collections Department, Marietta College Library, Marietta, Ohio, and were microfilmed by the FHL. Washington County was about one-third of the population of the old Northwest Territory in 1800. This sparse index was included in an *Early Ohio Censuses* index published by AIS. The portion of the District of Columbia census included with the Maryland side (Washington County, D.C.) survives and is part of the Maryland 1800 census. The portion for the Virginia side (Alexandria County, D.C.) is lost along with all of Virginia for 1800.

1800 U.S. Census Indexes

1800 State or Territory	State Population	Census exists?	AIS Index?	Other Index	Brøderbund CD #	Comments
Connecticut	251,002	yes	yes	—	CD#312	
Delaware	64,273	no	no	—	—	
District of Columbia	8,144	yes*	yes*	—	CD#312	* Washington County only, included with Maryland
Georgia	162,686	no*	no	(1)	—	* Oglethorpe County exists
Indiana Territory	5,090	no	no	—	—	
Kentucky	220,955	no	yes *	(2)	CD#312	* reconstructed from tax lists
Maine	151,719	yes	yes	—	CD#312	District of Massachusetts
Maryland	341,548	yes	yes	(3)	CD#312	includes Washington County, D.C.
Massachusetts	422,845	yes	yes	(4)	CD#312	
Mississippi Territory	7,600	no	no	—	—	
New Hampshire	183,858	yes	yes	(5)	CD#312	
New Jersey	211,149	no*	no	—	—	* Cumberland County exists
New York	589,051	yes	yes	(6)	CD#312	

1800 State or Territory	State Population	Census exists?	AIS Index?	Other Index	Brøderbund CD #	Comments
North Carolina	478,103	yes	yes	—	CD#312	
Northwest Territory	45,916	yes*	yes	(7)	CD#312	* Washington County only
Pennsylvania	602,365	yes	yes	(8)	CD#312	
Rhode Island	69,122	yes	yes	—	CD#312	
South Carolina	345,591	yes	yes	(9)	CD#312	
Tennessee	105,602	no	no	—	—	
Vermont	154,465	yes	yes	(10)	CD#312	
Virginia	886,149	no	no	—	—	incl. WV & Alexandria County, DC

U.S. total: 5,308,483

Other 1800 Published Indexes:

1. The only county which survives for Georgia's 1800 census is Oglethorpe County, which was published as *1800 Census of Oglethorpe County*, by Mary B. Warren (Athens, GA, 1965).

2. The 1800 Kentucky census name list was reconstructed from voters' lists, tax lists, and other sources and published as the *Second Census of Kentucky* by Glen Garrett (Baltimore: GPC, 1966). This index was then used by AIS and incorrectly called the *Kentucky 1800 Census Index*.

3. An alternate 1800 Maryland census index was compiled by Charlotte A. Volkel, et al. (Baltimore: GPC, 1967).

4. An alternate 1800 Massachusetts census index was compiled by Elizabeth Petty Bentley (Baltimore: GPC, 1978).

5. An alternate 1800 New Hampshire census index was compiled by John Brooks Threlfall in 1973.

6. An alternate 1800 New York Census index was compiled by Philip McMullin (Provo, UT: Gendex, Inc., 1971).

7. An *1800 Ohio Census Index* was compiled for Washington County, Northwest Territory, by Fay Maxwell (Columbus, OH, 1973). See also *Michigan Censuses, 1710-1830, Under the French, British, and Americans*, by Donna Valley Russell (Detroit: Detroit Society for Genealogical Research, 1982).

8. Two alternate 1800 Pennsylvania census indexes have been compiled: the first by John Stemmons in 1972; the second by Jeanne Robey Feldin (Baltimore: GPC, 1984).

9. Two alternate 1800 South Carolina census indexes have been compiled: a typescript by Mrs. Earl Rainwater, 1967; and another by Brent Holcomb (Baltimore: GPC, 1980).

10. An alternate 1800 Vermont census index was compiled by the Vermont Historical Society with J.R. Kearl as editor. (1938; reprint, Baltimore: GPC, 1981.)

1810 Federal Census

General Information: The 1810 federal census included the new state of Ohio, admitted to the union in 1803, bringing the total to 17 states in the Union. The 1810 census also included the District of Columbia, separated in the census schedules from Virginia and Maryland for the first time. In addition, six territories in the public domain were enumerated. Georgia ceded its western lands to the federal government in 1802. These were added to Mississippi Territory, doubling its size. In 1804, two new territories were created from the Louisiana Purchase: Louisiana Territory (renamed Missouri Territory in 1812); and Orleans Territory, which would become the state of Louisiana in 1812. The remainder of the old Northwest Territory left by the creation of the state of Ohio and a part of Indiana Territory was combined to become Michigan Territory in 1805. To complete the changes for the decade, Illinois Territory was created in 1809, reducing Indiana Territory to its present boundaries except for the northern peninsula of present-day Michigan.

Content: The 1810 census format included the name of a head of household, the number of free white males and free white females in specific age categories, the name of a slave owner, and number of slaves owned by that person.

Census losses: 1810 districtwide census losses include those for the District of Columbia, Georgia, Indiana Territory, Michigan Territory, Mississippi Territory, Louisiana (MO) Territory, New Jersey, and Tennessee. Partial losses include those for Illinois Territory, which had only two counties (Randolph is extant, St. Clair is lost), and Ohio, all lost except Washington County whose name list was included in the *Early Ohio Censuses* index published by AIS.

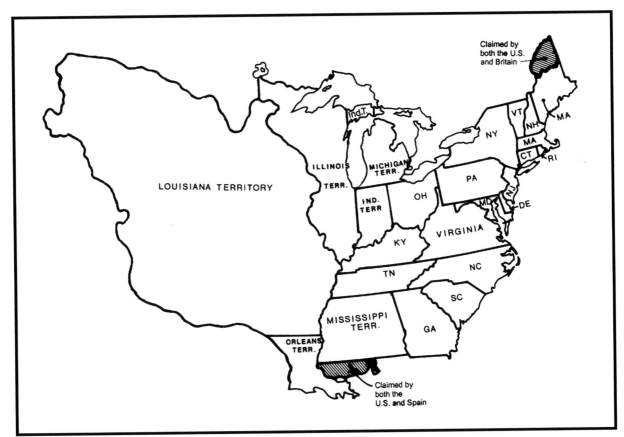

The United States in 1810

1810 U.S. Census Indexes

1810 State or Territory	State Population	Census exists?	AIS Index?	Other Index	Brøderbund CD #	Comments
Connecticut	261,942	yes	yes	—	CD#313	
Delaware	72,674	yes	yes	—	CD#313	
District of Columbia	15,471	no	no	—	—	
Georgia	251,407	no	no	—	—	
Illinois Territory	12,282	yes*	yes	(1)	CD#313	* Randolph County only
Indiana Territory	24,520	no	no	—	—	includes Michigan area
Kentucky	406,511	yes	yes	(2)	CD#313	
Louisiana Territory	19,783	no	no	—	—	renamed Missouri Territory in 1812
Maine	228,705	yes	yes	—	CD#313	District of Massachusetts
Maryland	380,546	yes	yes	—	CD#313	
Massachusetts	472,040	yes	yes	—	CD#313	
Michigan Territory	4,762	no	no	(3)	—	
Mississippi Territory	40,352	no	no	—	—	includes Alabama & Mississippi area
New Hampshire	214,460	yes	yes	—	CD#313	
New Jersey	245,562	no	no	—	—	
New York	959,049	yes	yes	—	CD#313	
North Carolina	556,526	yes	yes	—	CD#313	
Ohio	230,760	yes*	—	—	CD#313	* Washington County only
Orleans Territory	76,556	yes	yes	—	CD#313	became Louisiana in 1812
Pennsylvania	810,091	yes	yes	(4)	CD#313	
Rhode Island	69,122	yes	yes	—	CD#313	
South Carolina	415,115	yes	yes	—	CD#313	
Tennessee	261,727	no	no	—	—	
Vermont	217,895	yes	yes	—	CD#313	
Virginia	983,152	yes	yes	(5)	CD#313	includes West Virginia area

U.S. total: 7,239,881

Other 1810 Published Indexes:

1. An alternate 1810 census index for Randolph County, Illinois, and other sources were indexed by Margaret Cross Norton (Baltimore: GPC, 1969). See also "Illinois Census Returns, 1810, 1818" *Collections of the Illinois State Historical Library*, vol. 24, edited by Margaret Cross Norton (Springfield, IL, 1935).

2. Kentucky 1810 census index cards for heads of household were prepared by the Genealogical Society of Utah in 1936. An 1810 index was also compiled by Lowell M. Volkel of Springfield, IL, in 1971; and again by Ann T. Wagstaff (Baltimore: GPC, 1980).

3. The Michigan Territorial census for 1810 was reconstructed by Elizabeth Taft Harlan in 1977. See also *Michigan Censuses, 1710-1830, Under the French, British, and Americans,* by Donna

Valley Russell (Detroit: Detroit Society for Genealogical Research, 1982).

4. An alternate 1810 Pennsylvania census index was compiled by the Ohio Family Historians (Cleveland, 1966).

5. Two alternate 1810 Virginia census indexes were compiled: the first by Annie Walker Burns Bell in 1934; and a second version by Elizabeth Petty Bentley (Baltimore: GPC, 1980).

1820 Federal Census

General Information: By 1820, six new states had been formed bringing the total to twenty-three states in the Union. The six were: Louisiana, admitted in 1812; Indiana in 1816; Mississippi in 1817; Illinois in 1818; Alabama in 1819; and Maine in 1820. Orleans Territory became the state of Louisiana in 1812, and Louisiana Territory was renamed Missouri Territory the same year. Michigan Territory spanned the northern portion of the old Northwest Territory, north of the states of Ohio, Indiana, and Illinois. A new Arkansas Territory was created from the southern area of Missouri Territory in 1819.

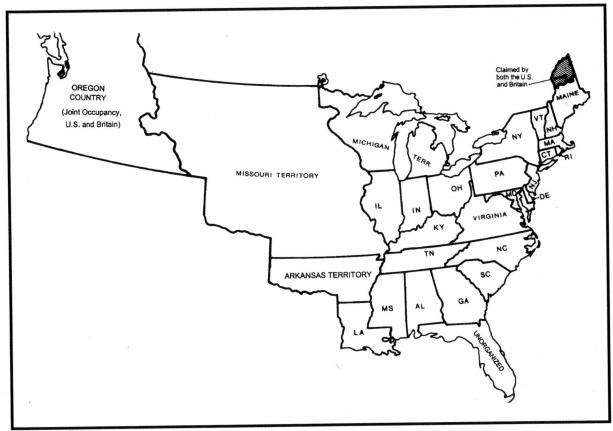

The United States in 1820

Content: The 1820 census format included the name of a head of household, the number of free white males and free white females in specific age categories, the name of a slave owner, the number of slaves owned by that person, the number of male and female slaves by age categories, and the number of foreigners (not naturalized) in a household.

Census losses: 1820 districtwide census losses include those for Arkansas Territory, Missouri Territory, and New Jersey. Partial losses were those for over half the counties of Alabama. In 1820, Tennessee had two federal court districts, one with an U.S Courthouse in Nashville, the other in Knoxville. The original censuses returned to Washington were from the Nashville District only, representing the western two-thirds of the state. The schedules for the twenty Eastern counties enumerated within the 1820 Federal Court District out of Knoxville were not received in Washington and are presumed lost.

1820 U.S. Census Indexes

1820 State or Territory	State Population	Census exists?	AIS Index?	Other Index	Brøderbund CD #	Comments
Alabama	127,901	yes*	yes	(1)	CD#314	* about 1/2 of Alabama counties
Arkansas Territory	14,273	no	yes*	(2)	CD#314	
Connecticut	275,248	yes	yes	—	CD#314	
Delaware	72,749	yes	yes	—	CD#314	
District of Columbia	23,336	yes	yes	(3)	CD#314	
Florida	—	no	yes*	(11)	CD#314	* taken from Spanish tax lists?
Georgia	340,989	yes	yes	(4)	CD#314	3 missing counties
Illinois	55,211	yes	yes	(12)	CD#314	
Indiana	147,178	yes	yes	ISL*	CD#314	* Indiana State Library
Kentucky	564,317	yes	yes	—	CD#314	
Louisiana	153,407	yes	yes	—	CD#314	
Maine	298,335	yes	yes	—	CD#314	
Maryland	407,350	yes	yes	(3)	CD#314	
Massachusetts	523,287	yes	yes	—	CD#314	
Michigan Territory	8,896	yes	yes	(5)	CD#314	
Mississippi	75,448	yes	yes	(6)	CD#314	
Missouri Territory	66,586	no	no	yes*	CD#314	* reconstructed from tax lists
New Hampshire	244,161	yes	yes	—	CD#314	
New Jersey	277,575	no	no	—	—	

1820 State or Territory	State Population	Census exists?	AIS Index?	Other Index	Brøderbund CD #	Comments
New York	1,372,812	yes	yes	—	CD#314	
North Carolina	556,526	yes	yes	—	CD#314	
Ohio	581,434	yes	yes	(7)	CD#314	
Pennsylvania	1,049,458	yes	yes	—	CD#314	
Rhode Island	83,059	yes	yes	—	CD#314	
South Carolina	502,741	yes	yes	(8)	CD#314	
Tennessee	422,823	part*	yes*	(9)	CD#314	* western 2/3 of the state only
Vermont	235,981	yes	yes	—	CD#314	
Virginia	1,075,069	yes	yes	(10)	CD#314	includes West Virginia counties

U.S. Total: 9,638,453

Other 1820 Published Indexes:

1. The *Alabama Territory 1820 Census Index* was compiled by the Idaho Genealogical Society, 1974. The original manuscripts are located at the Alabama Department of Archives and History in Montgomery. The 1820 territorial census, which exists for about half of Alabama's present counties, was also reproduced in the *Alabama Historical Quarterly* 6 (Fall 1944): 333-315.

2. The Arkansas Territorial census was reconstructed from tax lists, voter lists, and other sources by Bobbie Jones McLane in 1965 and again by James Logan in 1992.

3. An alternative 1820 census index for Maryland and the District of Columbia was compiled by Gary W. Parks (Baltimore: GPC, 1986).

4. Two alternative 1820 Georgia census indexes exist. For the first, the compilers name is unknown (Savannah, 1963). The second is a printed index compiled by Mrs. Eugene A. Stanley (Georgia Genealogical Society, 1969). The 1820 census for Georgia is missing Franklin, Rabun, and Twiggs counties.

5. An alternate 1820 Michigan Territorial census index was prepared by the Genealogical Society of Utah in 1973. Another version for 1820 was compiled by the Detroit Society for Genealogical Research in 1965. See also the index compiled by the Wisconsin State Historical Society for 1820 Michigan Territorial counties that later became part of Wisconsin. See also *Michigan Censuses, 1710-1830, Under the French, British, and Americans*, by Donna Valley Russell (Detroit: Detroit Society for Genealogical Research, 1982).

6. An alternate 1820 Mississippi census index was compiled by Irene S. Gillis in 1963.

7. An alternate 1820 Ohio Census was indexed by the Ohio Library Foundation in 1976 and reprinted in a new format by AGLL (dba Heritage Quest) in 1996.

8. An alternate 1820 South Carolina census index was compiled by Gwen Platt of Tustin, CA, in 1972.

9. Two alternate 1820 Tennessee census indexes to the surviving 1820 counties were compiled: a typescript by Martha Lou Houston; and a book by Elizabeth Petty Bentley (Baltimore: GPC, 1981).

10. An alternate 1820 Virginia census index was compiled by Jeanne Robey Feldin (Baltimore: GPC, 1976).

11. A so-called *1820 Florida Census Index* included on Brøderbund's CD#314 is most likely a list of Spanish land grant holders. The treaty with Spain in which Florida became part of the U.S. was not ratified until 1821. Florida was not included in the 1820 census.

12. See "Illinois Census Returns, 1820, published in *Collections of the Illinois State History Library* vol. 26, edited by Margaret Cross Norton (Springfield, IL, 1934).

1830 Federal Census

General Information: Missouri became a state in 1821, bringing the total number of states in the 1830 census to twenty-four. Florida was purchased from Spain in 1819, but treaty ratification did not occur until 1821. Florida became a territory in 1822, and its first census was taken in 1830. No other new territories were added to the U.S. before this census year.

Content: The 1830 census format included the name of a head of household; the number of free white males and free white females in specific age categories; the name of a slave owner and number of slaves owned by that person; the number of male and female slaves by age categories; the number of foreigners (not naturalized) in a household; and the number of deaf, dumb, and blind persons within a household.

Census losses: None for 1830 except some countywide losses in Massachusetts, Maryland, and Mississippi.

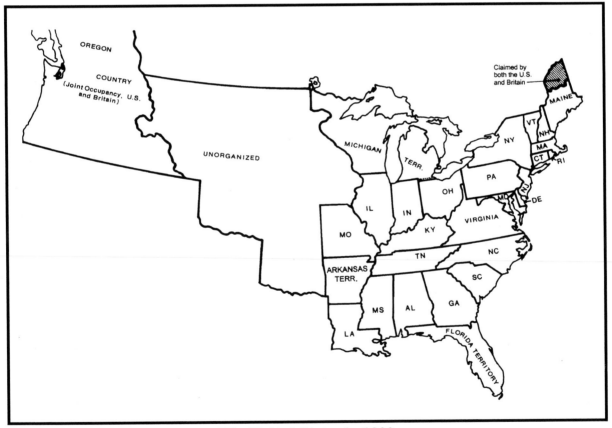

The United States in 1830

1830 U.S. Census Indexes

1830 State or Territory	State Population	Census exists?	AIS Index?	Other Index	Brøderbund CD #	Comments
Alabama	309,527	yes	yes	—	CD#315	
Arkansas Territory	30,388	yes	yes	(1,2)	CD#315	
Connecticut	297,675	yes	yes	—	CD#315	
Delaware	76,748	yes	yes	—	CD#315	
District of Columbia	30,261	yes	yes	—	CD#315	
Florida Territory	34,730	yes	yes	—	CD#315	
Georgia	516,823	yes	yes	—	CD#315	
Illinois	157,445	yes	yes	(3)	CD#315	
Indiana	343,031	yes	yes	(4)	CD#315	
Kentucky	687,917	yes	yes	—	CD#315	
Louisiana	215,739	yes	yes	(5)	CD#315	
Maine	399,455	yes	yes	—	CD#315	
Maryland	447,040	yes*	yes	—	CD#315	* 5 missing counties
Massachusetts	523,287	yes*	yes	—	CD#315	* most of Suffolk County lost
Michigan Territory	16,639	yes	yes	(6,7)	CD#315	includes Wisconsin & Minnesota areas
Mississippi	136,621	yes*	yes	—	CD#315	* Pike County lost
Missouri	140,455	yes	yes	(8)	CD#315	
New Hampshire	269,328	yes	yes	—	CD#315	
New Jersey	277,575	yes	yes	—	CD#315	
New York	1,918,608	yes	yes	—	CD#315	
North Carolina	737,989	yes	yes	—	CD#315	
Ohio	937,903	yes	yes	(9)	CD#315	
Pennsylvania	1,348,233	yes	yes	—	CD#315	
Rhode Island	97,199	yes	yes	—	CD#315	
South Carolina	581,185	yes	yes	(10)	CD#315	
Tennessee	681,904	yes	yes	(11)	CD#315	
Vermont	280,652	yes	yes	—	CD#315	
Virginia	1,220,978	yes	yes	—	CD#315	

U.S. total: 12,860,702

Other 1830 Published Indexes:

1. Miller County, Arkansas Territory, was reduced in size with the creation of the 1828 Indian Lands. The same line divided them as does now divide present-day Arkansas and Oklahoma. As a result, the entire 1830 area of Miller County was south of the Red River. The entire area was in Mexican Texas due to Arkansas's misinterpretation of the 1819 treaty line with Spain.

2. An Arkansas 1830 census index was compiled by Bobbie Jones McLane in 1965.

3. An 1830 Indiana census index was prepared by the Indiana State Historical Society. The original is at the Indiana State Library.

4. Two alternate 1830 Georgia census indexes were compiled, the first by Alvaretta K. Register (Baltimore: GPC, 1974); the second by Delwyn Associates of Albany, Georgia, in 1974.

5. An alternate 1830 census index for the Louisiana parishes of Catahoula, Concordia, Ouachita, Caldwell, Carroll, Madison, and Union (vol 1); and Caddo, Claiborne, and Natchitoches Parishes (vol 2) were compiled by Marleta Childs.

6. An alternate census index was compiled by the Wisconsin State Historical Society for 1830 Michigan counties that became part of Wisconsin.

7. See *Michigan Censuses, 1710-1830, Under the French, British, and Americans*, by Donna Valley Russell (Detroit: Detroit Society for Genealogical Research, 1982).

8. An alternate Missouri 1830 census index was compiled by Capitola H. Glazner of Hot Springs Nat'l Park, Arkansas, in 1983.

9. An 1830 Ohio Census Index was prepared by the Ohio Library Foundation in 1964. This book index was reprinted in a new format by AGLL (dba Heritage Quest) in 1997.

10. An alternate 1830 South Carolina census index was compiled in 1975 by Jean Park Hazelwood of Ft. Worth, Texas.

11. Alternates for the 1830 through 1870 Tennessee census indexes were compiled by Byron Sistler and Associates, 1969-1985. (These are considered more accurate indexes than the AIS versions for the same years.)

1840 Federal Census

General Information: Two new states were included in the 1840 federal census: Arkansas, admitted in 1836; and Michigan in 1837, bringing the total of states in the Union to twenty-six. Florida Territory was enumerated, as were two new territories: Wisconsin Territory, carved out of the bounds of Michigan Territory in 1836 including part of the area of present-day Minnesota; and Iowa Territory, created from the unorganized territory between the Mississippi and Missouri Rivers in 1838 and a northern area that later became Minnesota and Dakota Territories. The "Indian Territory" was created in 1828 from the western part of Arkansas Territory, but no federal census was taken in that area until 1860.

Content: The 1840 census format included the name of a head of household; the number of free white males and free white females in specific age categories; the name of a slave owner and number of slaves owned by that person; the number of male and female slaves by age categories; the number of foreigners (not naturalized) in a household; the number of deaf, dumb, and blind persons within a household; the number and age of each person receiving a military pension; and the number of persons attending school.

Census Losses: There were no substantial census losses for the 1840 census.

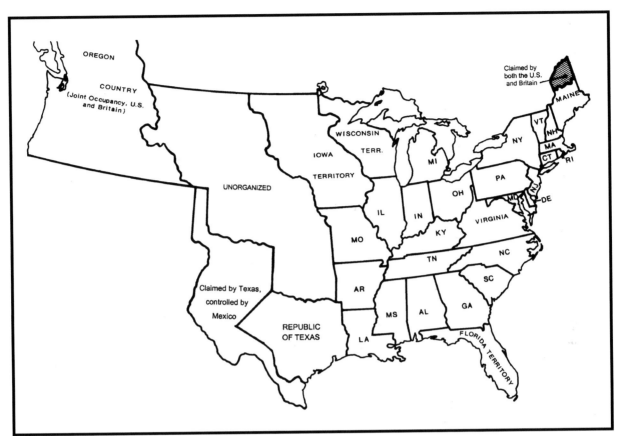

The United States in 1840

1840 U.S. Census Indexes

1840 State or Territory	State Population	Census exists?	AIS Index?	Other Index	Brøderbund CD #	Comments
Alabama	590,756	yes	yes	—	CD#316	
Arkansas	97,574	yes	yes	—	CD#316	
Connecticut	309,978	yes	yes	—	CD#316	
Delaware	78,085	yes	yes	—	CD#316	
District of Columbia	33,745	yes	yes	—	CD#316	
Florida Territory	54,477	yes	yes	(1)	CD#316	
Georgia	691,392	yes	yes	(2)	CD#316	
Illinois	476,183	yes	yes	(3)	CD#316	
Indiana	685,866	yes	yes	(4)	CD#316	
Iowa Territory	43,112	yes	yes	—	CD#316	
Kentucky	779,828	yes	yes	—	CD#316	

1840 State or Territory	State Population	Census exists?	AIS Index?	Other Index	Brøderbund CD #	Comments
Louisiana	352,411	yes	yes	(5)	CD#316	
Maine	501,793	yes	yes	—	CD#316	
Maryland	470,019	yes	yes	—	CD#316	
Massachusetts	737,699	yes	yes	—	CD#316	
Michigan	212,267	yes	yes	(6)	CD#316	
Mississippi	375,651	yes	yes	(7)	CD#316	
Missouri	383,702	yes	yes	—	CD#316	
New Hampshire	284,574	yes	yes	—	CD#316	
New Jersey	373,306	yes	yes	—	CD#316	
New York	2,428,921	yes	yes	—	CD#316	
North Carolina	753,419	yes	yes	—	CD#316	
Ohio	1,519,467	yes	yes	(8)	CD#316	
Pennsylvania	1,724,033	yes	yes	—	CD#316	
Rhode Island	108,830	yes	yes	—	CD#316	
South Carolina	594,398	yes	yes	—	CD#316	
Tennessee	829,210	yes	yes	(9)	CD#316	
Vermont	291,948	yes	yes	—	CD#316	
Virginia	1,249,764	yes	yes	—	CD#316	
Wisconsin Territory	30,945	yes	yes	(10)	CD#316	

U.S. total: 17,063,353

Other 1840 Published Census Indexes:

1. A substitute 1840 Florida census index was compiled from tax lists by Lucille S. Mallon.

2. Two alternate 1840 Georgia census indexes were compiled, one by Frances T. Ingmire in 1982, and another by Barbara Wood and Eileen Sheffield in 1969.

3. An alternate 1840 Illinois census index was compiled by Maxine Wormer in 1976.

4. An alternate 1840 Indiana census index was compiled by the Indiana Historical Society in 1975.

5. An alternate 1840 census index for the Louisiana Parishes of Catahoula, Concordia, Ouachita, Caldwell, Carroll, Madison, and Union (vol 1); and Caddo, Claiborne, and Natchitoches Parishes (vol 2) was compiled by Marleta Childs.

6. An alternate 1840 Michigan census index was compiled by Estelle A. McGlynn in 1987.

7. An alternate 1840 Mississippi census index was compiled by Thomas and Berniece Coyle of Lewisville, Texas, in 1991.

8. An alternate 1840 Ohio census index was compiled by Cleo Goff Wilkens (Ohio Library Foundation, 1976).

9. Alternates for the 1830 through 1870 Tennessee census indexes were compiled by Byron Sistler and Associates, 1969-1985 (They are considered more accurate indexes than the AIS versions for the same years.)

10. An alternate 1840 Wisconsin census index was compiled by the Wisconsin State Historical Society.

1850 Federal Census

General Information: Between 1840 and 1850, five new states were added to the Union: Florida and Texas, both admitted in 1845; Iowa in 1846; Wisconsin in 1848; and California in 1850 bringing the total to thirty-one states. In addition, four new territories were included: Oregon Territory, created in 1848; Minnesota Territory in 1849; and New Mexico Territory and Utah Territory, both created in 1850. No enumeration for the "Unorganized Territory" of the great plains was included in the 1850 census. This area later became all or part of the states of Nebraska, North Dakota, South Dakota, Montana, Wyoming, Colorado, Kansas, and Oklahoma.

Content: For the first time, the 1850 census schedules listed the names of every person in a household. The census was taken with a census day of 1 June 1850. The categories included the following for each person: name; age as of the census day; sex; color; birthplace; occupation; value of real estate; whether married within the previous year; whether deaf, dumb, blind, or insane; whether a pauper; whether able to read or speak English; and whether the person attended school within the previous year. No relationships were shown between members of a household.

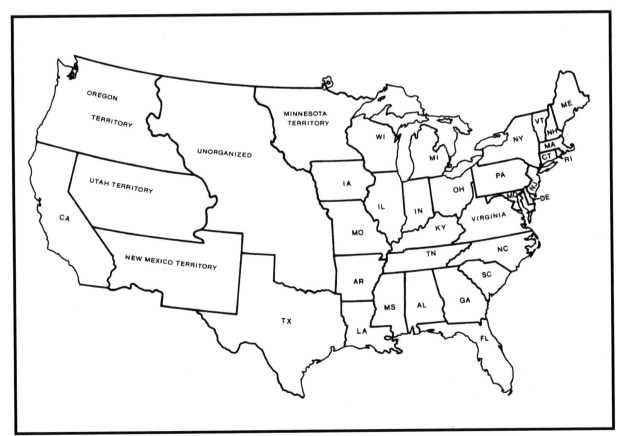

The United States in 1850

1850 U.S. Census Indexes

1850 State or Territory	State Population	Census exists?	AIS Index?	Other Index	Brøderbund CD #	Comments
Alabama	771,623	yes	yes	—	CD#317	
Arkansas	209,897	yes	yes	(1)	CD#317	
California	92,597	yes	yes	(2)	CD#317	
Connecticut	370,792	yes	yes	(3)	CD#317	
Delaware	91,532	yes	yes	(4)	CD#317	
District of Columbia	51,687	yes	yes	—	CD#317	
Florida	87,445	yes	yes	—	CD#317	
Georgia	906,185	yes	yes	(5)	CD#317	
Illinois	851,470	yes	yes	(6)	CD#317	
Indiana	988,416	yes	yes	(7)	CD#317	
Iowa	192,214	yes	yes	—	CD#317	
Kentucky	982,405	yes	yes	(8)	CD#317	
Louisiana	517,762	yes	yes	—	CD#317	
Maine	583,034	yes	yes	(9)	CD#317	
Maryland	583,034	yes	yes	—	CD#317	
Massachusetts	994,514	yes	yes	—	CD#317	
Michigan	397,654	yes	yes	(10)	CD#317	
Minnesota Territory	6,077	yes	yes	(11)	CD#317	includes Dakota area
Mississippi	606,526	yes	yes	(12)	CD#317	
Missouri	682,044	yes	yes	(13)	CD#317	
New Hampshire	317,976	yes	yes	—	CD#317	
New Jersey	489,555	yes	yes	—	CD#317	
New Mexico Territory	61,547	yes	yes	(14)	CD#317	includes Arizona area
New York	3,097,394	yes	yes		CD#317	
North Carolina	869,039	yes	yes	(15)	CD#317	
Ohio	1,980,329	yes	yes	(16)	CD#317	
Oregon Territory	12,093	yes	yes	(17)	CD#317	incudes Washington & Idaho areas
Pennsylvania	2,311,786	yes	yes	—	CD#317	
Rhode Island	147,545	yes	yes	—	CD#317	

1850 State or Territory	State Population	Census exists?	AIS Index?	Other Index	Brøderbund CD #	Comments
South Carolina	668,507	yes	yes	—	CD#317	
Tennessee	1,002,717	yes	yes	(18)	CD#317	
Texas	212,592	yes	yes	(19)	CD#317	
Utah Territory	11,380	yes	yes	(20)	CD#317	
Vermont	314,120	yes	yes	—	CD#317	
Virginia	1,421,661	yes	yes	(21)	CD#317	includes West Virginia counties
Wisconsin	305,945	yes	yes	(22)	CD#317	

U.S. total: 23,191,876

Other 1850 Published Census Indexes:

1. An "every name" census index for Arkansas 1850 was compiled by Bobbie Jones McLane and Desmond Walls Allen in 1995. An extract in family order for the 1850 Arkansas census was compiled by Mrs. Leister E. Presley of Searcy, Arkansas.

2. An alternate 1850 California census index was compiled by Alan P. Bowman (Baltimore: GPC, 1972). In addition, an index to *Ohioans in the California Census of 1850* was prepared. The 1850 California census is missing Contra Costa, San Francisco, and Santa Clara counties.

3. The Connecticut State Library prepared index cards for every head of household for Connecticut censuses, 1790-1850.

4. An alternate 1850 Delaware census index was compiled by Virginia Langham Olmsted (Baltimore: GPC, 1977).

5. A typescript, *New Englanders in the Georgia Census of 1850* was compiled by Frank Mortimer Hawes.

6. A name index to *Early Illinois Records, 1810-1855*, including state and federal censuses, is at the Illinois State Archives. It should be pointed out that in the Edgar County, Illinois, census, the enumerator there indicated the county of birth for each person in the county, information that was well beyond his requirements of state or country of birth. Some individuals from the 1850 Edgar County census were identified in two articles published in the National Genealogical Society Quarterly 38 (March 1950); 36 (Sept 1948).

7. An "every name" 1850 Indiana census index was prepared by the Indiana Historical Society in 1990.

8. An alternate 1850 Kentucky census index was compiled by Byron Sistler and Associates in 1995. In addition, a partial 1850 census index was compiled by Mrs. M.T. Parrish in 1973 for the East Kentucky counties of Breathitt, Carter, Clay, Floyd, Harlan, Johnson, Knox, Laurel, Lawrence, Letcher, Morgan, Perry, and Pike.

9. Maine census indexes for 1850, 1860, and 1870 are at the Maine Division of Vital Statistics, Augusta, Maine.

10. An alternate 1850 Michigan census index was compiled by the Michigan Genealogy Society and Michigan DAR in 1976.

11. The 1850 Minnesota Territory census was indexed for the Minnesota Historical Society in 1972 by Patricia C. Harpole and Mary D. Nagle. In addition, an 1850 census index for Itasco, Wahnahta, and Mankahta counties was prepared by Sharon Coe Pompey (Independence, CA: Historical and Genealogical Publishing Co., 1965).

12. An 1850 Mississippi census index was compiled by Irene S. Gillis of Shreveport, Louisiana, in 1972.

13. See *Pioneer Kentuckians with Missouri Cousins,* an index to the Missouri 1850 census for persons born in Kentucky, prepared by Linda Barber Brooks (St. Louis: Ingmire, 1985).

14. An 1850 New Mexico Territory census index was compiled by Margaret L. Windham (New Mexico Genealogical Society, 1976). The index includes the area which became Arizona Territory.

15. See *Index to Individuals Born Outside the U.S. as Enumerated in the 1850 Census of North Carolina,* compiled by the FHL in 1972.

16. An 1850 Ohio census index was compiled by Linda F. Harshman (Ohio Family Historians, 1972).

17. An 1850 Oregon Territory census index was compiled by Mildred E. Porter and Jo Landers (Clark County Washington Genealogical Society, 1972) including Clark County (later Washington Territory). In addition, an Oregon 1850 census index was prepared by William Bowen (San Fernando Valley State College, 1972). See also the index prepared by Shirley Buirch for the following counties of Oregon in 1850: Benton, Clark, Clatsop, Lewis, Linn, Marion, Polk, Washington, and Yamhill (1977).

18. Alternates for the 1830 through 1870 Tennessee census indexes were compiled by Byron Sistler and Associates, 1969-1985. The names from the 1850 Tennessee census were extracted for every family and includes an index to every head of household for that year.

19. An 1850 Texas census index was compiled by Mrs. V. K. Carpenter (Huntsville, AL: Century Enterprises, 1969).

20. The 1850 census for Utah Territory had a census day of 1 April 1851. A census index was prepared by the Genealogical Society of Utah (FHL) in 1950. In addition, an 1850, 1860, and 1870 Utah census index was prepared by J. R. Kearl, et al (Baltimore: GPC, 1981).

21. An 1850 Virginia census index exists for the progeny counties of Lincoln, McDowell, and Mingo and their parent counties of Summers, Tazewell, Boone, Cabell, Fayette, Greenbrier, Kanawha, Logan, Mercer, Monroe, Raleigh, Wayne, and Wyoming Counties in areas of present-day West Virginia.

22. The AIS 1850 Wisconsin census index was taken from the federal copy microfilmed by the National Archives. However, an 1850 Wisconsin census index to the state copy of the federal census was prepared by the Wisconsin State Historical Society. The state copy differs from the federal copy often and the volume and page numbers do not always agree with each other. Nevertheless, Wisconsin's original copy of its 1850 federal census is superior to the federal copy as to accuracy and completeness. Researchers comparing the state copy with the federal copy will find many differences including different name spellings, omissions, etc., since the federal copy was made from the state copy and transcription errors were common.

1860 Federal Census

General Information: Between 1850 and 1860, two new states were added to the Union for a total of thirty-three states: Minnesota was admitted in 1858 and Oregon in 1859. The existing territories of New Mexico and Utah were included in the 1860 census as were three new territories: Washington Territory, created in 1853 from Oregon Territory; and Nebraska and Kansas Territories, created from the "Unorganized Territory" in 1854. Washington Territory increased in size in 1859 when Oregon became a state, adding the area of present-day Idaho plus the portions of present-day Montana and Wyoming lying west of the continental divide. The region matching the present bounds of Oklahoma was unofficially called the "Indian Territory." In 1860, for the first time, a census was taken there, but only for non-Indians living in that region. The name lists for the non-Indians in the "Indian Territory" were added to the end of the Arkansas name lists. The remainder of the "Unorganized Territory" left by the creation of Nebraska Territory and the state of Minnesota was included in the 1860 census, enumerated as "Unorganized Dakota Territory."

Content: The 1860 census schedules listed the name of every person in a household with a census day of 1 June 1860. The categories included the following for each person: name; age as of the census day; sex; color; birthplace; occupation; value of real estate; value of personal estate; whether married within the previous year; whether deaf, dumb, blind, or insane; whether a pauper; whether able to read or speak English; and whether the person attended school within the previous year. No relationships between members of a household were given.

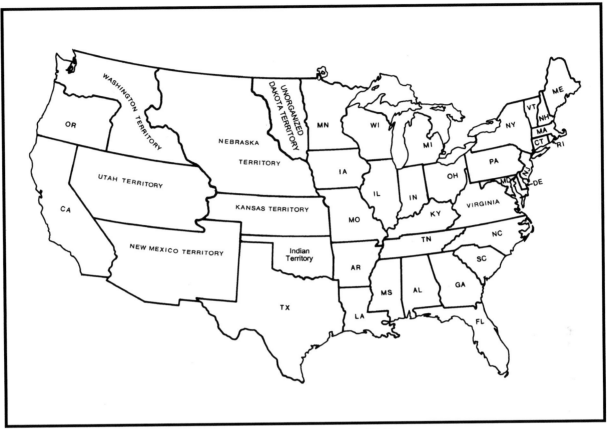

The United States in 1860

1860 Census Indexes

1860 State or Territory	State Population	Census exists?	AIS Index?	Other Index	Brøderbund CD #	Comments
Alabama	996,992	yes	yes	—	CD#318	
Arkansas*	435,450	yes	yes	(8)	CD#318	* includes non-Indians in Indian Terr.
California	379,994	yes	yes	(1)	CD#318	
Connecticut	460,147	yes	yes	(2)	CD#318	
Unorg. Dakota Terr.	4,837	yes	yes (3)	—	CD#318	
Delaware	61,073	yes	yes	(4)	CD#318	
District of Columbia	75,080	yes	yes	(5)	CD#318	
Florida	140,424	yes	yes	(6)	CD#318	
Georgia	1,057,286	yes	yes	(7)	CD#318	
Illinois	1,711,951	yes	yes	—	CD#318	
Indian Territory	—	yes*	yes	(8)	CD#318	* non-Indians included with AR census
Indiana	1,350,428	yes	yes	(9)	CD#318	
Iowa	674,913	yes	yes	(10)	CD#318	

1860 State or Territory	State Population	Census exists?	AIS Index?	Other Index	Brøderbund CD #	Comments
Kansas Territory	107,206	yes	yes	(11)	CD#318	includes portion of present-day CO
Kentucky	1,155,684	yes	yes	—	CD#318	
Louisiana	708,002	yes	yes	—	CD#318	
Maine	628,279	yes	yes	(12)	CD#318	
Maryland	687,049	yes	yes	—	CD#318	
Massachusetts	1,231,066	yes	yes	—	CD#318	
Michigan	749,113	yes	yes	(13)	CD#318	
Minnesota	172,023	yes	yes	(14)	CD#318	
Mississippi	791,305	yes	yes	(15)	CD#318	
Missouri	1,182,012	yes	yes	—	CD#318	
Montana area	—	yes*	yes	(16)	CD#318	Bitterroot Valley of WA Territory
Nebraska Territory	28,841	yes	yes	(17)	CD#318	includes CO, WY, MT, ND, SD areas
New Hampshire	326,073	yes	yes	—	CD#318	
New Jersey	489,555	yes	yes	—	CD#318	
New Mexico Territory	93,516	yes	yes	(18)	CD#318	includes Arizona area
New York	3,880,735	yes	yes	—	CD#318	
North Carolina	992,622	yes	yes	—	CD#318	
Ohio	2,339,511	yes	yes	(19)	CD#318	
Oregon	52,465	yes	yes	(20)	CD#318	
Pennsylvania	2,906,215	yes	yes	—	CD#318	
Rhode Island	174,260	yes	yes	(21)	CD#318	
South Carolina	703,708	yes	yes	(22)	CD#318	
Tennessee	1,109,801	yes	yes	(23)	CD#318	
Texas	604,215	yes	yes	—	CD#318	
Utah Territory	40,273	yes	yes	(24)	CD#318	includes NV/CO/WA areas
Vermont	315,098	yes	yes	—	CD#318	
Virginia	1,596,318	yes	yes	—	CD#318	AIS index has no WV counties
Washington Territory	11,594	yes	yes	(25)	CD#318	includes ID & western MT & WY areas
WV counties *	—	yes	yes	—	CD#318	WV counties of 1860 Virginia
Wisconsin	775,881	yes	yes	(26)	CD#318	

U.S. total: 31,443,321

Other 1860 Published Indexes:

1. An alternate 1860 California census index was compiled by Bryan Lee Dilts (Index Publishing, 1984). It is available from Heritage Quest.

2. An alternate 1860 Connecticut census index was compiled by Bryan Lee Dilts (Index Publishing, 1985). It is also available from Heritiage Quest.

3. The so-called 1860 AIS "Dakota Territory" census index lists every name. In the census, the area was called "Unorganized Dakota," but the area was not an official territory of the United States. "Unorganized Dakota" was confined to the region west of Minnesota and Iowa and extended west to the Missouri River. Included in its enumeration were the communities of Medary, Sioux Falls, Vermillion, and Yankton Agency. In addition, several military forts along the Missouri River were enumerated, most of which were on the west side of the river, and therefore, were technically in Nebraska Territory, not in the Unorganized Dakota Territory. The forts enumerated along the Missouri River were as follows: Ft. Union, Ft. William, Ft. Berthold, Ft. Clark, Dirtville, Ft. Pierre, Old Ft. George, Ft. Lookout, Old Cedar Fort, and Ft. Randall.

4. An alternate 1860 Delaware census index was compiled by Bryan Lee Dilts (Index Publishing, 1984) and is also available from Heritiage Quest.

5. An alternate 1860 District of Columbia census index was compiled by Bryan Lee Dilts (Index Publishing, 1983) and is also available from Heritiage Quest.

6. An alternate 1860 Florida census index was compiled by Bryan Lee Dilts (Index Publishing, 1984) and is also available from Heritiage Quest.

7. An alternate 1860 Georgia census index was compiled by Arlis Acord of LaGrange, Georgia, in 1986.

8. Non-Indians living in the so-called "Indian Territory" were enumerated and the lists added to the end of the Arkansas 1860 census lists. The printed AIS index for the so-called "1860 Oklahoma Census" was the Special Federal Census taken for the five civilized tribes of 1860, and included on CD#318. Another index to the Indian Territory was published as, *1860 Federal Population Schedules of the U.S. Census: Indian Lands West of Arkansas: Creek, Cherokee, Chickasaw, Choctaw, and Seminole Nations* (Tulsa, OK: Oklahoma Yesterday Publ. Co., c 1980). The Arkansas 1860 census is missing Little River County.

9. An every-name index to the 1860 Indiana census was prepared by the Indiana Historical Society in 1990 for the Indiana State Library. In addition, an 1860 Indiana census index (heads of household) was compiled by Kratz Indexing of Salt Lake City in 1987.

10. An alternate 1860 Iowa census index was compiled by David Paul Davenport.

11. An 1860 census index was compiled for *Kansas Territory Settlers Who Were Born in Tennessee, Virginia, North Carolina, and South Carolina*, by Clara Hamlett Robertson (Baltimore: GPC, 1976). Kansas Territory's Arapahoe County in 1860 included a portion of present-day Colorado.

12. Maine census indexes for 1850, 1860, and 1870 are at the Maine Division of Vital Statistics, Augusta, Maine.

13. An alternate 1860 Michigan census index was compiled by Evelyn M. Sawyer (Western Michigan Genealogical Society, 1987).

14. An 1860 Minnesota census index was prepared on index cards from the Minnesota state original copy of their 1860 federal census and is located at the Minnesota Historical Society Library in St. Paul. Researchers comparing the state copy with the federal copy will find many differences, including different name spellings, omissions, etc., since the federal copy was made from the state copy and transcription errors were common. Useful for comparing the federal and state copies is Dennis E. Meissner's *Guide to the Use of the 1860 Minnesota Population Census Schedules and Index* (Minnesota Historical Society, 1978).

15. An 1860 Mississippi census index was compiled by Kathryn R. Bonner of Marianna, Arkansas, in 1983.

16. The so-called "1860 Montana Territory" census index by AIS is a list of 551 persons from the 1860 Washington Territory census for the "Bitter Root Valley" and "Ponderay Mountains" region of present-day Montana west of the continental divide. Montana did not become a territory until 1864.

17. An 1860 Nebraska Territory census index was compiled by E. Evelyn Cox (Ellensburg, WA: Ancestree, 1973). See note three regarding certain military forts in Nebraska Territory enumerated with "Unorganized Dakota" in 1860. Nebraska Territory also included the mining camps near present-day Boulder, Colorado.

18. See the 1965 U.S. Government publication, 89th Congress, 1st Session, *Territory of New Mexico and Territory of Arizona: Excerpts from the Federal Census of 1860 for Arizona County in the Territory of New Mexico, the special federal census of Arizona Territory in 1864, and the Arizona Territory Federal Census for 1870.*

19. An 1860 Ohio census index was compiled by Linda Flint Harshman, (Ohio Library Foundation, 1979).

20. An alternate 1860 Oregon census index was compiled by Bryan Lee Dilts (Index Publishing, 1985). It is also available from Heritiage Quest.

21. An alternate 1860 Rhode Island census index was compiled by Bryan Lee Dilts (Index Publishing, 1985). It is available from Heritiage Quest.

22. Two alternate 1860 South Carolina census indexes exist: the first by Jonnie P. Arnold (Greenville, SC: A Press, 1972); and another by Bryan Lee Dilts (Index Publishing, 1985). The latter is also available from Heritiage Quest.

23. Alternates for the 1830 through 1870 Tennessee census indexes were compiled by Byron Sistler and Associates, 1969-1985 (and are considered more accurate indexes than the AIS versions for the same years).

24. 1850, 1860, and 1870 Utah census indexes were prepared by J. R. Kearl, et al (Baltimore: GPC, 1981). See also 1860 Washington Territory.

25. An 1860 Washington Territorial census index was compiled by J. V. Stucki (Huntsville, AL: Century Gen. Serv., 1972). Researchers should be aware that the 1860 census for Utah Territory included households in Washington Territory, living just above the present-day Utah/Idaho boundary near the Bear Lake region of Idaho.

26. The AIS 1860 Wisconsin census index was taken from the federal copy microfilmed by the National Archives. However, an 1860 Wisconsin census index to the state copy of the federal census was prepared by the Wisconsin State Historical Society. The state copy differs from the federal copy often and the volume and page numbers do not always agree with each other. Researchers comparing the state copy with the federal copy will find many differences, including different name spellings, omissions, etc., since the federal copy was made from the state copy and transcription errors were common.

1870 Federal Census

General Information: Between 1860 and 1870—the decade of the Civil War—four new states were added to the Union for a total of thirty-seven states: Kansas became a state in 1861, West Virginia in 1863, Nevada in 1864, and Nebraska in 1867. In addition, six new territories were created: Dakota and Colorado Territories in 1861, Arizona and Idaho Territories in 1863, Montana Territory in 1864, and Wyoming Territory in 1868. New Mexico Territory was reduced to its present size with the creation of Arizona and Colorado Territories, as was Washington Territory with the creation of Idaho, Wyoming, and Montana Territories. Kansas was reduced to its present size with the creation of Colorado Territory, as was Nebraska with the creation of Dakota, Montana, Wyoming, and Dakota Territories. Utah Territory was reduced to its present size with the creation of the state of Nevada and Colorado Territory. The "Unorganized Territory," unofficially called the "Indian Territory" was not enumerated for non-Indians in 1870.

Content: The 1870 census schedules listed the name of every person in a household with a census day of 1 June 1870. The categories included the following for each person: name; age as of the census day; month of birth if born during the year; sex; color; birthplace; occupation; value of real estate; value of personal estate; whether married within the previous year; month of marriage if married within the previous year; whether deaf, dumb, blind, or insane; whether able to read or write; whether father or mother of foreign birth; and whether the person attended school within the previous year. No relationships between members of a household were shown.

The United States in 1870

1870 Census Indexes

1870 State (1) or Territory	State Population	Census exists?	AIS Book Index?	Other Book Index	Broder-bund CD#	Heritage Quest CD#	Comments
Alabama	996,992	yes	yes	(2)	CD#319	ACD-0036	HQ book X131
Alaska area	—	no	yes*	(3)	CD#319*	—	* compiled town lists
Arizona Territory	9,658	yes	yes	(21)	CD#319	ACD-0024	HQ book X144
Arkansas	484,471	yes	yes	(4)	CD#319	ACD-0017	HQ book X121
California	560,247	yes	yes	—	CD#319	ACD-0024	HQ book X144
Colorado Territory	39,864	yes	yes	(5)	CD#319	ACD-0024	HQ book X144
Connecticut	537,454	yes	no	—	—	ACD-0023	HQ book X137
Dakota Territory	14,181	yes	no	—	—	ACD-0040	HQ book X133
ND area	2,405	—	yes*	(6)	CD#319*	—	* ND counties only
SD area	11,776	—	yes*	(6)	CD#319*	—	* SD counties only

1870 State (1) or Territory	State Population	Census exists?	AIS Book Index?	Other Book Index	Broder-bund CD#	Heritage Quest CD#	Comments
Delaware	125,015	yes	yes	(7)	CD#319	ACD-0033	HQ book X117
District of Columbia	131,700	yes	yes	(8)	CD#319	ACD-0016	HQ book X118
Florida	187,784	yes	yes	(9)	CD#319	ACD-0021	HQ book X131
Georgia	1,184,109	yes	yes*	(10)	CD#319* CD#291	ACD-0021	*3 counties only HQ book X108
Idaho Territory	14,999	yes	yes	(11)	CD#319	ACD-0024	HQ book X146
Illinois	2,539,891	yes	yes*	(12)	CD#319* CD#288*	ACD-0013	* Chicago/Cook Co. only HQ book X114
Indiana	1,680,637	yes	yes*	(13)	CD#319*	ACD-0038	* Indianapolis only HQ book X124
Iowa	1,194,020	yes	yes	—	CD#319	ACD-0020	HQ book X128
Kansas	364,399	yes	yes	—	CD#319	ACD-0040	HQ book X126
Kentucky	1,321,011	yes	yes	—	CD#319	ACD-0035	HQ book X121
Louisiana	726,915	yes	yes	—	CD#319	ACD-0017	HQ book X132
Maine	626,915	yes	yes*	(14)	CD#319*	ACD-0041	*646 names only HQ book X138
Maryland	780,894	yes	no	(15)	CD#288*	ACD-0016	*Baltimore City/Co. only HQ book X119
Massachusetts	1,457,351	yes	no	(16)	CD#284	ACD-0042	HQ book X135
Michigan	1,184,059	yes	no	(17)	—	ACD-0022	HQ book X135
Minnesota	439,706	yes	yes*	(34)	CD#319	ACD-0040	HQ book X134
Mississippi	827,922	yes	no	—	—	ACD-0019	HQ book X129
Missouri	1,721,295	yes	no	—	CD#288*	ACD-0019	*St. Louis City/Co. only HQ book X103
Montana Territory	20,595	yes	yes*		CD#319	ACD-0024	*an "every-name" index HQ book X147
Nebraska	122,993	yes	no	(18)	—	ACD-0040	HQ book X127
Nevada	42,941	yes	yes	(19)	CD#319	ACD-0024	HQ book X148
New Hampshire	318,300	yes	no	—	—	ACD-0041	HQ book X140
New Jersey	906,096	yes	yes*	(20)	—	ACD-0033	HQ book X120
New Mexico Terr.	91,874	yes	yes*	(21)	CD#319	ACD-0024	*an "every-name" index HQ book X149
New York City	1,022,245	yes*	no	(22)	CD#287*	—	*plus Suffolk Co. HQ book X111 (NYC)

1870 State (1) or Territory	State Population	Census exists?	AIS Book Index?	Other Book Index	Broder-bund CD#	Heritage Quest CD#	Comments
New York State	4,382,759	yes	no	(22)	—	ACD-0018	HQ books: Long Island, X104 Upstate NY, X123
North Carolina	1,071,361	yes	yes	(23)	CD#319 CD#289*	ACD-0029 w/SC	HQ book X100 *w/South Carolina
Ohio	2,665,260	yes	no	(24)	—	ACD-0014	HQ book X116
Oregon	90,923	yes	yes	(25)	CD#319	ACD-0024	HQ book X150
Pennsylvania	3,521,951	yes	no	(26)	CD#285 CD#286 excl. PA central	ACD-0028	HQ books: Philadelphia, X102 PA East, X110 PA West, X109 PA Central, X112
Rhode Island	217,353	yes	yes*	(27)	—	ACD-0023	*AIS book only HQ book X141
South Carolina	705,606	yes	no	(28)	CD#289 w/NC	ACD-0029 w/NC	HQ book X107
Tennessee	1,258,520	yes	no	(29)	—	ACD-0034	HQ book X115
Texas	818,579	yes	yes	—	CD#319	ACD-0043	HQ book X151
Utah Territory	86,336	yes	yes*	(30)	—	ACD-0024	*AIS book only HQ book X152
Vermont	330,551	yes	no	—	—	ACD-0041	HQ book X142
Virginia	1,225,163	yes	no	(31)	CD#319 CD#290 w/WV	ACD-0015 w/WV	HQ book X101
Washington Terr.	23,955	yes	yes	—	CD#319	ACD-0024	HQ book X153
West Virginia	442,014	yes	no	(32)	CD#319 CD#290 w/VA	ACD-0006 w/VA	HQ book X106
Wisconsin	1,054,670	yes	yes	(33)	CD#319	ACD-0039	HQ book X136
Wyoming Territory	9,118	yes	yes	—	CD#319	ACD-0024	HQ book X154

U.S. total: 38,558,371

Other 1870 Published Census Indexes:

1 Census indexes published by AIS/Brøderbund typically include the surname and given name of a head of household, a name of a county and subdistrict of residence, and a reference to a page number on the microfilmed census schedules. However, the 1870 statewide census indexes prepared by Heritage Quest include a surname, given name, age, sex, race, and birthplace for each head of household, all males over 50 years old, and all females over 70 years old, plus any person in a household with a different surname than the head of house. The residence for each person is broken

down by county and subdistrict, such as a town, village, or post office. In addition, the microfilm series, roll number, and page number are indicated for each person in the index. Heritage Quest recently developed the Family Quest Archives™ Index CDs, which make it possible for more comprehensive searching of this added information, e.g., searching a database for all persons with a specific surname, then by a person's age, sex, race, or place of birth. The use of wild card searching is also possible, such as * or ? characters replacing one or more letters. Heritage Quest's Family Quest Archives™ CDs are indicated in a separate column in the 1870 table.

2. In the late 1930s, the WPA produced a card index to the 1870 census names for twenty-five Alabama counties. Counties NOT included were Cherokee, Cleburne, Coffee, Covington, Fayette, Franklin, Sanford (now Lamar), Limestone, Marion, Morgan, and Winston counties. All other AL counties were included. The card index was microfilmed and is now available at the FHL in Salt Lake City.

3. The U.S. purchased Alaska from Russia in 1867, but it did not become organized as a territory until 1912. For the 1870 census, a few residents were counted by the military but no names were recorded. No official federal census was taken there until 1880. Apparently, AIS produced lists of residents from a few villages of Alaska (a total of 1,240 names) and incorrectly called it the "1870 Census of Alaska Territory." These names were included on Brøderbund's CD#319.

4. An extract of the 1870 Arkansas census names, listed in family order, was compiled in the 1970s by Mrs. Leister E. Presley of Searcy, Ark. A microfilm copy of the typescript is at the FHL in Salt Lake City.

5. A research guide to Brøderbund CD-ROMs says there are 73,087 entries for 1870 Colorado Territory on CD#319. However, according to census reports, the entire territory in 1870 had a total population of 39,864 people. The possibility exists that AIS included the names from an 1870 census of miners taken by the territory in 1870, which may account for the larger number of entries. Meanwhile, an alternate 1870 Colorado Territory census index was compiled by the Weld County Genealogical Society in 1977; and a microfilmed copy is at the FHL in Salt Lake City.

6. The counties that were later part of North Dakota and South Dakota were indexed by AIS in separate publications for each state — though neither became states until 1889. In the 1870 and 1880 censuses, they were part of Dakota Territory. The numbers given for 1870 North and South Dakota add up to 75,962

entries supposedly on CD#319. However, since the entire Dakota Territory in 1870 had a population of 14,181 people, according to census reports, something is clearly wrong with their figures.

7. An alternate 1870 Delaware census index was compiled by Bryan Lee Dilts (Index Publishing, 1985).

8. An alternate 1870 District of Columbia census index was compiled by Bryan Lee Dilts (Index Publishing, 1985).

9. An "every-name" 1870 Florida census index was compiled by Bryan Lee Dilts (Index Publishing, 1984).

10. A complete 1870 Georgia census index was published in 1991 by Precision Indexing/AGLL, Inc. and licensed to Brøderbund in 1995, who converted it to CD-ROM as CD#291. The AGLL index was not repeated on CD#319. CD#291 has 334,000 entries and includes all Georgia counties. No AIS statewide index in book form was prepared for Georgia 1870; however, Brøderbund's CD#319 includes AIS indexes prepared for Chatham, Fulton, and Richmond counties with a total of 37,342 names. Meanwhile, Heritage Quest released a new version of Georgia and Florida 1870 as ACD-0021.

11. There are supposedly 47,011 names from 1870 Idaho Territory included on CD#319. However, there is something wrong with this figure—since the entire territory in 1870 had a population of only 14,999. Fortunately, researchers should know that an "every-name" 1870 Idaho Territory census index was compiled by the Idaho Genealogical Society in 1973. The original is at the Idaho State Library in Boise, and a microfilm copy is at the FHL in Salt Lake City.

12. An AIS census index for 1870 Cook County is included on Brøderbund's CD#319. In addition, a Chicago/Cook County census was published by Precision Indexing/ AGLL, Inc. in 1990 that was then licensed to Brøderbund, who converted it to CD-ROM along with the cities of Baltimore and St. Louis. AGLL's census list has 121,500 Chigaco/Cook County entries on Brøderbund's CD#288. The Brøderbund CD#319 has 121,000 plus entries from the AIS Cook County index, but does not include AGLL's alternate name list from CD#288. Meanwhile, Heritage Quest has completed the census index for the entire state of Illinois 1870, which is ACD-0013.

13. CD#319 includes 44,242 entries for "Marion County," Indiana, which apparently came from the AIS index printed in 1991. However, the AIS index book was for the 1870 city of Indianapolis only, which is within Marion County, but not for the entire

population of Marion County. In addition to Heritage Quest's statewide index to Indiana 1870, several counties have been indexed separately by various historical and genealogical groups. Available at the Indiana State Library are countywide 1870 census indexes for the following counties: Adams, Boone, Hancock, Jefferson, Kosciusko, LaPorte, Miami, Orange (partial), Owen, Pike, Porter, Posey, Ripley, Scott, Shelby, Tipton, Vigo, Wabash, and Warrick. Another publication for Indiana is "Index to Blacks, Mulattos, and Indians in the 1870 Indiana Census," compiled by Audrey Clare Werle. Index cards for this index are found at the Indiana State Library, and a microfilm copy is at the FHL in Salt Lake City.

14. CD#319 includes 614 entries for Cumberland County, Maine. No AIS statewide census index exists for 1870 Maine, and the source of the names for Brøderbund's CD is not known. However, researchers need to know that Maine census indexes for 1850, 1860, and 1870 are at the Maine Division of Vital Statistics, Augusta, ME and were filmed by the FHL in Salt Lake City. In addition, the Heritage Quest statewide Maine 1870 index is on ACD-0041.

15. An early census index for Maryland 1870 was for Baltimore City/County, prepared by Precision Indexing/AGLL, Inc. This index was licensed to Brøderbund in 1995, who converted it to CD-ROM along with the cities of Chicago and St. Louis as CD#288. The Baltimore names are not included on Brøderbund's CD#319 for 1870 censuses. Meanwhile, a printed version of the Baltimore 1870 City/County census index was published by AGLL, Inc. in 1997; and the entire state was published by Heritage Quest as ACD-0016.

16. An 1870 Massachusetts census index was released in 1997 by Brøderbund as CD#284, and another version of the entire state was indexed by Heritage Quest as ACD-0042.

17. A statewide 1870 Michigan heads-of-household census index exists (Lansing, MI: Library of Michigan, 1991) and a copy is at the FHL in Salt Lake City.

18. A statewide 1870 Nebraska heads-of-household census index was compiled by E. Evelyn Cox (Ellensburg, WA: Ancestree, 1980), a copy of which is at the FHL in Salt Lake City.

19. A statewide 1870 Nevada heads-of-household census index was compiled by volunteers of the Las Vegas Family History Center in 1979. A microfilm copy is at the FHL in Salt Lake City.

20. AIS recently printed 1870 indexes for Essex, Passaic, and Mercer Counties, plus Jersey City and Hoboken city. These recent AIS indexes do not appear on Brøderbund's CD#319. The Heritage Quest statewide index to 1870 New Jersey appears on ACD-0033.

21. See the 1965 U.S. Government publication, "Territory of New Mexico and Territory of Arizona: Excerpts from the Federal Census of 1860 for Arizona County in the Territory of New Mexico, the special federal census for Arizona Territory in 1864, and the Arizona Territory Federal Census for 1870," a copy of which is on film at the FHL in Salt Lake City.

22. Heritage Quest's first printed census index for New York 1870 was for the current counties of greater New York City: New York (which included today's Bronx County in 1870), Kings, Queens (which included today's Nassau County in 1870), and Richmond County (Staten Island); plus the remainder of Long Island (Suffolk County). An earlier printed index was prepared by Precision Indexing/AGLL, Inc. in 1989 as "Long Island, New York." The first printed index included Richmond County but did not include New York County. In 1995, the 1870 New York City/County census index was completed by Precision Indexing and all the greater New York City counties were then combined and licensed to Brøderbund in 1995, who converted it to CD-ROM as CD#287. Meanwhile, an 1870 census index to the entire state of New York was released by Heritage Quest as ACD-0018.

23. A heads-of-household 1870 North Carolina census index was prepared by Precision Indexing/AGLL, Inc. in 1989. This index was licensed to Brøderbund in 1995, who converted it to CD-ROM along with 1870 South Carolina as CD#289. Precision Indexing's 1870 North Carolina names are not included on Brøderbund's CD#319, which includes the AIS 1870 North Carolina index. Meanwhile, Heritage Quest has released a new ACD-0029 which includes South Carolina on the same disk.

24. The AIS 1870 printed census index is for Stark, Summit, and Lucas Counties; plus the cities of Cleveland, Columbus, Dayton, and Toledo; but the names do not appear on any Brøderbund CD-ROM publication. In addition, a census index was compiled by Pamela Miller and Richard Rees (San Francisco: Egeon Enterprises, 1988). An index for Warren County, Ohio, was compiled in 1993 by Ellen Van Houten and Florence Cole (Address in 1993: 9500 Creekside Dr., Cleveland, OH 45140). Meanwhile, Heritage Quest's CD-ROM census index for the entire state of Ohio 1870 was released as ACD-0014.

25. An alternate 1870 Oregon census index was compiled by Bryan Lee Dilts (Index Publishing, c1985).

26. An 1870 census index for about 3/4ths of the heads of household in the state of Pennsylvania was published in 1989 by Precision Indexing, a division of AGLL, Inc., in three sets, comprising seven printed volumes: Philadelphia, Pennsylvania East, and Pennsylvania West. The 4th set (PA Central) was released in 1997, completing the 1870 PA census for the entire state. The data for the first three sets of the PA 1870 index was licensed to Brøderbund in 1995, who converted the data into two (2) CD-ROM publications: "1870 PA West" (CD#285) and "1870 PA East" (CD#286), which includes the city of Philadelphia. Counties included in the 4th set by Precision Indexing (and not part of either CD#285 or CD#286) are the central Pennsylvania counties of Adams, Bradford, Centre, Clinton, Columbia, Cumberland, Franklin, Fulton, Huntingdon, Juniata, Lycoming, Miffin, Montour, Northumberland, Perry, Potter, Snyder, Sullivan, Tioga, Union, and York. Meanwhile, Heritage Quest has released the 1870 census index for the entire state of Pennsylvania as ACD-0028.

27. An alternate 1870 Rhode Island census index was compiled by Bryan Lee Dilts (Index Publishing, c1985).

28. A heads-of-household 1870 South Carolina census index was prepared by Precision Indexing/AGLL, Inc. in 1989. This index was licensed to Brøderbund in 1995, who converted it to CD-ROM along with 1870 North Carolina as CD#289. Precision Indexing's 1870 South Carolina names are not included on Brøderbund's CD#319. Meanwhile, Heritage Quest has released the 1870 census index for both North and South Carolina as ACD-0029.

29. An 1870 Tennessee printed census index was compiled by Byron Sistler and Associates in 1985. Meanwhile, Heritage Quest has released its version of the 1870 Tennessee census index as ACD-0034.

30. A printed 1870 AIS index exists for Utah, but the data is apparently not included on CD#319. Meanwhile, Heritage Quest has released its statewide index to 1870 Utah as ACD-0024, which includes several western states.

31. An index to all 1870 Virginia counties is supposed to be included on CD#319; however, there is no known AIS printed index to VA 1870, and the source of the data is unknown. In 1989, Precision Indexing/AGLL prepared an 1870 Virginia census index, and in 1995 it was licensed to Brøderbund, who converted it to CD-ROM along with West Virginia as CD#290. The Brøderbund CD#319 does not include the names from CD#290. Meanwhile, Heritage Quest has released ACD-0015 which includes Virginia and West Virginia.

32. In 1990, Precision Indexing, AGLL prepared an 1870 West Virginia census index; and in 1995 it was licensed to Brøderbund, who converted it to CD-ROM along with the Virginia 1870 census index as CD#290. The Brøderbund CD#319 does not include the names from CD#290. Meanwhile, Heritage Quest has released ACD-0015 which includes West Virginia and Virginia.

33. An 1870 Wisconsin census index to the state copy of the federal census was prepared by the Wisconsin State Historical Society, and a microfilmed version is at the Family History Library in Salt Lake City. The state copy differs from the federal copy often, and the volume and page numbers do not always agree with each other. Researchers comparing the state copy with the federal copy will find many differences, including different name spellings, omissions, etc., since the federal copy was made from the state copy and transcription errors were common. Meanwhile, Heritage Quest has released a statewide census index to the 1870 Wisconsin census as ACD-0039.

34. The original 1870 census schedules for Minnesota were involved in the January 1921 fire in the Commerce Building in Washington, DC. The destroyed schedules pertained to counties with names running alphabetically from Aitkin to Sibley. The surviving counties, Stearns, Steele, Stevens, St. Louis, Todd, Wabasha, Wadena, Waseca, Washington, Watonwan, Wilkin, Winona, and Wright counties, were microfilmed as series M-593, rolls 716 thru 719. The National Archives obtained a state copy of the entire Minnesota 1870 census schedules from the Minnesota State Historical Society, and this latter set was microfilmed as series T-132 (13 rolls). The AIS printed census index for Minnesota 1870 was taken from the federal set, since the index omits the counties of Aitkin through Sibley. As a result, the Minnesota names on CD#319 are from Stearns through Wright counties only. See 1860, note 26, for information about the 1860 Minnesota state copy, which applies to 1870 as well. Meanwhile, Heritage Quest has released a statewide census index for 1870 Minnesota as ACD-0040.

1880 Federal Census

General Information: One new state was admitted to the Union between 1870 and 1880 (Colorado in 1876) bringing the total to thirty-eight states. Eight territories were enumerated: Arizona, Dakota, Idaho, Montana, New Mexico, Utah, Washington, and Wyoming territories. Unorganized Alaska was enumerated, but the "Indian Territory" was not enumerated for non-Indians. Unlike any previous censuses, after microfilming, the original 1880 census schedules for several states were transferred from the National Archives to various state archives, state libraries, or universities libraries. Only the original 1880 schedules for Pennsylvania remain at the National Archives. Several statewide 1880 originals were transferred to the National Society Daughters of the American Revolution in Washington, DC. They are: Alaska Territory, Arizona Territory, Connecticut, Iowa, Mississippi, Missouri, Nebraska, New Hampshire, New Mexico Territory, and Rhode Island.

Content: The 1880 census schedules listed the name of every person in a household with a census day of 1 June 1880. The categories included the following for each person: name; age as of the census day; month of birth if born during the year; relationship to the head of house; name of street and number of house; sex; color; birthplace; occupation; marital

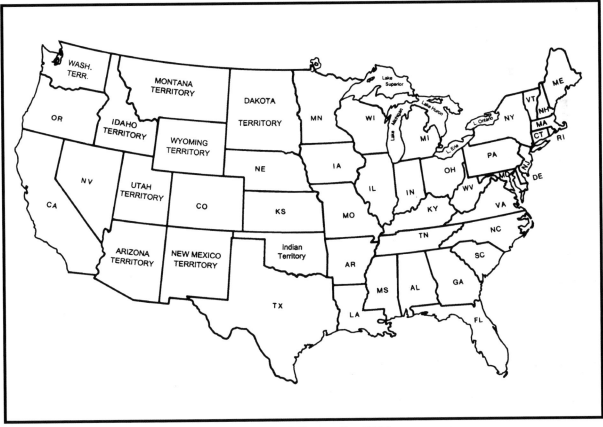

The United States in 1880

status; whether married within the previous year; whether temporarily or permanently disabled; whether crippled, maimed, or deformed; time unemployed during the census year; whether deaf, dumb, blind, or insane; whether able to read or write; birthplace of father and mother; and whether the person attended school within the previous year.

1880 Soundex Index: Soon after the creation of the Social Security Administration in 1935, clerical workers from the Works Progress Administration (WPA) were called upon to create an index to the 1880 census. A special system of coding names was created, called "Soundex." 3" x 5" cards were prepared for each household which included children ten years old or younger. Older children were not indexed, nor were persons living alone, or any household with no children. A person ten or under in 1880 would have been born between 1869 and 1880. The same person in 1935 would have been about 55 to 65 years old. The WPA Soundex index was prepared for the purpose of confirming a person's age after he or she applied for Social Security benefits in the mid to late 1930s. The information on the Soundex index cards was extracted from the full census schedules and included the full name, age, and birthplace for a head of household, and for any other person living in the household, along with a relationship to the head of household. A citation to the original census schedules—which were bound into large books—indicated a state, county, volume, enumeration district, page, and line from which the family names were extracted. Each head of household's surname was given a Soundex code, and the cards were then arranged in alphabetical order by the Soundex code number and after that by the first name of the head of the household. After the 1880 census and 1880 Soundex cards were microfilmed in the 1940s, the need for knowing the volume number was eliminated since the census schedules were microfilmed in numerical order by Enumeration District. Therefore, the pertinent information one needs from the 1880 Soundex index is the state, county, E.D. number, and page number to find a family in the census schedules.

1880 U.S. Census Indexes

1880 State or Territory	State Population	Census & Soundex exists?	AIS book Index?	Other book Index	Brøderbund CD#	Comments
Alabama	1,262,505	yes	no	—	—	
Alaska area	33,426	yes	no	—	CD#320	1,316 names, source unknown
Arizona Territory	40,440	yes	yes	(1)	CD#320	
Arkansas	802,525	yes	no	—	—	
California	864,694	yes	no	—	—	
Colorado	194,327	yes	yes	—	CD#320	
Connecticut	622,700	yes	no	—	—	
Dakota Territory	135,177	yes	no	—	—	

1880 State or Territory	State Population	Census & Soundex exists?	AIS book Index?	Other book Index	Brøderbund CD#	Comments
North Dakota area	36,909	—	yes	—	CD#320	North Dakota counties
South Dakota area	98,268	—	yes	—	CD#320	South Dakota counties
Delaware	146,608	yes	no	—	—	
District of Columbia	177,624	yes	no	—	—	
Florida	269,493	yes	no	(2)	—	
Georgia	1,542,180	yes (3)	no	—	—	
Idaho Territory	32,610	yes (4)	yes*	—	—	* an "every-name" index
Illinois	3,077,871	yes	no	(5)	CD#320	Cook County only, source unknown
Indiana	1,978,301	yes	no	(6)	—	
Iowa	1,624,615	yes	no	—	—	
Kansas	996,096	yes	no	—	—	
Kentucky	1,648,690	yes	no	—	—	
Louisiana	939,943	yes	no	—	—	
Maine	648,936	yes	no	—	—	
Maryland	934,946	yes	no	—	—	
Massachusetts	1,783,085	yes	no	—	—	
Minnesota	780,773	yes	yes (7)	—	—	several counties missing
Mississippi	1,131,597	yes	no	—	—	
Missouri	2,168,380	yes	no	—	—	
Montana Territory	39,159	yes	no	—	—	
Nebraska	452,402	yes	no	—	—	
Nevada	62,266	yes	yes	—	CD#320	
New Hampshire	346,991	yes	no	—	—	
New Jersey	1,131,116	yes	no	—	—	
New Mexico Territory	119,565	yes	no	—	—	
New York	5,082,871	yes	no	—	—	see note 11
North Carolina	1,399,750	yes	no	—	—	
Ohio	3,198,062	yes	no	(8)	CD#20	HQ Book X930
Oregon	174,768	yes	no	—	—	

1880 State or Territory	State Population	Census & Soundex exists?	AIS book Index?	Other book Index	Brøderbund CD#	Comments
Pennsylvania	4,282,891	yes	no	—	—	
Rhode Island	276,531	yes	no	—	—	
South Carolina	995,577	yes	no	—	—	
Tennessee	1,542,359	yes	no	—	—	
Texas	1,591,749	yes	yes	—	CD#320	
Utah Territory	143,963	yes	yes	(9)		names not on any CD
Vermont	332,286	yes	no	—	—	
Virginia	1,512,565	yes	no	—	—	
Washington Territory	75,116	yes	no	—	CD#320	an "every-name" index
West Virginia	618,457	yes	no	(10)	—	
Wisconsin	1,315,497	yes	no	—	—	
Wyoming Territory	20,789	yes	yes	—	CD#320	

U.S. total: 50,189,209

Other 1880 Published Census Indexes:

1. An 1880 Arizona Territorial census index was compiled by the Southern Arizona Genealogical Society in 1970.

2. An index to *Florida's Unfortunate: the 1880 census of Defective, Dependent, and Delinquent Classes* was compiled by Donna Rachel Mills in 1993.

3. The original 1880 Soundex cards for the entire state of Georgia are located at the Gwinnett Historical Society in Lawrenceville, Georgia. The staff will conduct brief "look up" services. Contact them at 21 N. Clayton St., zip 30245. Phone: (770) 822-5174. See also *Lists of Persons Enumerated in the 1880 Federal Census for Georgia* at the Georgia State Archives, which indexes Crawford and Franklin Counties only.

4. The original 1880 Soundex cards for Idaho are found at the Idaho Historical Society/State Library in Boise.

5. The National Archives' microfilmed Soundex cards for the 1880 Illinois census omitted names coded O-200 to O-240. Photocopies of the missing cards were indexed by Nancy Frederick in 1981, and a microfiche copy of her work is available at the FHL in Salt Lake City.

6. See *The Dutch in the Indiana 1880 Census*, extracted and published by Robert Swierenga in 1994. See also *Index to Blacks, Mulattos, and Indians in the 1880 Census*, for which a card index is at the Indiana State Library in Indianapolis.

7. An 1880 Minnesota "every-name" printed index was published by AIS; however, several counties of Minnesota were omitted (Lincoln to Redwood County). This 1880 name list does not appear on Brøderbund's CD#320.

8. An 1880 Ohio Census Index was compiled by the Ohio Genealogical Society. This printed index was reformatted and published in 1991 by Precision Indexing/AGLL, Inc.; and an electronic version was licensed to Brøderbund, who published the 1880 Ohio index as CD#20.

9. Besides the AIS 1880 Utah Territorial index, an 1880 Utah Territory Census Index was compiled by the BYU Research Center. Unfortunately, no name lists for the 1880 Utah census appear on any CD-ROM publication.

10. An *1880 Census of West Virginia Compiled Alphabetically by Counties* was created by William A. Marsh (Parsons, WV: McClain Printing Co., 1979-1993). Volume 14 is a name

index for all counties. The families in each county are arranged in alphabetical order by the head of house; but the family groupings are retained as they were shown on the census schedules, along with age, birthplace, birthplace of parents, etc. for each person. This index is an outstanding piece of work, a unique tool for researchers using the West Virginia 1880 census.

11. Brøderbund's Resource Guide indicates that CD#320 contains names from the 1880 New York census. As it turns out, ONE person from Montgomery County and TWO persons from Onondaga county are all that are listed. (If someone purchased a copy of CD#320 based on the label's statement that it included 1880 census entries for New York, they would be grossly misled.)

Location of 1880 Census Originals

The census originals, 1790-1870, remain in Washington, D.C. at the National Archives. After they were microfilmed in the 1940s, the original 1900 through 1920 censuses were destroyed. However, in 1956 the National Archives transferred the original 1880 censuses to state archives, state libraries, historical societies, university libraries, or other repositories willing to take them. This was the only census which was handled in this way. Although the original 1880 census schedules are said to be very fragile, a set of

original manuscript volumes acts as a better alternate than the microfilmed version. In many cases, the microfilmed copies may be unreadable; but the original documents can be viewed in person for confirmation of the census data if a genealogist is willing to visit a repository where the originals are located.

The states for which the 1880 census schedules are extant, the number of state volumes transferred, and the repository holding original 1880 census schedules are listed below:

State	Volumes	Repository holding original 1880 census schedules
Alabama	23	Dept. of Archives and History, Montgomery, AL
Arizona	1	DAR Library, Washington, DC
Arkansas	15	Arkansas History Commission, Little Rock, AR
California	18	California State Archives, Sacramento, CA
Colorado	4	Colorado Div. of State Archives and Public Records, Denver, CO
Connecticut	10	DAR Library, Washington, DC
Delaware	3	Hall of Records, Dover, DE
District of Columbia	16	Historical Society of Washington, Washington, DC
Florida	5	Florida State University, Tallahassee, FL
Georgia	26	Georgia Dept. of Archives and History, Atlanta, GA
Idaho	1	Idaho State Historical Society, Boise, ID
Illinois	59	Illinois State Archives, Springfield, IL
Indiana	38	Indiana State Library, Indianapolis, IN
Iowa	33	DAR Library, Washington, DC
Kansas	21	Kansas Genealogical Society, Dodge City, KS

State	Volumes	Repository holding original 1880 census schedules
Kentucky	30	Kentucky Dept. of Libraries and Archives, Frankfort, KY
Louisiana	17	Louisiana State University, Baton Rouge, LA
Maine	13	Maine Division of Vital Statistics, Augusta, ME
Maryland	19	Maryland State Law Library, Annapolis, MD
Massachusetts	40	Archives of the Commonwealth, Boston, MA
Michigan	31	Michigan Department of State, Lansing, MI
Minnesota	15	Minnesota Historical Society, St. Paul, MN
Mississippi	23	DAR Library, Washington, DC
Missouri	45	DAR Library, Washington, DC
Montana	1	Montana Historical Society, Helena, MT
Nebraska	10	DAR, Washington, DC
Nevada	2	Nevada State Museum, Carson City, NV
New Hampshire	3	DAR Library, Washington, DC
New Jersey	22	Rutgers University, New Brunswick, NJ
New Mexico	3	DAR Library, Washington, DC
New York	105	New York State Library, Albany, NY
North Carolina	24	North Carolina State Archives, Raleigh, NC
North Dakota	1	State Historical of North Dakota, Bismarck, ND
Ohio	68	Ohio State Museum, Columbus, OH
Oregon	4	Oregon State Library, Salem, OR
Pennsylvania	92	National Archives, Washington, DC
South Dakota	1	South Dakota Historical Society, Pierre, SD
Tennessee	35	Tennessee State Library and Archives, Nashville, TN
Texas	34	Texas State Library, Austin, TX
Utah	3	Utah State Archives, Salt Lake City, UT
Vermont	3	Law and Documents, Vermont State Library, Montpelier, VT
Virginia	32	Virginia State Library, Richmond, VA
Washington	2	Washington State Library, Olympia, WA
West Virginia	14	West Virginia Historical Society, Charleston, WV
Wisconsin	32	State Historical Society of Wisconsin, Madison, WI
Wyoming	1	Wyoming State Archives, Cheyenne, WY

1885 Censuses Taken With Federal Assistance

General Information: Congress allowed any state or territory to take a census in 1885 and have the federal government pay for part of the expense. Only five states or territories took up the government's offer. The 1885 census followed the same format as the 1880 census schedules, except that the names usually give an initial letter instead of a first name for a person.

Those federal copies of the 1885 census that have been micro-filmed include population sched-ules (list of inhabitants), inter-filed with other schedules, such as agriculture schedules (lists of farmers and farm products), manufacturer schedules (lists of companies, description of businesses, etc.), and mortality schedules (lists of persons who died within the previous twelve months).

1885 Census Indexes

State or Territory w/1885 census	Federal copy exists?	State copy exists?	Book index?	
Colorado	yes	yes	no	see note 1
Dakota Territory	partial	no	yes	see note 2
Florida	yes	no	yes	see note 3
Nebraska	yes	no	no	see note 4
New Mexico Territory	yes	yes	no	see note 5

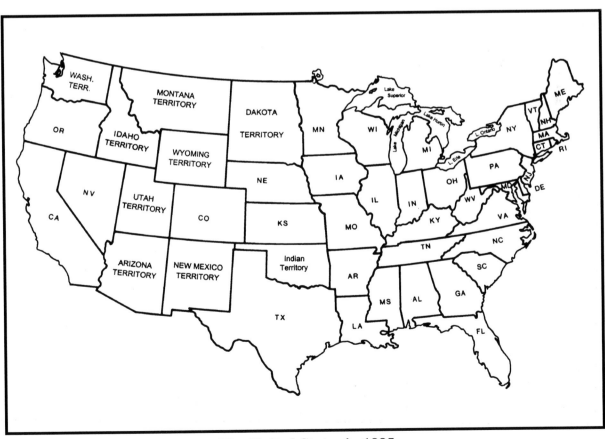

The United States in 1885

1885 Notes:

1. The state copy of the Colorado 1885 census is located at the Colorado State Archives. The federal copy is at the National Archives and was microfilmed as series M158 (8 rolls). The federal copy is missing Fremont and Garfield counties, while the state copy has Fremont, but is missing Garfield and eighteen other counties.

2. The Dakota Territorial 1885 census survives for just 37 of the 132 counties that existed in 1885, 17 in the present-day North Dakota portion and 20 in the present-day South Dakota portion. There are AIS printed indexes to the 1885 Dakota census separated into North and South Dakota, even though neither became a state until 1889. The surviving 1885 counties for present-day North Dakota are Allred, Bowman, Buford, Dunn, McIntosh, McKenzie, Mercer, Mountrail, Oliver, Renville, Stanton, Towner, Villard, Wallace, Ward, Wells, and Wynn. The surviving 1885 counties of present-day South Dakota are Beadle, Butte, Charles Mix, Edmunds, Fall River, Faulk, Hand, Hanson, Hutchinson, Hyde, Lake, Lincoln, Marshall, McPherson, Moody, Roberts, Sanborn, Spink, Stanley, and Turner. The original manuscripts for all surviving North Dakota counties are located today at the State Historical Society of North Dakota, which reproduced the 1885 census lists in *Collections of the State Historical Society of North Dakota* 4 (1913):338-448, which includes a name index to all enumerated persons as part of the general index to the 1913 volume. The South Dakota State Historical Society holds the 1885 original manuscripts for surviving South Dakota counties. These were microfilmed by the National Archives as series GR27, 3 rolls. (Rolls 4 and 5 of that same series include an 1895 state census taken in South Dakota.)

3. The Florida State Archives reported having no state manuscript of the 1885 census, just the microfilmed federal copy (microfilm series M845, 14 rolls). Missing from the 1885 Florida census are Alachua, Clay, Columbia, and Nassau counties. An index to the 1885 Florida census was compiled by William and Patricia Martin of Miami, Florida, in 1991.

4. The federal copy of the Nebraska 1885 census was microfilmed by the National Archives as series M352 (56 rolls). Missing are Blaine and Chase counties.

5. The federal copy of the New Mexico 1885 census (microfilm series M846, 6 rolls) is complete for all counties. The state copy microfilmed at the University of New Mexico - Albuquerque is missing Bernalillo, Rio Arriba, Santa Fe, and San Miguel counties.

1890 Federal Census Schedules and Union Veterans' Census Indexes

General Information: Six new states were added to the Union between 1880 and 1890: Montana, North Dakota, South Dakota, and Washington, all in 1889; plus Idaho and Wyoming in 1890, bringing the total to forty-four states. In 1889, Oklahoma Territory was created but represented only a part of the present-day state, as Indian tribal areas made up the rest of that area. In addition, the territories of Arizona, New Mexico, and Utah were enumerated in 1890, as was unorganized Alaska.

Over 99 percent of the 1890 population schedules were destroyed in a fire which took place in January 1921 at the Commerce Building in Washington, D.C. Of the 62,979,766 persons enumerated in 1890, a total of 6,160 names could be extracted from the surviving schedules. These names were all indexed and microfilmed by the National Archives as Series M496 on two rolls of film. In addition, a special census listing was extracted from the population schedules for surviving Union soldiers, sailors, and marines, (or their widows). Of the forty-nine states and territories enumerated in 1890, sixteen of the states' Union veterans' schedules were apparently lost in the fire, as were about half of the names for Kentucky. See the *Index to Surviving 1890 Population Schedules and Register of Film Numbers to the Special Census of Union Veterans*, compiled by Ken Nelson in

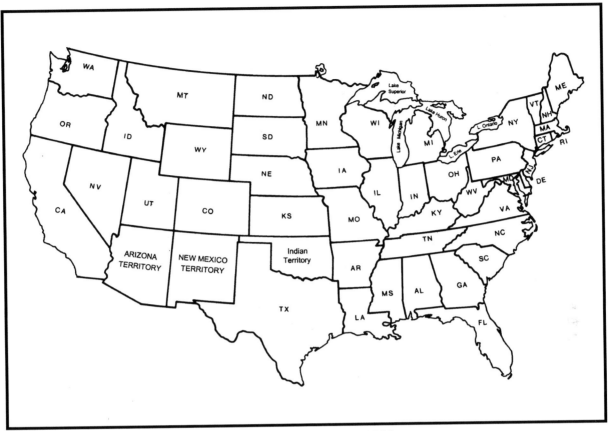

The United States in 1890

1991, which is an unpublished 177-page typescript available at the FHL in Salt Lake City and through interlibrary loan at the various Family History Centers across the country. The index includes all 6,100 surviving names, plus a listing and film numbers of all the surviving Union Veterans' schedules for 1890. In addition, an AIS printed index to the 6,160 names was published. The surviving fragments of 1890 population schedules came from the following states and subdistricts:

Alabama: Perry County (Perryville Beat No. 11 and Severe Beat No. 8).

District of Columbia: Dwellings on "Q" St., "S" St., "R" St., 13th St., 14th St., 15th St., Riggs St., and Johnson Ave.

Georgia: Muscogee County (Columbus).

Illinois: McDonough County (Mound Twp).

Minnesota: Wright County (Rockford).

New Jersey: Hudson County (Jersey City).

New York: Westchester County (Eastchester); Suffolk County (Brookhaven Twp).

North Carolina: Gaston County (So. Point Twp and River Bend Twp); Cleveland County (Twp No. 2).

Ohio: Hamilton County (Cincinnati) and Clinton County (Wayne Twp).

South Dakota: Union County (Jefferson Twp).

Texas: Ellis County (J.P. #6, Mountain Peak, and Ovilla Precinct); Hood County (Precinct #5); Rusk County (Precinct #6, and J.P. #7); Trinity County (Trinity Town, and Precinct #2); and Kaufman County (Kaufman).

Content of the schedules: Unlike any earlier census, the 1890 format was one sheet for one household. The detailed information captured for every household was extensive, including the address of the house; the number of persons in the household; each individual by name; whether a soldier, sailor, or marine during the Civil War and whether Union or Confederate, or whether the widow of a veteran; relationship to head of family; race; sex; age; marital status; whether married during the previous year; if a mother, mother of how many children, and how many living; place of birth of the individual and his/her father and mother; if foreign born, how many years in the U.S.; whether naturalized or in the process of naturalization; a profession, trade, or occupation; the number of months unemployed during the previous year; ability to read and write; ability to speak English, if not, language or dialect spoken; whether suffering from an acute or chronic disease, if so, name of disease and length of time afflicted; whether defective in mind, sight, hearing, or speech, or whether crippled, maimed, or deformed, with the name of defect; whether a prisoner, convict, homeless child, or pauper; whether the home was rented or owned by the head or other member of the family, and whether it was mortgaged; whether a farmer, and if so, whether the farm was rented or owned; and if mortgaged, the post office address of the owner.

Content of 1890 Union Veterans' Census: The schedules listed the name of each soldier, sailor, marine, or widow of a veteran in a household; the veteran's rank; company; regiment or vessel; dates of enlistment and discharge; length of service in years, months, and days; post office address; nature of disability, if any; and remarks.

1890 Census Indexes

1890 State or Territory	State Population	Surviving Union Vet. census?	AIS Vet. book Index?	Other Vet. book Index	1890 census	Comments
Alabama	1,513,401	no	no	—	—	
Alaska area	32,052	no	no	—	—	
Arizona Territory	88,243	no	no	—	—	
Arkansas	1,128,211	no	no	—	—	
California	1,213,398	no	no	—	—	
Colorado	413,249	no	no	—	—	
Connecticut	746,258	no	no	—	—	
Delaware	168,493	no	no	—	—	
Georgia	1,837,353	no	no	—	(1)	

1890 State or Territory	State Population	Surviving Union Vet. census?	AIS Vet. book Index?	Other Vet. book Index	1890 census	Comments
Idaho	88,548	no	no	—	—	
Illinois	3,837,352	no	no	—	—	
Indiana	2,192,404	no	no	—	—	
Iowa	1,912,297	no	no	—	—	
Kansas	1,428,108	no	no	—	—	
Kentucky	1,858,635	partial	yes	—	—	
Louisiana	1,118,588	yes	yes	—	(22)	
Maine	661,086	yes	no	(2)	—	
Maryland	1,042,390	yes	yes	(3)	—	
Massachusetts	2,238,947	yes	no	(4)	—	
Michigan	2,093,890	yes	no	(5)	—	
Minnesota	1,310,283	yes	no	(6)	—	
Mississippi	1,289,600	yes	yes	(7)	—	
Missouri	2,679,185	yes	no	(8)	—	
Montana	142,924	yes	yes	—	—	
Nebraska	1,062,656	yes	yes	—	—	
Nevada	47,355	yes	yes	—	—	
New Hampshire	376,530	yes	yes	—	—	
New Jersey	1,444,933	yes	yes	—	—	
New Mexico Territory	160,282	yes	yes	—	—	
New York	6,003,174	yes	no	(9)	—	
North Carolina	1,617,949	yes	yes	(10)	—	
North Dakota	190,282	yes	yes	(11)	—	
Ohio	3,672,329	yes	no	—	—	
Oklahoma Territory	258,657	yes	yes*	(12)	(13)	* includes Indian Territory
Oregon	317,704	yes	no	—	—	(14)
Pennsylvania	5,258,113	yes	no	—	—	
Rhode Island	345,506	yes	yes	—	—	
South Carolina	1,151,149	yes	yes	—	—	

1890 State or Territory	State Population	Surviving Union Vet. census?	AIS Vet. book Index?	Other Vet. book Index	1890 census	Comments
South Dakota	345,506	yes	yes	—	—	
Tennessee	1,767,518	yes	yes	(15)	(16)	
Texas	2,235,527	yes	yes	(17)	—	
Utah Territory	210,779	yes	yes	—	—	
Vermont	332,422	yes	yes	—	—	
Virginia	1,655,980	yes	yes	(18)	—	
Washington	357,232	yes	yes	—	—	
West Virginia	762,794	yes	yes	(19)	—	
Wisconsin	1,693,330	yes	yes	(20)	—	
Wyoming	62,555	yes	yes	(21)	—	
Army Forts & Prisons	—	yes	no	—	—	
U.S. Vessels & Navy Yards	—	yes	yes	—	—	

U.S. total: 62,979,766

1890 Published Censuses:

1. Washington County, Georgia, officials copied the name lists from their copy of the 1890 federal census into their county court records. These have been microfilmed. This is one of only two known counties in the United States to have made a copy of their census records for 1890. (The other was Ascension Parish, Louisiana, see item 22.)

2. An 1890 Maine Union Veterans' index was compiled by Bryan Lee Dilts (Index Publishing, 1984) and is available from Heritage Quest.

3. An 1890 Maryland Union Veterans index was compiled by Bryan Lee Dilts (Index Publishing, 1984) and is available from Heritage Quest. A partial index was compiled by Jody Powell of Roanoke, Texas in 1993, *Eastern Shore of Maryland - 1890 Census of Civil War Veterans*.

4. An 1890 Massachusetts Union Veterans' index was compiled by Bryan Lee Dilts (Index Publishing, 1984) and is available from Heritage Quest.

5. An 1890 Michigan Union Veterans' index was compiled by Bryan Lee Dilts (Index Publishing, 1985) and is available from Heritage Quest.

6. An 1890 Minnesota Union Veterans' index was compiled by Bryan Lee Dilts (Index Publishing, 1985) and is available from Heritage Quest. In addition, see *Wisconsin and Minnesota Veterans Census* compiled by Martin William Johnson in 1980.

7. An 1890 Mississippi Union Veterans' index was compiled by Bryan Lee Dilts (Index Publishing, 1985) and is available from Heritage Quest.

8. An 1890 Missouri Union Veterans' index was compiled by Bryan Lee Dilts (Index Publishing, 1985) and is available from Heritage Quest. In addition, see the 1890 Missouri Veterans' index by Harold DeGood (Columbia, MO: Missouri State Genealogical Association, 1994). A complete extraction and index was compiled by the Ozarks Genealogical Society in 1980.

9. An 1890 New York Union Veterans' index was compiled by Bryan Lee Dilts (Index Publishing, 1984) and is available from Heritage Quest.

10. An 1890 North Carolina Union Veterans' index was compiled by Sandra L. Almasy (Joliet, IL: Kensington Glen Publ. Co., 1980).

11. An 1890 North Dakota Union Veterans' index was compiled by Edith Helmer, et al. (Lewistown, MT: Lewistown Genealogical Society, 1986).

12. An 1890 Oklahoma Territory Union Veterans' index was compiled by the Oklahoma Genealogical Society in 1970. In addition, an 1890 veterans' index for *Oklahoma and Indian Territory* was compiled by Linda Norman Garrison (Lawton, OK: Southwest Oklahoma Genealogical Society, 1991).

13. Oklahoma Territory took a census in 1890 (in addition to the federal census), and there are extant 1890 census schedules for the various tribes of the Indian Territory. The original schedules for the 1890 territorial census are located at the Oklahoma Historical Society. An extraction of the 1890 Indian population was done by Joyce A. Rex (Purcell, OK: McClain County Historical Society, 1990). An 1890 Cherokee Nation census was indexed by Rosalie Wagner (Vinita, OK: Northeast Oklahoma Genealogical Society, 1986).

14. A complete extract of the 1890 Oregon Veterans' census was arranged by county, E.D., and enumerator, with veterans and enumerators indexed by Jane A. Myers (Cottage Grove, OR: Cottage Grove Genealogical Society, 1993).

15. An 1890 Tennessee Union Veterans' census extract and index was compiled by Byron Sistler in 1978. Sistler also compiled a list of *Tennesseans in Texas* from the Texas 1890 Veterans' census in 1978.

16. A substitute census for Tennessee is the 1891 state census taken for all males 21 years of age or older. This list was extracted and indexed by Sue S. Reed of Houston, Texas, in 1989.

17. An 1890 Texas Union Veterans' index was compiled by Bryan Lee Dilts (Index Publishing, 1984) and is available from Heritage Quest. A list of *Tennesseans in Texas* was compiled by Byron Sistler in 1978.

18. An 1890 Virginia Union Veterans' index was compiled by Bryan Lee Dilts (Index Publishing, 1986) and is available from Heritage Quest.

19. An 1890 Washington Union Veterans' index was compiled by Bryan Lee Dilts (Index Publishing, 1986) and is available from Heritage Quest.

20. See *Wisconsin and Minnesota Veterans' Census* compiled by Martin William Johnson in 1980.

21. An 1890 Wyoming Union Veterans' index was compiled by Bryan Lee Dilts (Index Publishing, 1986) and is available from Heritage Quest.

22. The original work copies of the 1890 population schedules for Ascension Parish, Louisiana, survives. The 20,000+ name list was extracted and indexed in book form, a copy of which can be found at the Family History Library in Salt Lake City (FHL book 976.319 X2b).

1900, 1910, and 1920 Federal Censuses

General Information: After the 1890 census, the states added to the Union were: Utah in 1896; Oklahoma in 1907; and Arizona and New Mexico in 1912, bringing the total to forty-eight states. Hawaii was annexed to the U.S. in 1898, became a territory in 1900, and a state in 1959; while Alaska became a territory in 1912 and a state in 1959.

Content: The 1900-1920 census schedules listed the name of every person in a household and included the name and age of each person; relationship to the head of house; name of street and number of house; sex; color; birthplace; occupation; marital status; number of years in the U.S.; birthplace of father and mother; whether parents were of foreign birth; whether able to read or write, speak English, or attended school within the previous year. One question unique to the 1900 census was the month of birth for a person; while the 1900 and 1910 censuses added questions for number of years in a marriage, number of children born to a mother, and number of children still living at the time of the census.

Soundex Indexes, 1900 and 1920: There are hand-entered WPA Soundex indexes for 1900 and 1920 which are complete for every head of household and for all states.

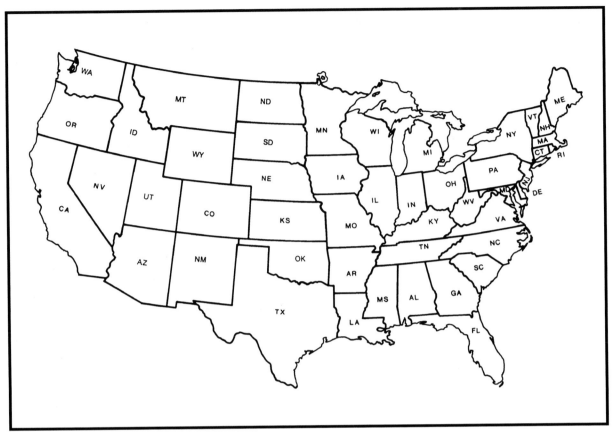

The United States in 1900-1920

Soundex/Miracode Indexes, 1910: The 1910 Soundex and Miracode indexes were compiled in 1962 for twenty-one states by the staff of the Personal Census Search section of the Bureau of the Census. The Miracode indexes were done using computers, while the Soundex indexes were done on hand-entered index cards, similar to all of the other Soundex indexes.

There have been reports that the reason only twenty-one states were indexed and others were not is that the Personal Census Search staff (now called the Age Search Group) only needed an index for those states that did not have statewide birth registration by 1910, and that these were the states that received a Miracode or Soundex index. (This explanation cannot be confirmed.

For example, California had statewide vital statistics registration by 1905, yet California has a 1910 Miracode index.)

1910 Soundex states: Alabama, Georgia, Louisiana (except Shreveport and New Orleans), Mississippi, South Carolina, Tennessee, and Texas.

1910 Miracode states: Arkansas, California, Florida, Illinois, Kansas, Kentucky, Louisiana (Shreveport and New Orleans only), Michigan, Missouri, North Carolina, Ohio, Oklahoma, Pennsylvania, Virginia, and West Virginia.

The phonetic coding method for the Miracode index is identical to the Soundex coding system. The two differ only in the citation given for a household being indexed. For each of the Miracode printouts, the citation includes the Volume number, Enumeration District Number, and Visitation Number (house number) taken from the original census schedules pages; while the 1910 Soundex cards cite the Volume Number, Enumeration District Number, and Sheet Number.

1900-1920 U.S. Census Indexes

State or Territory	1900 Population	1910 Population	1920 Population	1900 1920 Sndx?	1910 Sndx/ Mira.	Other 1900 Index	Other 1910 Index	Other 1920 Index	Comments
Alabama	1,828,697	2,138,093	2,348,174	yes	Sndx	—	—	—	
Alaska Terr. *	63,592	64,356	55,036	yes	—	—	—	—	* terr., 1912; state, 1959
Arizona Terr.*	122,931	204,354	334,162	yes	—	—	—	—	* state, 1912
Arkansas	1,311,564	1,574,449	1,752,204	yes	Mira.	—	(1)	—	
California	1,485,053	1,574,449	1,752,204	yes	Mira.	—	—	—	
Colorado	539,700	799,024	939,629	yes	—	—	—	—	
Connecticut	908,420	1,114,756	1,380,631	yes	—	—	—	—	
Delaware	184,735	202,322	223,003	yes	—	—	—	—	
Distr. Columbia	278,718	331,069	437,571	yes	—	—	—	—	
Florida	528,542	752,619	968,470	yes	Mira.	—	—	—	
Georgia	2,216,331	2,609,121	2,895,832	yes	Sndx	—	—	—	
Hawaii Territory *	154,001	191,874	255,881	yes	—	—	(2)	—	* state, 1959
Idaho	161,772	325,594	431,866	yes	—	—	(3)	—	
Illinois	4,821,550	5,638,591	6,485,280	yes	Mira.	—	—	—	
Indiana	2,516,462	2,700,876	2,930,390	yes	—	(4)	—	—	
Iowa	2,231,853	2,224,771	2,404,021	yes	—	—	—	—	
Kansas	1,470,495	1,690,949	1,769,257	yes	Mira.	—	—	—	
Kentucky	2,147,174	2,289,905	2,416,630	yes	Mira.	—	—	—	
Louisiana	1,381,625	1,656,388	1,798509	yes	both*	—	—	—	* certain cities Soundex
Maine	694,466	742,371	768,014	yes	—	—	—	—	
Maryland	1,188,044	1,295,346	1,449,661	yes	—	—	(5)	—	
Massachusetts	2,805,346	3,366,416	3,852,356	yes	—	—	—	—	
Michigan	2,420,982	2,810,173	3,668,412	yes	Mira.	—	(6)	—	
Minnesota	1,751,394	2,075,708	2,387,356	yes	—	—	—	—	

State or Territory	1900 Population	1910 Population	1920 Population	1900 1920 Sndx?	1910 Sndx/ Mira.	Other 1900 Index	Other 1910 Index	Other 1920 Index	Comments
Mississippi	1,551,270	1,797,114	1,790,618	yes	Sndx.	—	—	—	
Missouri	3,106,665	3,293,335	3,404,055	yes	Mira.	—	—	—	
Montana	243,329	376,053	548,889	yes	—	—	—	—	
Nebraska	1,066,300	1,192,214	1,296,372	yes	—	—	—	—	
Nevada	42,335	81,875	77,407	yes	—	—	(7)	—	
New Hampshire	411,588	430,572	443,083	yes	—	—	—	—	
New Jersey	1,883,669	2,537,167	3,155,900	yes	—	—	—	—	
New Mexico *	195,310	327,301	360,350	yes	—	—	—	—	* state, 1912
New York	7,268,894	9,113,614	10,385,227	yes	—	—	—	—	
North Carolina	1,893,810	2,206,287	2,559,123	yes	Mira.	—	—	—	
North Dakota	319,146	577,056	646,872	yes	—	—	—	—	
Ohio	4,157,545	4,767,121	5,759,394	yes	Mira.	—	—	—	
Oklahoma Terr.*	790,391	1,657,155	2,028,283	yes	Mira.	—	—	—	* state, 1907
Oregon	413,536	672,765	783,389	yes	—	—	—	—	
Pennsylvania	6,302,115	7,655,111	8,720017	yes	Mira.	—	—	—	
Rhode Island	428,556	542,610	604,397	yes	—	—	—	—	
South Carolina	1,340,316	1,515,400	1,683,724	yes	Sndx.	—	—	—	
South Dakota	401,570	583,888	636,547	yes	—	—	—	—	
Tennessee	2,020,616	2,184,789	2,337,885	yes	Sndx.	—	—	—	
Texas	3,048,710	3,896,542	4,663,228	yes	Sndx.	—	—	—	
Utah	276,749	373,351	449,396	yes	—	—	—	—	
Vermont	343,641	355,956	352,428	yes	—	—	—	—	
Virginia	1,854,184	2,061,612	2,309,187	yes	Mira.	—	—	—	
Washington	518,103	1,141,990	1,356,621	yes	—	—	—	—	
West Virginia	958,800	1,221,119	1,463,701	yes	Mira.	—	—	—	
Wisconsin	2,069,042	2,333,860	2,632,067	yes	—	—	—	—	
Wyoming	92,531	145,965	194,402	yes	—	—	(8)	—	

U.S. Totals: 76,212,168 92,228,496 106,021,537

1900-1920 Notes:

1. A partial substitute for the 1910 census of Arkansas is the census of Arkansas Confederate veterans taken in 1911, which was indexed by Bobbie Jones McLane (Arkansas Ancestors, 1988).

2. A 1910 printed census index for all islands of Hawaii was compiled by AIS; however, the list of names does not appear on any known CD-ROM.

3. An "every-name" 1910 Idaho census index was compiled by volunteers of the Upper Snake River Valley Family History Center and McKay Library employees of Ricks College. The index contains over 320,000 entries. A printed version was published by Precision Indexing, a division of AGLL, Inc. in 1993, and the same index was licensed to Brøderbund in 1995, which converted the index to CD-ROM as CD#335. It is now available on CD-ROM from Heritage Quest as Family Quest Archives™ Index ACD-0025.

4. See *The Dutch in the Indiana 1900 Census*, extracted and published by Robert Swierenga in 1994.

5. An index to *People of Polonia*, a listing of Polish/Americans from the 1910 Maryland census schedules was published.

6. The 1910 Michigan Miracode index for the surname Cooke/Cook was extracted and published by Quantic of Casselberry, Florida, in 1989.

7. A 1910 Nevada census index was compiled by Bryan Lee Dilts (Index Publishing, 1984) and is available from Heritage Quest.

8. A 1910 Wyoming census index was compiled by Bryan Lee Dilts (Index Publishing, 1985) and is available from Heritage Quest.

Summary

For the censuses, 1790-1920, genealogists have several alternative choices for census indexes. It is hoped that the facts concerning census indexes shown in the tables—particularly the alternate publications that are not available in any electronic format—will allow any genealogist another shot at locating an elusive ancestor.

It is widely known by genealogists that census indexes are prone to errors and omissions, due mostly to the difficult task of reading old, and sometimes illegible, handwriting found on the census pages. Rather than fault the poor indexer, who is, after all, subject to human errors, genealogists should thank the indexers—but be aware of alternative publications where another indexer may have seen the old handwriting differently.

Street Indexes to 1910 Cities

In 1984, the National Archives produced a *Cross Index to Selected City Streets and Enumeration Districts, 1910 Census*, (publication M1283) which is a typescript (fifty-one microfiche cards) available at the FHL in Salt Lake City. It is an index to the city streets for 39 U.S. cities in 1910:

Akron, OH	Chicago, IL	Elizabeth, NJ
Atlanta, GA	Cleveland, OH	Erie, PA
Baltimore, MD	Dayton, OH	Fort Wayne, IN
Brooklyn, NY	Denver, CO	Gary, IN
Canton, OH	Detroit, MI	Grand Rapids, MI
Charlotte, NC	District of Columbia	Indianapolis, IN

Kansas City, MO

Long Beach, CA

Los Angeles City and County, CA

Newark, NJ

New York City, NY (Manhattan Borough, Bronx Borough, and Richmond Borough)

Oklahoma City, OK

Omaha, NE

Patterson, NJ

Peoria, IL

Philadelphia, PA

Phoenix, AZ

Reading, PA

Richmond, VA

San Antonio, TX

San Diego, CA

San Francisco, CA

Seattle, WA

South Bend, IN

Tampa, FL

Tulsa, OK

Researchers can use this street index to determine a census Enumeration District for a known address in one of the cities. This can shorten the time needed to locate a particular family in the census schedules for certain unindexed 1910 cities.

In 1993, volunteers at the Family History Library (FHL) in Salt Lake City compiled a street index to various 1910 cities with no Miracode or Soundex index, adding cities not included in the National Archives publication above, entitled *Street Indexes to Unindexed Cities in the U.S. 1910 Federal Census*. The street indexes are for the following cities:

Boston, MA

Des Moines, IA

Minneapolis, MN

Queens Borough, New York City

The street indexes are arranged by the city and then by the street name and street numbers. It gives the page number, enumeration district, and FHL microfilm number for most addresses. The typescript is not available outside the FHL in Salt Lake City, but the microfiche version is available via interlibrary loan to the many Family History Centers across the country.

Census Research Aids

Enumeration District Descriptions: Geographic areas forming census districts were formally described in writing and used by the census takers in their door-to-door rounds. These written descriptions cover rural areas as well as towns and cities. The earliest of these descriptions which survive are for the 1830 census and continue thereafter for each decennial census. They have been microfilmed by the National Archives and are available. The earliest descriptions are not complete and are fairly sparse. By the time of the 1880 census, the Enumeration Districts are precisely defined for the numbered E.D.s for every county in all states.

Explanation of the Soundex and Miracode Index Systems

The Soundex is a filing system for surnames which reduces the sound of a name to a few hard consonants, rather than using all of the soft vowels and extra letters that may be found in the spelling of a name. The hard consonants are what causes a name to sound a certain way. All consonants are grouped into categories for letters that have a similar sound, and coded.

With the advantage of census indexes prepared by the Works Progress Administration (WPA) for the Census Bureau in the late 1930s, genealogists have partial Soundex indexes for 1880 (families with children of age ten and younger), partial Soundex and Miracode indexes for 1910 (twenty-one states total) and complete Soundex indexes (heads of household) for the 1900 and 1920 censuses. The indexes were originally hand-prepared on 3" x 5" index cards, each card showing a head of household by full name and a list of all other persons residing in a household. Persons with a different surname than the head of household usually have a separate index card, coded under their own surname, as well as the one for the household in which they were listed. Included was each person's age and nativity and a reference to the location in the census schedules where that family appears. The cards were organized by the Soundex code for the head of household's surname, then alphabetized by that person's first name. As a result, all names with the same Soundex codes are inter-filed, such as Lee, Leigh, Low, Law, Liem, or Lieh, all surnames with the Soundex code L000. But these cards were filed alphabetically by the first names of all persons with the same Soundex code. The Soundex cards were microfilmed and appear on the roll of film one card after another in Soundex code order. Therefore, the names of people are not in a strict alphabetical order, but if one knows the Soundex code and the first name of a person, it is possible to go directly to that person's index card. However, these rules were sometimes ignored; and a Soundex user should search an entire Soundex code for a first name. In some cases, Soundex codes are inter-filed and then alphabetical by first name, e.g., codes D400 through D466 are inter-filed, and then alphabetized for the entire group of codes by the first names of heads of household.

In indexing several states for the 1910 census, a slightly different method was used, called Miracode; but the principles for coding a name in both the Soundex and Miracode systems are the same.

Soundex and Miracode Coding Guide

Code	Key letters and equivalents
1	b, p, f, v
2	c, s, k, g, j, q, x, z
3	d, t
4	l
5	m, n
6	r

The letters a, e, i, o, u, y, w, and h are not coded, and the first letter of a surname is not coded. Also, any two or more letters together with the same code are coded as one letter. For example, if the letters c-s appear together (as in the name Tricse), they are coded as one letter; or if the letters c-s-k appear together (as in Coussacsk), they are coded as one letter. In both cases, the code for c-s or c-s-k would be the number 2.

Every Soundex number must be a 3-digit number. A name yielding all vowels after the first letter, such as Lee, would thus be L000. A name yielding only one code number would have two zeros added, such as Kuhne, coded as K500. And a name yielding only two code letters would have one zero added, as Ebell, coded as E140. Not more than three digits are used, so Ebelson would be coded as E142, not E1425.

The coding of a name should start with each letter from left to right. Eliminating all vowels or double letters before coding may cause an inaccurate code. For example, code the name Ebbettson in the following steps:

1. Keep the first letter "E"

2. Code the first "b" as 1

3. Ignore the second letter "b"

3. ignore the "e," a vowel

4. Code the first "t" as 3

5. Ignore the second "t"

6. Code the letter "s" as 2

Letters coded: Ebts

Soundex code: E132

An inaccurate code for the name Cousscack would occur if all double letters and vowels were removed first: Cousscack could be reduced first to Csscck, then Csck, which would give an incorrect code of C200 since the s, c, and k remained and the rule of coding multiple letters as one was used.

The correct way to code the name Cousscack is to start from left to right:

1. Keep the "C"

2. Ignore the "o," a vowel

3. Ignore the "u," a vowel

4. Code the first "s," second "s," and first "c" as one letter (2)

5. Ignore the "a," a vowel

6. Code the second "c" and "k" as one letter (2)

Letters coded: Csc-

Soundex code: C220

The Soundex coding system solves the problem of indexing names which sound alike. The example of Cousscack, would share the same code with many different spellings, all with the same basic sounds, such as Cussack, Cossack, Causich, Coosich, Cawsach, or Cooshick, all names that would code as C220.

The example of Cousscack gives another possibility: what if the name were spelled Kousscack? Because the Soundex code does not covert the first letter of a name to a code number, one must know the first letter is correct, or look for other possibilities. In this case, the code would be the same, but in the "K" section of the Soundex listings under K220. A genealogist should think of the possible variations for spelling all names. For example, Needham may be spelled Kneedham in the census. Philoman may be spelled Filoman in the census, and so on.

Coding Anomalies

In the late 1930s and early 1940s when the WPA workers were indexing the 1880, 1900, and 1920 censuses, there were some workers who did not understand the Soundex coding system completely. There are numerous examples of names being coded by one person one way and coded another way by another person. Here are some examples of these anomalies:

Lloyd, coded L430 includes the second "l", while L300 does not. Someone looking for the surname Lloyd should use both Soundex codes.

van Buren, coded as Brn- (B650). Prefixes such as "van", "Von", "Di", "le", "D", "dela", or "du" are sometimes disregarded in alphabetizing and coding. Therefore, one should look for both Brn- (B650) and Vnbr (V516) for the name van Buren.

McGee, is correctly coded as Mc (M200) because the "c" and the"g" are coded as one letter. But a coder might have interpreted Mc; separate from Gee and coded the name as Mc g (M220).

Sister Magdelaine, a nun, was usually coded as if her surname were "Sister" (S236).

Shinka-Wa-Samay, a native American, was coded as if the surname were "Shinka" (Snk—, S520), but could also have been coded as if the surname were "Samay" (Sm—, S500). A genealogist needs to investigate the possibilities of coding such a name.

Locating a Family in the Census Schedules Using the Soundex System

The Soundex index is secondary evidence, copied from the census schedules. The primary evidence is the census schedules themselves. Therefore, the primary use of the Soundex indexes is to locate a family on the pages of the census schedules. For the 1880, 1900, and 1920 Soundex indexes, each card gives the state, county, volume, enumeration district (E.D.), page number, and line number for the head of household. This is the information needed to access the exact page on which a family appears in the census schedules, right down to the line.

After each census was taken, the original census schedules were bound into books for each state. When the Soundex index cards were first created, the books had not been microfilmed; and it was necessary to know the state and volume number first. After microfilming, the need to know the volume was eliminated, since each book was microfilmed page by page in order; and often, several books were microfilmed on a single roll of film. The organization within the books was in numerical order by the enumeration districts. When the schedules were microfilmed, this order was maintained. The page numbers in the volumes were related to the enumeration district, not the volume. So, the information a genealogist needs is the state, county, the E.D. number, the page number, and finally, the line number on the page to locate a family. Capturing just the state, E.D., and page is usually sufficient to locate a family, since there are never more than fifty lines on a typical census page.

With the citation to the name of the state, county, E.D., and page number, the microfilmed census schedules can be easily found. All census schedules are organized by a microfilm series number (for the census year) and then assigned roll numbers for the states, organized generally in alphabetical order for each county. For example, if a genealogist finds a reference using a 1900 Soundex card for a family, the card indicates the State and County, plus the E.D., page, and line number where that family appears in the census schedules, say Baldwin County, Alabama. The next step is to go to the National Archives film catalog for the 1900 census and learn that the 1900 census is film series T623, and that the Baldwin County, Alabama, census schedules are on roll #1. With this roll of film on a microfilm projector, a researcher can move quickly to Baldwin County, then to the correct E.D. number, page number, and the actual line number on a page where the head of household's name is written.

Locating a Family in the Census Schedules Using the Miracode System

In the 1910 census index, only twenty-one states were indexed. Of this number, fifteen of the states were indexed using the Miracode systems, while five states used the Soundex system, plus Louisiana, which was indexed using both Miracode and Soundex. The two systems differ only in the citation to the page where a family appears in the census schedules. While the Soundex system uses the volume, enumeration district, then the page number and line number, the Miracode system refers to the volume, enumeration district, then the **visitation number**, and the line number on a page. The visitation number is the number for a house assigned in the order a census taker followed from house to house. In both the Soundex and Miracode indexes, the most important references are to the state, county, and enumeration district (E.D.), followed by the page number or visitation number, depending on whether it is a Soundex or Miracode reference.

1930 and Later Censuses

In anticipation of the 2002 release of the 1930 census, genealogists will have a much smaller Soundex index than was done for 1920. Only ten southern states were completely indexed by the WPA: Alabama, Arkansas, Florida, Georgia, Louisiana, Mississippi, North Carolina, South Carolina, Tennessee, and Virginia, plus seven counties in Kentucky and seven more in West Virginia. The 1940 and 1950 censuses have no index at all.

In reporting the 1960 census statistics, the Census Bureau employed electronic computers for the first time; but rumors abound that the stored magnetic tapes of the 1960 census are now disintegrating. It is expected that computer-generated, name indexes might be possible for the 1970 and later censuses. But, unfortunately, genealogists may have to wait until the year 2042 to find out.

Relationship Terms and Abbreviations Used in the Soundex and Miracode Indexing Systems

Adopted	Ad		Bartender	Bar
Adopted Child	Ad.Cl		Boarder	Bo
Adopted Daughter	Ad.D		Bound Girl	B.Girl
Adopted Grandchild	Ad.Gcl		Bound Boy	B.Boy
Adopted Mother	Ad.M		Boy	Boy
Adopted Son	Ad.S		Brother	B
Apprentice	Ap		Brother-in-law	Bl
Attendant	At		Butler	Bu
Assistant	Asst		Captain	Cap
Aunt	A		Chamber Maid	Cha
Aunt-in-law	Al		Child	Cl

Coachman	Coa	Great Grandmother	Ggm
Companion	Com	Great-Great-Grandfather	Gggf
Cook	Cook	Great-Great-Grandmother	Gggm
Cousin	C	Guardian	Gua
Cousin-in-law	Cil	Guest	Guest
Daughter	D	Half Sister	H.Si
Daughter-in-law	Dl	Half Brother	Hb
Day Laborer	Dla	Half Brother-in-law	Hbl
Dish Washer	Dw	Help	Help
Domestic	Dom	Herder	He
Employee	Emp	Hired Girl	H.Gi
Engineer	En	Hireling	Hlg
Farm Hand	Fa.H	Housekeeper	Hk
Farm Laborer	Fa.L	Housemaid	H.maid
Farm Worker	Fa.W	House Worker	Hw
Father	F	Husband	Husband
Father-in-law	Fl	Inmate	Inmate
Fireman	Fi	Laborer	La
First Cousin	First C	Laundry	L
Foster Brother	Fo.B	Maid	Maid
Foster Sister	Fo.Si	Manager	Man
Foster Son	Fo.S	Matron	Mat
God Child	God Cl	Mother	M
Governess	Go	Mother-in-law	Ml
Grand Child	Gcl	Nephew	N
Grand Daughter	Gd	Nephew-in-law	Nl
Grand Father	Gf	Niece	Ni
Grand Mother	GM	Niece-in-law	Nil
Grand Mother-in-law	Gml	Nurse	Nu
Grand Son	Gs	Officer	O
Grand Son-in-law	Gsl	Partner	Pa
Grand Niece	Gni	Patient	P
Great Niece	Gni	Physician	Ph
Grand Nephew	Gn	Porter	Por
Great Nephew	Gn	Principal	Pri

Prisoner .... Pr

Private .... Prv

Pupil .... Pu

Roomer .... R

Sailor .... Sa

Saleslady .... Sal

Servant .... Se

Servant's Child .... Se.Cl

Sister .... Si

Son .... S

Son-in-law .... Sl

Step Brother .... Sb

Step Brother-in-law .... Sbl

Step Child .... Scl

Step Daughter .... Sd

Step Daughter-in-law .... Sdl

Step Father .... Sf

Step Father-in-law .... Sfl

Step Granddaughter .... Sgd

Step Grandson .... Sgs

Step Mother .... Sm

Step Mother-in-law .... Sml

Step Sister .... Ssi

Step Sister-in-law .... Ssl

Step Son .... Ss

Step Son-in-law .... Ssl

Superintendent .... Su

Tenant .... Ten

Uncle .... U

Uncle-in-law .... Ul

Visitor Vi

Waiter .... Wt

Waitress .... Wai

Ward .... Ward

Warden .... Wa

Wife .... W

Workman .... Wkm

Section 3

Countywide Census Indexes

There have been many census indexes prepared by local genealogical groups or individuals, in most cases, published for one U.S. county. A review of the countywide federal census indexes that can be found at the Family History Library in Salt Lake City are shown below. These census indexes are separate from any statewide indexes described in the previous section. However, these county indexes can give a genealogical researcher an alternate compiled list of names for a particular county in the United States.

Shown below are just those states and counties for which a countywide published census index exists, with the census year and Family History Library (FHL) call number for a book or microform publication. Most of the publications identified below were gathered for a special project conducted by staff members of the Family History Library in 1986. A comprehensive review of census indexes for any other counties published since 1986 was not completed for this list.

Alabama

County	City or Township	Year	FHL Call Number
Baldwin		1860	book 976.121 X2p; film 924,431, item 2
Butler		1860	book 976.137 X2p
Colbert		1870	book 976.1 B2v, Vol. 11, pp1-3
Cullman		1880	film 1,026,261, item 1
Jefferson		1870	book 976.178 X2p
Washington		1860	book 976.1 X2p
Wilcox		1860	book 976.1 A1, No. 41

Arkansas

County	City or Township	Year	FHL Call Number
Benton		1860	book 976.7 A1, No. 91
Benton		1870	book 976.713 X2p; film #982,168, item 8
Carroll		1860	book 976.717 X2p
Clark		1860	book 976.749 X22f
Clark		1880	book 976.7 X22i

Arkansas (continued)

County	City or Township	Year	FHL Call Number
Columbia		1860	book 976.7 X22f
Columbia		1860	book 976.X22i
Conway		1860	book 976.731 X22f; 976.7 X22i
Dallas		1860	book 976.731 Xx2t
Desha		1860	book 976.785 X2d
Hempstead		1860	book 976.754 X2p
Independence		1870	book 976.726 X22t
Madison		1860	book 976.715 X2p
Madison		1870	book 976.715 X2p
Madison		1880	book 976.715 X2p
Miller		1880	book 976.756 X2s
Mississippi	Slave schedules	1860	book 976.7 A1, No. 86
Mississippi		1860	book 976.7 A1, No. 86
Newton		1850	book 976.716 X22d
Newton		1860	book 976.716 X22d
Newton		1870	book 976.716 X22d
Newton		1880	book 976.716 X22d
Newton		1900	book 976.716 X22d
Pope		1860	book 976.732 X2pa
Pope		1870	book 976.732 X2p
Pope		1880	book 976.732 X2p
Pope		1900	book 976.732 X22i
Randolph		1870	film 907,977, item 4
Sebastian		1860	book 976.736 X2s
Sevier		1860	book 976.747 X2p
Washington		1860	book 976.714 X22s
White		1860	book 976.714 X22s
Woodruff	Augusta	1880	book 976.792/A1 X2p
Yell		1860	book 976.738 X2d

California

County	City or Township	Year	FHL Call Number
Humboldt		1860	book 979.4 A1, No. 23; film 924,680
Los Angeles	Santa Ana	1870	book 979.496 B2q, Vol. 9, p. 101
San Diego		1900	book 979.498 X22w
San Luis Obispo		1870	book 929.478; film 944,282, item 13
Tulare		1860	book 979.4 A1 No. 65; film 1,036,747
Tulare		1870	book 979.4 A1 No. 66

Colorado

County	City or Township	Year	FHL Call Number
Boulder	Altoona, Boulder, Boulder Creek, & Gold Hill	1860	film 1,294,357, item 1, p. 1
Boulder		1870	film 1,294,357, item 1, p. 19
Boulder		1880	film 1,294,357, item 1, p. 55
Gunnison	Rock Creek	1880	book 978.841 X2c, pp 3-4
Gunnison	Rock Creek	1900	book 978.841 X2c, pp 7-12

Florida

County	City or Township	Year	FHL Call Number
Alachua		1830-1870	book 975.965/T1 X2b, p. 66
Hillsborough		1830-1870	book 975.965/T1 X2b, p. 79
Hillsborough	Tampa	1860	book 975.965/T1 X2b, p. 16
Hillsborough	Tampa	1870	book 975.965/T1 X2b, p. 36
Monroe		1830-1870	book 975.965/T1 X2b, p. 77

Georgia

County	City or Township	Year	FHL Call Number
Appling		1860	book 975.8784 X2m
Bleckley		1860	book 975.852 X2P; film 1,036,798, item 5
Brooks		1860	book 975.8874 X2e
Bullock		1860-1870	book 975.8766 X2p; film 1,036,726, item 12
Chatham		1860	book 975.8724 X2e
Chattahooche		1880	film 423,493
Clarke		1880	film 214,556
Carroll		1860	book 975.839 X28c
Clayton		1860	book 975.8432 X2ca
Clayton		1870	book 975.8432 X2p
Dade		1860-1880	book 975.8342 X2p
Fayette		1880	film 209,383
Glascock		1840-1880	book 975.8666 X2c; film 432,645
Heard		1860-1870	book 975.8422 X2e
Jefferson		1880	film 180,897
Jones		1850-1870	film 007,137
Newton		1880	film 325,765
Pickens		1860	book 975.852 H2t, p. 93
Pulaski		1860	book 975.852 X2p; film 1,036,798
Taliaferro		1880	film 220,569, item 3
Ware		1870	book 975.8794 X2e

Idaho

County	City or Township	Year	FHL Call Number
Oneida	Lincoln Valley	1870	book 976.6 X2p

Illinois

County	City or Township	Year	FHL Call Number
Adams		1860	book 977.344 X2e
Bond		1860	book 977.3873 X2ub
Cass		1880	book 977.3465
Christian		1880	film 986,508, item 1
Clark		1860	book 977.371 X2e
Clark		1870	book 977.371 X22s
Clay		1860	book 977.3795 X2sc
Coles		1860	book 977.372 X2p
Cook		1860	book 977.31
DeKalb		1860	book 977.328 X2f
DeWitt		1860	book 977.3685 X2p
Douglas		1860	book 977.368 X2c
DuPage		1860	book 977.324 X2r
Edwards		1860	book 977.3791 X2e
Effingham		1860	book 977.3796 X2c
Franklin		1860	book 977.394 X2ur
Franklin		1870	book 977.394 X2u
Grundy		1860	book 977.325 X2e
Hamilton		1860	book 977.395 X2p; 977.395 X2ur
Hamilton		1870	book 977.395 X28r
Hancock		1860	book 977.343 X28r
Hardin		1860	book 977.398 X2d
Iroquois		1860	book 977.364 X2f
Jo Daviess		1860	book 977.3343 X22c
Jo Daviess		1870	book 977.3343 X22i
Kane		1860	book 977.323 X2k
La Salle	Grand Rapids	1860	book 977.327/G1 X2c
Lawrence		1860	book 977.376 X2m
Lawrence		1870	book 977.376 X2sa
Logan		1860	book 977.357 X2us
McDonough		1860	book 977.342 X2us
Macon		1860	book 977.3582 X2h; 977.3582 X2u
Marion		1860	book 977.3794 X2m
Menard		1860	book 977.3555 X2us

Illinois (continued)

County	City or Township	Year	FHL Call Number
Menard		1870	book 977.3555 X2m
Montgomery		1860	book 977.382 X2m
Moultrie		1860	book 977.3675; film 1,036,844
Moultrie		1870	book 977.3675 X2p
Piatt		1860	book 977.3673 X2fe
Piatt		1870	book 977.3673 X2f
Pope		1860	book 977.3991 X2af
Pulaski		1860	book 977.3998 X2p
Richland		1860	book 977.377 X2p; film 1,033,751, item 8
St. Clair		1860	book 977.389 X2j
Scott		1860	book 977.3455 X2e
Stark		1860	book 977.3513
Stark		1870	book 977.3513 X2b
Wabash		1860	book 977.378 X2s
Wayne		1860	book 977.3792 X2be, Vol. 1-2
White		1860	book 977.396 X2sh
Winnebago		1860	book 977.331 X2j

Indiana

County	City or Township	Year	FHL Call Number
Jasper		1880	film 462,703, item 3
Jefferson		1870	book 977.213/M1 X2p
Shelby		1880	film 549,293
Vermillion	Newport and Vermillion	1860	book 977.2462/N1 H2n, p. 294
Vermillion	Newport and Vermillion	1870	book 977.2462/N1 H2n p. 301
Vermillion	Newport and Vermillion	1880	book 977.2462/N1 H2n, p. 311
Wayne		1880	film 549,294

Iowa

County	City or Township	Year	FHL Call Number
Cedar		1860	book 977.7 A1 No. 15; film 982,664, item 2
Clay		1860	book 977.715 X2p; film 1,000,026, item 7
Dallas		1860	book 977.757 V2s; film 908,874, item 2; 962,131
Fremont		1870	book 977.777 X2p; film 973,096, item 1
Union	Pleasant	1860-1870	book 977.785/P1 X2p
Union	Platte	1860	book 977.785/P2 X2p; film 538,092, item 7

Kansas

County	City or Township	Year	FHL Call Number
Davis		1870	book 978.129 X2b
Hunter		1860	book 978.189 X2p
Labette	Parsons	1880	book 978.196 P1 X2; film 982,391, item 12
Marion		1860	book 978.157 X2p
Mead		1880	book 978.1 X2p; film 1,035,840
Pottawatomie		1860	book 978.132 X2k
Salina		1870	book 978.1545 X2k
Shawnee		1860	book 978.1 A1, No. 69
Wabaunsee		1860	book 978.161 X2kt
Wichita		1880	book 978.1 X2a; film 1,035,840, item 4
Wilson		1860	book 978.1 X2
Wilson		1880	book 978.1 A1 no. 31; film 928,096, item 15

Kentucky

County	City or Township	Year	FHL Call Number
Bell		1890	book 976.9 A1, No. 210
Breckinridge		1860	book 976.9854 X2c
Breckinridge		1870	book 976.9854 X2m
Butler		1870	book 976.9755 X2p; film 982,223
Crittendon		1870	book Q976.989 X2p; film 982,051
Cumberland		1860	book 976.968 X2ps
Cumberland		1870	book 976.968 X2ps
Cumberland		1880	book 976.968 X2ps
Daviess		1870	book 976.9864 X2m
Floyd		1860	book Q976.922 X2p; film 982,223, item 9
Floyd		1870	book Q976.922 X2p; film 982,223, item 10
Green		1850-1860	book 976.9695 X2p, p. 144; film 982,245, item 2
Hardin		1870	book 976.9845 X2d
Hickman		1870	book 976.998 X2l
Hopkins		1860	film 982,131, item 1
Hopkins		1880	book 976.982 X2p; film 982,102, items 2 &3
Knott		1880	book 976.9 A1, No. 18
Letcher		1880	book 976.9 A1, No. 18
Logan		1850	book 976.976 H2m
Maggofin		1860	book Q976.9215 X2p; film 982,223, item 6
Maggofin		1870	book 976.9215 X2p; 976.9 A1, No. 44; film 924,561, item 3; 982,223, item 7.
Maggofin		1880	book 976.9 A1, No. 176

Kentucky (continued)

County	City or Township	Year	FHL Call Number
Mc Lean		1870	book 976.9 A1, No. 172
Meade		1860	book 976.9852 X2c
Metcalfe		1870	book 976.9693 X2c; film 1,035,840, item 1
Monroe		1870	book 976.9685 X28a; film 1,035,840, item 3
Montgomery		1870	book 976.9553 X28a; film 1,035,840, item 2
Nelson		1860	book 976.9495 X2p; film 897,098, item 2
Nelson		1870	book 976.9495 X2p; film 908,024, item 3
Ohio		1860	book 976.9835 X2o
Perry		1860	book 976.1 A1, No. 186
Pulaski		1870	book 976.963 X2c
Powell		1860	book 976.9585 X2p; film 982,207, item 2
Rockcastle		1880	book 976.9623 X2p; film 982,207
Rowan		1860	book 976.957 X2c; film 1,036,012, item 11
Washington		1860	book 976.9493 X2s
Wayne		1810-1880	book 976.964 X2c; film 1,036,791, item 4
Webster		1860	book 976.988 X2p; film 982,369
Webster		1870	book 976.9883 X2f

Louisiana

Parish	City or Township	Year	FHL Call Number
Ascension		1860	book 976.319 X2w
Ascension		1890	book 976.319 X2b
Calcasieu		1860	book 976.354 X2e
East Baton Rouge		1860	book 976.318 X21

Maine

County	City or Township	Year	FHL Call Number
Androscoggin		1880	film 010,521
Aroostook	Sherman	1880	film 012,076
Cumberland		1860-1870	film 009,734
Hancock		1860-1870	film 009,735
Hancock	Deer Island	1860-1880	film 1,033,591 item 1, pp 6, 110, 239
Hancock	Benjamin Lake	1870	film 1,033,591 item 1, p 249
Hancock	Stonington	1880	film 1,033,591, item 1, p 249
Kennebec	Gardner, Belgrade, Hllowell, Litchfield, Waterville	1860-1870	film 009,734

Maine (continued)

County	City or Township	Year	FHL Call Number
Knox	Isle au Haut	1860	film 1,033,591, item 1, p 85
Knox	Vinal Haven, North haven, Isle au Haut, Matinicus Island	1870	film 1,033,591, item 1, pp 186, 202, 206, 277
Knox	Isle au Haut	1880	film 1,033,591, item 1, p 236
Penobscot		1860-1870	film 009,736
Somerset		1860-1880	film 009,734; 009,737
Somerset		1880	film 205,624
Waldo		1880	film 012,414
Washington		1860-1870	film 009,738

Maryland

County	City or Township	Year	FHL Call Number
Caroline		1860	book 975.231 X2p: film 1,036,671

Michigan

County	City or Township	Year	FHL Call Number
Allegan (eastern)		1860	film 927,683, item 1
Allegan (western)		1860	film 927,683, item 2
Allegan		1870	film 927,680, item 2 and 5
Barry	Cities A-K	1880	film 915,282, item 1
Barry	Cities L-Y	1880	film 915,282, item 2
Genesee		1860	book 977.437 X2c
Hillsdale	Allen	1840-1900	book 977.429 X22a; film 1,033,839, item 1
Houghton		1880	film 915,277, item 2
Ingham	Lansing	1860	book 977.426/L1 X2ph; film 926,724, item 4
Ionia		1880	film 915,310
Kalamazoo		1880	film 915,313
Kent		1880	film 984,115
Keweenah		1880	film 915,274
Lapeer		1880	film 915,317
Macomb		1880	book 977.439 X22w
Manistee		1860	film 926,734, item 2
Mason		1860	film 927,691, item 2
Mason		1870	film 926,734, item 6; 927,691, item 3
Mecosta		1880	film 915,321, item 2
Oceana		1880	film 915,328
Ottawa		1880	film 915,330
Shiawassee		1860	film 927,443, item 2

Michigan (continued)

County	City or Township	Year	FHL Call Number
Van Buren		1860-1870	book 977.413 X2p; film 392,702, item 6; 927,447, item 2 & 3
Wastenaw		1880	film 955,815
Wayne		1860	book 977.433 X22i
Wayne	Livonia	1870	book 977.433/L1 X29w

Minnesota

County	City or Township	Year	FHL Call Number
Aitkin		1860	book 977.6 X2p; film 1,000,270, item 6
Cottonwood		1860	book 977.6 X2p
Itasca		1860	book 977.6 X2p; film 1,000,270, item 6
Jackson		1860	book 977.6 X2p; film 1,000,270, item 6
Kanabec		1860	book 977.6 X2p; film 1,000,270, item 9
Mille Lacs		1860	book 977.6 X2p; film 1,000,270, item 6
Murray		1860	book 977.6 X2p, film 1,000,270, item 6

Mississippi

County	City or Township	Year	FHL Call Number
Amite		1860	book 976.2 A1, No. 2
Chickasaw		1860	book 976.2942 X2f
Clairborne		1860	book 976.2 A1, No. 23
Copiah		1860	book 976.2 A1, No. 24
Harrison		1860	book 976.213 X2h
Hinds		1860	book 976.2 A1, No. 25
Issaquena		1860	book 976.2 A1, No. 26
Itawamba		1860-1870	book 976.2982 X2f
Marion		1860	book 976.221 X2pw; film 1,036,508, item 4
Monroe		1860	book 976.2975 X2p; film 873,817, item 6
Neshoba		1860	book 976.2 A1, No. 27
Newton		1860	book 976.2 A1, No. 28
Noxubee		1860	book 976.2 A1, No. 29
Oktibbeha		1880	film 900,518
Simpson		1860	book 976,2585 X2f
Tunica		1860	book 976.2 A1, No. 30

Missouri

County	City or Township	Year	FHL Call Number
Barton		1860	book 977.871 X2k
Barton		1870	book 977.871 X2kb

Missouri (continued)

County	City or Township	Year	FHL Call Number
Boone		1860-1880	book 977.829 X22p
Buchanan		1860	book 977.8132
Buchanan	St. Joseph, Washington	1860	book 977.8132/S1 X2p
Buchanan		1880	book 977.8132 X28p
Buchanan	St. Joseph	1880	book 977.8132/S1 X2p
Butler		1860	book 977.8 A1, No. 4
Camden		1860	book 977.854 X2c
Cass		1860	book 977.852 X2c
Christian		1860	book 977.8792 X2c
Dade		1860	film 908,783, item 5
Dade		1870	book 977.8745; film 908,783, item 4
Dent		1860	book 977.886 X2d
Dunklin		1860	book 977.8993 X2p; film 982,409, item 19
Dunklin		1870	book 977.8993 X2p; film 982,409, item 20
Dunklin		1880	book 977.8993 X2p
Gasconade		1860	book 977.861 X2k
Greene	Springfield	1880	book 977.878/S1 D2h
Grundy		1860	book 977.8215 X2p
Grundy		1860	book 977.8215/S1; film 873,984, item 2
Jackson		1860	book 977.841 X2p; film 1,000,309
Jasper		1860	book 977.872 X21
Jasper		1870	book 977.872 X2k
La Clede		1860	book 977.8 A1, No. 111
Lafayette		1860	book 977.8453 X2b
Maries		1870	book 977.8592 X2k
McDonald		1860	book 977.8736 X2m
New Madrid		1860	book 977.8985 X2p
Pulaski		1860	book 977.857 X2p
Ray		1860	book 977.819 X2p; film 873,983, item 4
Ray		1860	book 977.819 X2ph
Reynolds		1860	book 977.8885 X2p
Ripley		1860	book 977.8894 X2p
Ripley		1870	book 977.8 A1, No. 49; film 924,688, item 11
Ripley		1880	book 977.889 X2p
Schuyler		1880	film 1,012,039
Scotland		1860	film 1,000,310, item 4
Stone		1860	book 977.8794 X2p

Missouri (continued)

County	City or Township	Year	FHL Call Number
Sullivan		1860	book 977.8235 X2p
Taney		1860	book 977.879 X2p; film 873,984, item 9
Texas		1860	book 977.884 X2p; film 897,025, item 7
Wayne		1860	book 977.892 X2p
Webster		1860	book 977.882 X2p
Wright		1860	book 977.882 X2p

Montana

County	City or Township	Year	FHL Call Number
Washington Territory, west of Continental Divide	Bitter Root Valley and Ponderay Mountain Area	1860	book 978.6 A1, No. 8
Bighorn		1870	book 978.638 X2p
Dawson		1880	book 978.624 X2p

Nebraska

County	City or Township	Year	FHL Call Number
Bath		1860	book 978.2 A1, No. 20
Call		1860	book 978.2 A1, No. 20
Calhoun		1860	book 978.2 A1, No. 20
Custer		1880	book 978.247; film 1,036,052, item 2
Merrick		1860	book 978.2 A1, No. 20
Polk		1860	book 978.2 A1, No. 20
Richardson		1890	book 978.2282 X28c

Nevada

County	Notes	Year	FHL Call Number
Churchill	(Missourians in the county)	1870	book 979.35 X2p; film 823,651
Douglas	(Missourians in the county)	1870	book 979.35 X2p; film 823,651

New Hampshire

County	City or Township	Year	FHL Call Number
Grafton	Enfield	1790-1870	film 015,781

New Jersey

County	City or Township	Year	FHL Call Number
Atlantic		1860	book 974.984 X29c
Cumberland	Millville	1830-1880	book 974.994 X2p; film 1,036,662, item 2

New York

County	City or Township	Year	FHL Call Number
Albany	City of Albany, wards 1-5	1880	film 521,940
Albany	City of Albany, wards 1-5	1880	film 521,941
Albany	Guilderland, Knox, New Scotland, Rensselaerville, Westerlo, Bethlehem, Berne, Caeymans	1880	film 521,942
Albany	Cohoes, West Troy, Watervliet, Green Island	1880	film 521,943
Allegany		1880	film 506,765
Broome		1860	film 808,827
Broome	Binghamton	1880	film 808,832; 808,833
Cattaraugus		1880	film 584,493; 584,494
Cayuga	Summerhill	1860-1880	book Q974.7 A1, No. 5; film 982,242, item 5
Cayuga		1880	film 853,208; 853,209
Columbia		1880	film 479,103; 479,104
Cortland	Cincinnatus	1860	film 017,605
Cortland	Cortlandville	1860	film 017,610
Cortland	Cuyler	1860	film 017,612
Cortland	Harford	1860	film 017,704
Cortland	Homer	1860	film 017,702
Cortland	Lapeer	1860	film 017,741
Cortland	Marathon	1860	film 017,861
Cortland	Preble	1860	film 017,771
Cortland	Scott	1860	film 017,957
Cortland	Taylor	1860	film 017,978
Cortland	Virgil	1860	film 017,994
Cortland	Willet	1860	film 018,025
Erie	City of Buffalo	1880	film 825,691, item 2
Erie	Hamburg thru West Seneca	1880	film 825,692
Fulton		1880	film 465,984
Livingston		1880	film 510,546; 510,549, item 1
Madison		1880	film 408,499; 408,500
Montgomery		1870	film 982,388, item 4
Montgomery	Palatine	1870	film 982,388, item 8
Niagara		1880	film 878,327; 878,328

New York (continued)

County	City or Township	Year	FHL Call Number
Ontario		1880	film 590,812; 590,813
Rensselaer	Troy, wards 1-6	1880	film 549,900
Rensselaer	Troy, wards 7-13	1880	film 550,436
Rensselaer	Berlin, Brunswick, East Greenbush, Grafton, North Greenbush, Green-bush, Petersburg	1880	film 549,901
Rensselaer	Hoosick, Lansingburg, Nassau	1880	film 549,902
Rensselaer	Pittstown, Poestenkill, Schaghticoke, Schodack, Stephen-town, Sand Lake	1880	film 549,903
Richmond		1880	film 946,691, item 6
Rockland		1880	film 564,819, item 1
Schenectady		1880	film 513,833
Schoharie		1860	film 982,388, item 12
Steuben	Addision, Avoco, Bath, Cameron, Campbell, Canisteo	1880	film 519,415
Steuben	Caton, Cohocton, Corning, Dansville, Erwin, Fremont, Greenwood, Hartsville, Hornby	1880	film 519,416
Steuben	Hornellsville, Howard, Jasper, Lindley, Prattsburg, Pulteney, Rathbone, Thurston, Troupsburgh, Tuscorora, Urbana, Wayland, Wayne, West Union, Wheeler, Woodhull	1880	film 519,417
Tioga	Barton, Candor (Persons over 70 years)	1880	book 974.7 A1, No. 129; film 908,967, item 13
Tompkins		1880	film 853,062
Wayne	Wayne (Master Index, all censuses	1790-1880	film 813,649, items 1 & 2
Wayne		1860	film 843,650, item 3
Wayne		1870	film 843,650, item 5
Wayne		1880	film 843,650, item 7
Wyoming		1880	film 817,071, item 2

North Carolina

County	City or Township	Year	FHL Call Number
Carteret		1860	book 975.6197 X2s
Carteret		1870	book 975.6197 X2s
Cleveland		1870	book 975.6775 X2d
Jackson		1860	book 975.6 A1, No. 121
Nash		1860	book 975.6 A1, No. 122
Randolph		1860	book 975.661 X2x
Rowan		1880	film 019,821
Rutherford		1860	book 975.6913 X2d
Rutherford		1870	book 975.6913 X2j
Union		1860	book 975.6755 X2s
Wake		1880	film 020,003; 020,004
Wilkes		1860	book 975.682 X2p; film 982,178, item 4

North Dakota

County	City or Township	Year	FHL Call Number
Benson	Fort Totten	1870	book 978.4 B2h, Vol. 3, p. 226
Ramsey	Devils Lake Mission	1880	book 978.4 B2h, Vol. 3, p. 229

Ohio

County	City or Township	Year	FHL Call Number
Ashtabula		1870	film 960,583
Clermont		1880	film 393,286, item 2
Columbian		1860	book 977.163; film 897,342
Delaware	Scioto	1860	film 859,787, item 5
Fairfield		1870	book 977.158 K22f
Hancock		1860	book 977.1 A1, No. 102; film 982,099, item 12
Hancock		1870	book 977.1 A1, No. 101; film 982,104, item 4
Knox		1860	book 977.1 A1, No. 44
Monroe		1860	book 977.196 X2p
Pickaway		1880	film 288,402, item 2
Pike		1870	book 977.1 A1, No. 114; film 982,235, item 7
Portage		1880	film 960,602
Prebel		1870	book 977.171 X2gi
Scioto		1870	book 977.1 A1, No. 165

Oregon

County	City or Township	Year	FHL Call Number
Baker		1870	book 979.5 X2h
Benton		1860	book 979.5 A1, No. 11; film 873,818, item 6

Oregon (continued)

County	City or Township	Year	FHL Call Number
Benton		1870	book 979.53 X2i
Clackamas		1870	book 979.541 X2h
Clatsop		1870	book 979.54 X2h
Columbia		1870	book 979.54 X2h
Coos		1870	book 979.5 A1, No. 43
Curry		1860-1870	book 979.5 A1, No. 43
Douglas		1860	book 979.5 A1, No. 43
Douglas		1870	book 979.529 X2h
Douglas		1880	book 979.529 X2h
Grant		1870	book 979.5 X12h
Grant		1880	book 979.578 X2p
Jackson		1860	book 979.527 X2p; film 873,822, item 8
Jackson		1870	book 979.527 X2p
Jackson		1880	book 979.527 X2p
Josephine		1860	book 979.5 A1, No. 26; film 982,338, item 5
Josephine		1880	book 979.5 A1, No. 27
Lane		1860	book 979.631 X2p
Lane		1870	book 979.531 X2p; film 1,036,826, item 2
Lane		1880	book 979.531 X2p
Linn		1870	book 979.535 X2h
Marion		1860	book 979.537 X2h
Marion		1870	book 979.537 X2h
Marion		1880	book 979.537 X2h; film 1,206,429, item 15
Multnomah	Portland	1870	book 979.549/P1 X2h
Polk		1870	book 979.53 X2h
Tillamook		1860	book 979.544 X2ps
Tillamook		1860-1870	book 979.54 X2h
Umatilla		1870	book 979.5 X2h
Umpqua		1851-1860	book 979.5 A1, No. 43
Union		1870	book 979.5 X2h
Wasco		1870	book 979.5 A1, No. 45
Wasco		1880	book 979.562 X2h
Washington		1860	book 979.5 A1, No. 28; film 982,409
Washington		1870	book 979.54 X2h
Washington		1880	book 979.543 X2h
Yamhill		1860	book 979.539 X2h
Yamhill		1870	book 979.539 X2h
Yamhill		1880	book 979.539 X2h

Pennsylvania

County	City or Township	Year	FHL Call Number Maine
Berks		1860	book 974.816 X22h
Berks		1870	book 974.816 X22i
Greene	Allepo, Center, Carmichaels	1880	book 974.883 X2p, Vol. 1; p.25, Vol 2; p. 90, Vol. 3, p. 17

Rhode Island

County	City or Township	Year	FHL Call Number
Newport	Little Compton	1760	film 022,397, p. 51

South Carolina

County	City or Township	Year	FHL Call Number
Chester		1870-1880	film 599,050
Fairfield		1870-1880	film 599,049
Laurens		1880	film 599,050, item 2

South Dakota

County	City or Township	Year	FHL Call Number
Hutchinson		1880	book 978.3384 X2h; film 1,033,841, item 4

Tennessee

County	City or Township	Year	FHL Call Number
Bledsoe		1870	book 976.876 X2c
Campbell		1870	book 976.872 X2t
Dyer		1860	book 976.8 A1, No. 62
Fayette		1860	book 976.8 A1, No. 63
Humphreys		1870	book 976.837 X2c
Lawrence		1840-1860	book 976.842 X2pa; film 1,036,764, item 3
Lawrence		1880	book 976.842 X21
Maury		1860	book 976.859 X2m
Maury		1880	book 976.859 X2s
McNairy		1860	book 978.8 A1, No. 24; film 962,242, item 4
Tipton		1860	book 976.8 A1, No. 64
Wayne		1850-1860	book 976.839 X2p
Williamson		1880	film 454,093
Wilson		1860	book 976.854 X2p, Vols. 1 & 2; film 928,209, items 4-5

Texas

County	City or Township	Year	FHL Call Number
Bosque		1860	book 976.4 A1, No. 84
Bosque		1860	book 976.4 B2c, Vol. 19, Nos. 1-4

Texas (continued)

County	City or Township	Year	FHL Call Number
Bowie		1860	book 976.4 A1, No. 85; 976.4197 X2e
Bowie		1860-1880	film 1,033,772, item 7
Brazoria		1860	book 976.4 A1, No. 86
Brazos		1860	book 976.4 A1, No. 87
Brown		1860	book 976.4 A1, No. 88
Burnet		1860	book 976.4 A1, No. 89
Calhoun		1860	book 976.4 A1, No. 90
Calhoun		1860	book 976.4121 X2u; film 1,035,899, item 7
Calhoun		1870	book 976.4121; film 1,035,899, item 8
Calhoun		1880	book 976.4121 X2u; film 1,035,899, item 9
Cherokee		1880	book 976.4183 X22b
Comanche		1860	book 976.4554 X2h
Coryell		1860	book 976.4515 X2t
Erath		1860-1870	book 976.4551 X2h
Fannin		1870	book 976.4265 X29u
Franklin		1880	book 976.4213 X2p; film 982,409, item 18
Galveston	City of Galveston	1880	film 1,009,547, items 1-2
Hood		1880	book 976.4522 X2p; film 824,294, item 4
Hunt		1880	book 976.4272 X29u
Jack		1870	book 976.4 A1, No. 126
Jackson		1870	book 976.4 A1, No. 125
Jefferson		1870	book 976.4 A1, No. 124
Mason		1860-1880	book 976.4 A1, No. 123
Matagorda		1860	book 976.4132 X2e
Matagorda		1870	book 976.4132 X2e
Matagorda		1880	book 976.4 A1, No. 92
McLennan		1860	book 976.4 B2c, Vol. 18, Nos. 1-4
Menard		1880	book 976.4 A1, No. 93
Milam		1880	book 976.4 A1, No. 94
Nacogdoches		1860	book 976.4182 x2e
Nacogdoches		1870	book 976.4182 X2ep
Nacogdoches		1880	book 976.418 X2o; film 928,079, item 7
Presidio		1870	book 976.4933 X2p
Red River		1860	book 976.4212 X21
Runnels		1880	book 976.4724 D3b; film 928,564, item 6
Sabine		1860	book 976.4177 X2s
Sabine		1870	book 976.4177 X2to

Texas (continued)

County	City or Township	Year	FHL Call Number
Sabine		1880	book 976.4177 X2t
Smith		1870	book 976.4229 X2f
Travis		1860	book 976.43 X2p; film 1,000,609, item 9
Young		1860-1880	book 976.4545 X2h; film 982,025

Vermont

County	City or Township	Year	FHL Call Number
Bennington	Arlington	1860	book 974.3 A1, No. 13; film 962,911, item 8
Bennington	Sunderland	1860	book 974.3 A1, No. 14; film 962,517, item 7

Virginia

County	City or Township	Year	FHL Call Number
Warwick		1860-1880	book 975.5416 X2p
Russell		1870	book 975.5755 X2p

Washington

County	City or Township	Year	FHL Call Number
Columbia		1900	book 979.746 X2m
Klickitat		1860-1880	book 979.753 X2p
Lewis		1880	book 979.753 X2p
Mason (Swamish)		1860	book 979.7 X2p
Mason		1880	book 979.7 A1, No. 9
Pacific		1880	book 979.7 A1, No. 8
Skamania		1860	book 979.7 X2p
Snohomish		1860	book 979.7 X2p
Spokane		1880	book 979.737 X2p; film 940,013, item 3
Stevens		1880	book 979.7 A1, No. 17; film 940,013, item 4
Walla Walla		1880	book 979.748 X2p; film 824,055, item 3
Whatcom	incl. present-day San Juan & Skagit counties	1860	book 979.773 X2w 1860
Whatcom	incl. present-day San Juan & Skagit counties	1870	book 979.755 X2w 1870
Whatcom		1900	book 979.773 X2wgs
Whatcom		1910	book 979.773 X22w
Whitman		1880	book 979.739 X20; film 824,055
Yakima		1880	book 979.755 X2p

West Virginia

County	City or Township	Year	FHL Call Number
Barbour		1850-1860	book 975.5 X2pw; film 982,213, item 3
Calhoun		1860	book 974. X2p
Calhoun		1860	book 974.X2t
Hampshire		1850-1860	book 975.5 X2pw; film 982,213, item 3
Hardy		1860	book 975.5 X2pw
Lewis		1860	book 975.5 X2pw
Marion		1860	book 975.4 A1, No. 15
McDowell		1860	book 975.449 D2e; film 6,018,779
Pendleton		1850-1860	book 975.5 X2pw; film 982,213, item 3
Pleasants		1870	book 975.421 X2c
Pocahontas		1850-1860	book 975.5 X2pw; film 982,213, item 3, p 83
Preston		1880	film 827,556
Randolph		1860	book 975.5 X2pw
Ritchie		1860	book 975.424 X2c
Roane		1870	book 975.436 X2c
Wirt		1860	book 975.426 X2c
Wirt		1870	book 975.426 X2cw
Wyoming		1860	book 975.445 X2c

Wisconsin

County	City or Township	Year	FHL Call Number
Douglas		1860	film 848,698

Section 4

Non-population
Census Schedules

Experienced genealogists are well aware of the U.S. federal censuses, 1790-1920, because they are primary genealogical sources. Genealogists use the population schedules, since these schedules list names of residents of the United States for each census year. Yet, for every census year since 1800, other census schedules were produced, such as the special census lists of Union Veterans and Widows prepared in 1890, or the slave schedules compiled for 1850 and 1860. The status of the surviving 1890 Union Veterans' schedules were identified earlier and are not included in this report. This review identifies all known surviving copies of the following non-population census schedules.

1. **Agricultural Schedules** for 1850, 1860, 1870, and 1880

2. **Defective, Dependent, Delinquent Classes** for 1880

3. **Industry and Manufacturing Schedules** for 1800 thru 1880 censuses

4. **Mortality Schedules** for 1850, 1860, 1870, and 1880

5. **Slave Schedules** for 1850 and 1860

6. **Social Statistics Schedules** for 1850, 1860, and 1870

7. **1885 Non-population Schedules** (for those states with an 1885 federal census)

All of the special census schedules are called "non-population schedules" and are not as well known to researchers. It is not surprising that many genealogists know little about these special census schedules because the non-population schedules are not as complete or as readily available as the population schedules. Like the population schedules, the non-population schedules have lists of names. Any document that lists names of people has great value to genealogists and may confirm the home of a person living in the United States back in time.

Unlike most of the population schedules, the non-population schedules are not all in one place. The National Archives long ago decided to return the originals of most of the non-population schedules to any state agency that wanted them. The original manuscripts for most of the non-population schedules were distributed to various state libraries, state historical societies, state archives, or university libraries. Sometimes, the original manuscripts were transferred to some unlikely locations. Original non-population schedules relating to a particular state may be found today in a completely different state. One example is the original 1850-1880 Agricultural Schedules for Georgia which are not in Georgia, but at the Duke University Library in Durham, North Carolina. As it turns out, Duke University has microfilmed all of Georgia's agricultural schedules. Knowing this, a genealogist may borrow rolls of film from the Duke University Library through the national interlibrary loan system and then use the film at his or her local library. An address for the Duke University Library is at the end of this report, along with the telephone number for their interlibrary loan librarian.

Some non-population schedules were microfilmed by the National Archives; and the film can be obtained on loan by Heritage Quest members. Heritage Quest has virtually every National Archives microfilm series of interest to genealogists, including most, if not all, of the non-population schedules filmed by the National Archives. Several statewide non-population schedules were microfilmed by the repository that holds the originals outside the National Archives. An identification of forty-four different repositories holding original manuscripts or microfilm copies is shown later, along with a full address and telephone number. We will identify all of the non-population schedules that exist for every state, 1800-1880; identify where the original manuscripts are physically located today; and identify where any microfilm versions of the schedules may exist today. In addition, several statewide sched-

ules have never been microfilmed. These can be seen in the Location Table that follows on page 102.

Below, a description of the non-population schedules is given. Following that, a complete list of the schedules taken from various reports (compiled over the last few years) is given. The main source of this information came from a 1995 report of non-population schedules compiled by Claire Prechtel-Kluskens, a staff archivist/genealogy specialist at the National Archives in Washington, D.C. An earlier report produced by the National Archives in 1972 listed population and non-population Schedules, although the 1972 report was mostly superceded by the 1995 report. A check of Heritage Quest's microform catalog confirmed that the existence of most NARA films are in the hands of Heritage Quest and available for loan to its members. Heritage Quest is also acquiring non-population schedules from other repositories. So, if a person needs a particular schedule, check with Heritage Quest first to see if they have it. Other microfilm prepared by an institution other than the National Archives is also shown in this report, giving the name of the repository.

Description of Non-population Census Schedules

The non-population schedules were taken separately from the population schedules. They were all organized in the same manner as the population schedules, that is, by state, county, and subdistrict of a county.

Agricultural Schedules

For the 1850, 1860, 1870, and 1880 censuses, a separate schedule was prepared listing the production for all farms in America. These

schedules show the name of the farm owner, agent, or manager, along with details about his livestock and produce. The types of questions on the 1850 agricultural schedules form are shown below. Each of the other census years had a similar layout:

- Name of owner, agent, or manager of a farm
- Number of improved acres
- Number of unimproved acres
- Cash value of a farm

- Value of farming implements and machinery
- Number of horses, milk cows, working oxen, other cattle, sheep, and swine
- Value of livestock
- Bushels produced during the census year ending June 1, of wheat, rye, Indian corn, oats, rice, tobacco, clover seed, other grass seed, hops, flax seed, and hemp
- Pounds produced during the census year ending June 1, of butter, cheese, flax, cane sugar, maple sugar, beeswax, and honey
- Value of orchard products, in dollars
- Wine produced, in gallons
- Hay produced, in tons
- Gallons of molasses
- Value of homemade manufactures
- Value of slaughtered animals

Defective, Dependent, and Delinquent Classes (1880 census only)

A total of seven supplementary schedules under the title *Defective, Dependent, and Delinquent Classes* were prepared for the 1880 census as they applied to each county's census enumeration. These were: Insane Inhabitants, Idiots, Deaf-mutes, Blind, Homeless Children, Inhabitants in Prison, and Pauper and Indigent Inhabitants.

1. Insane Inhabitants. This supplemental schedule lists the following information:

- Page number (from population schedule)
- Line number (from population schedule)
- Name of insane person
- City or town of residence
- County of residence
- Whether an inmate of an institution or a day patient
- Form of disease
- Duration of current attack
- Number of attacks
- Age at first attack
- Whether person must be kept in a cell
- Whether person must be restrained
- Whether person is an inmate in a hospital or asylum
- Total length of time in institution
- Date of discharge
- Whether the person is epileptic
- Whether the person is suicidal
- Whether the person is homicidal

2. Idiots. (In 1880, an *idiot* was the common term for someone who was mentally deficient.) The supplemental schedule listed the following information for each person:

- Page number (from population schedule)
- Line number (from population schedule)
- Name of person
- City or town of residence
- County of residence
- Whether person is self-supporting or partly so
- Age at which idiocy occurred
- Supposed cause of idiocy
- Size of person's head (large, small, or normal)
- Whether person ever in training school. If yes, name of school
- Time spent during life in training school
- Year of discharge from training school
- Whether the person is also insane
- Whether the person is also blind

- Whether the person is also deaf
- Whether the person is also epileptic
- Whether the person is paralyzed. On left or right side?

3. Deaf-mutes. This schedule listed the following information:

- Page number (from population schedules)
- Line number (from population schedules)
- Name of person
- City or town of residence
- County of residence
- Whether person is self-supporting, or partly so
- Supposed cause of deafness, if known
- Age at which deafness occurred
- Whether person is semi-mute
- Whether person is semi-deaf
- Whether person was ever in an institution for deaf-mutes
- Total length of time in an institution
- Year of discharge
- Whether person is also insane
- Whether person is also idiotic
- Whether person is also blind

4. Blind Inhabitants. This schedule listed the following information:

- Page number (from population schedule)
- Line number (from population schedule)
- Name of person
- City or town of residence
- County of residence
- Whether person is self-supporting or partly so
- Age at which blindness occurred
- Form of blindness

- Supposed cause of blindness, if known
- Whether totally blind
- Whether semi-blind
- Whether an inmate at an institution for the blind. If so, name of institution.
- Total length of time in such an institution
- Year of discharge
- Whether this person is also insane
- Whether this person is also idiotic
- Whether this person is also deaf-mute

5. Homeless Children. This schedule listed the following information:

- Page number (from population schedule)
- Line number (from population schedule)
- Name of person
- City or town of residence
- County of residence
- Whether child's father is deceased
- Whether child's mother is deceased
- Whether the child was abandoned by his/her parents
- Whether the child was surrendered to an institution by parents
- Whether the child was born in an institution
- Year admitted to an institution
- Whether the child is illegitimate
- Whether the child is separated from his/her mother
- Whether the child was arrested. If so, for what offense?
- Whether the child was convicted or sentenced
- Whether the origin of the child was respectable
- Whether the child was removed from criminal surroundings

- Whether the child is blind
- Whether the child is deaf-mute
- Whether the child is an idiot

6. Inhabitants in Prison. This schedule listed the following information:

- Line number (from population schedules)
- Name of person
- City or town of residence
- County of residence
- Place of imprisonment
- Whether imprisoned by U.S., State, or City
- Whether person is awaiting trail
- Whether person is serving a term of imprisonment
- Whether person is serving out a fine
- Whether person is awaiting execution (death)
- Whether person sentenced to higher prison and awaiting transfer
- Whether person is held as a witness
- Whether imprisoned for debt
- Whether imprisoned for insanity
- Date incarcerated
- Alleged offense
- Amount of fine imposed
- Number of days in jail or workhouse
- Number of years in penitentiary
- Whether at hard labor. If yes, what kind of work
- If at hard labor, inside or outside work
- If at hard labor, whether labor contracted out

7. Pauper and Indigent Inhabitants in Institutions, Poor-houses or Asylums, or Boarded at Public Expense in Private Houses. This schedule listed the following information:

- Page number (from population schedules)
- Line number (from population schedules)
- Name of person
- City or town of residence
- County of residence
- Supported at cost of city or town
- Supported at cost of county
- Supported at cost of state
- Supported at cost of institution
- Whether person is able-bodied
- Whether person is habitually intemperate (alcoholic)
- Whether person is epileptic
- Whether person ever convicted of a crime
- Whether person disabled. If so, describe disability
- Whether person was born in an institution
- Date of admission to institution
- Whether husband is also in this establishment
- Whether wife is also in this establishment
- Whether mother is also in this establishment
- Whether father is also in this establishment
- Whether sons in this establishment. If so, how many?
- Whether daughters in this establishment. If so, how many?
- Whether brothers in this establishment. If so, how many?
- Whether sisters in this establishment. If so, how many?
- Whether person is also blind
- Whether person is also deaf and dumb
- Whether person is also insane

Industry and Manufacturing Schedules

The 1850, 1860, and 1870 Products of Industry census schedules each had special lists prepared showing manufactured products and other statistics about businesses in general. Any business producing articles valued at $500 or more per year is listed. In doing so, the name of the business owner, agent, or manager was listed as well as the following information:

- Name of business
- Capital invested in the business
- Raw materials used
- Kind of motive power used
- Average number of hands employed
- Average monthly cost for male wages
- Average monthly cost for female wages
- Annual product: quantities, kind, values

The 1880 Manufactures Schedules added special lists by the category of the business, including the following:

- Boot and shoe factories; and leather and tanning /curing works
- Flouring and grist mills; and cheese or butter processing plants
- Salt works
- Lumber mills, sawmills; and brickyards and tile works
- Coal mines
- Agricultural implement works
- Quarries

Mortality Schedules

These special lists were prepared for the 1850, 1860, 1870, and 1880 censuses. The mortality schedules were taken separately from the population schedules and list the names of any person who died within one year before the census day. For example, in the 1850 census, which had a census day of 1 June 1850, the mortality schedule for that year lists the name of any person who died between 1 June 1849 and 31 May 1850. The information listed on the 1850 and 1860 Mortality Schedules was as follows:

- Name of deceased
- Age
- Sex
- Color
- Free or slave
- Married or widowed
- Birthplace
- Month of death
- Occupation
- Disease or cause of death
- Number of days ill

The 1870 Mortality Schedule included the following information:

- Name of deceased
- Age, last birthday
- Sex
- Color
- Married or widowed
- Birthplace
- Whether father of foreign birth
- Whether mother of foreign birth
- Month of death
- Occupation
- Disease or cause of death

The 1880 Mortality Schedule included the following information:

- Page number (from population schedule)
- Family Number (from population schedule)
- Name of deceased
- Age
- Sex
- Color
- Whether single, married, widowed, or divorced
- Birthplace of deceased
- Birthplace of deceased's father
- Birthplace of deceased's mother
- Occupation
- Month of death
- Disease or cause of death
- Months in county
- Place disease contracted
- Name of attending physician

Slave Schedules

Slave schedules were extracted only for the 1850 and 1860 censuses. In all cases, the schedules list the name of a slave owner and numbers of slaves held by that slave owner. Virtually all of the original manuscripts for all applicable states were retained by the National Archives and all surviving schedules were microfilmed by the National Archives. Heritage Quest currently lists all extant slave schedules in its microform catalog as available for sale to the general public and loan to its members. The information listed on the 1850 and 1860 Slave Schedules was as follows:

- City, town, or subdistrict of slave owner
- Name of slave owner
- Number of slaves, listed by age, sex, and color

- Whether a fugitive
- Whether manumitted (granted freedom)
- Whether deaf, dumb, insane, or idiotic

Most of the countywide slave schedules list the names of slave owners only; however, some enumerators chose to list the first names of individual slaves on their lists. A researcher must view each countywide slave schedule to see if the names of slaves are shown or not.

Social Statistics Schedules

For the 1850, 1860, and 1870 censuses, a special set of forms was used to gather statistics concerning a particular geographic area within a county. The divisions are described on each schedule page, such as "North Half Fulton County," and the divisions in rural areas do not follow any strict rules. Most divisions are easily identified as townships, towns, cities, or parts of a county. As an example of the type of statistics gathered, the listings for the 1850 Social Statistic Schedules are shown below:

- Total value of real estate for the division
- Total value of personal property for the division
- Names and numbers of colleges, academies, and schools in the division; the number of pupils and number of teachers; and facts about endowments, taxation, etc.
- Names and number of libraries in the division, with description, and number of books
- Names and number of newspapers in the division, with description, publication dates, and circulation
- Poor Houses (pauperism) with a count of the number of native and foreign paupers, and the cost to support them

- Number of criminals in the division, native and foreign
- Average monthly wage for a farmhand in the division
- Average monthly wage for a day laborer in the division
- Average monthly wage for a carpenter in the division
- Average weekly wage for a male domestic
- Average weekly wage for a female domestic
- Average price of board to a laboring man for a week

1885 Non-population Census Schedules

In 1885, Congress allowed any state or territory to take a census with Federal assistance. Only five states or territories opted to take advantage of this provision. The states and territories that took an 1885 census were Colorado, Dakota Territory, Florida, Nebraska, and New Mexico Territory. The format of the 1885 census was nearly the same as the 1880 and added the same types of non-population schedules as well. The table below lists which of the non-population schedules exist. In addition, the current location of the schedules for each of the five states/territories that had an 1885 census taken is given.

Location of Non-population Census Schedules

State /Year/ Schedules	Nat'l Archives and Heritage Quest Film Numbers	Other Microfilm at	Original Manuscripts Located at (No. in Address List)
Alabama			
1850 Agricultural	—	U of NC, Chapel Hill (1)	AL Dept. Arch./Hist. (2)
1860 Agricultural	—	U of NC, Chapel Hill (1)	AL Dept. Arch./Hist. (2)
1870 Agricultural	—	U of NC, Chapel Hill (1)	AL Dept. Arch./Hist. (2)
1880 Agricultural	—	U of NC, Chapel Hill (1)	AL Dept. Arch./Hist. (2)
1850 Industry	—	U of NC, Chapel Hill (1)	AL Dept. Arch./Hist. (2)
1860 Industry	—	U of NC, Chapel Hill (1)	AL Dept. Arch./Hist. (2)
1870 Industry	—	U of NC, Chapel Hill (1)	AL Dept. Arch./Hist. (2)
1880 Manufactures	—	U of NC, Chapel Hill (1)	AL Dept. Arch./Hist. (2)
1850 Mortality	—	U of NC, Chapel Hill (1)	AL Dept. Arch./Hist. (2)
1860 Mortality	—	U of NC, Chapel Hill (1)	AL Dept. Arch./Hist. (2)
1870 Mortality	—	U of NC, Chapel Hill (1)	AL Dept. Arch./Hist. (2)
1880 Mortality	—	U of NC, Chapel Hill (1)	AL Dept. Arch./Hist. (2)
1880 Def/Dep/Del	—	U of NC, Chapel Hill (1)	AL Dept. Arch./Hist. (2)
1850 Slave	M432, rolls 17-24	—	NARA, Wash., DC (3)
1860 Slave	M653, rolls 27-36	—	NARA, Wash., DC (3)
Arizona			
1870 Mortality	T655, roll 1	—	NARA, Wash., DC (3)
1880 Mortality	T655, roll 2	—	NARA, Wash., DC (3)

State /Year/ Schedules	Nat'l Archives and Heritage Quest Film Numbers	Other Microfilm at	Original Manuscripts Located at (No. in Address List)
Arkansas			
1850 Agricultural	—	AR Hist. Commission (4)	U of AR, Fayetteville (5)
1860 Agricultural	—	AR Hist. Commission (4)	U of AR, Fayetteville (5)
1870 Agricultural	—	AR Hist. Commission (4)	U of AR, Fayetteville (5)
1880 Def/Dep/Del	—	AR Hist. Commission (4)	U of AR, Fayetteville (5)
1880 Manufactures	—	AR Hist. Commission (4)	U of AR, Fayetteville (5)
1850 Mortality	—	AR Hist. Commission (4)	U of AR, Fayetteville (5)
1860 Mortality	—	AR Hist. Commission (4)	U of AR, Fayetteville (5)
1870 Mortality	—	AR Hist. Commission (4)	U of AR, Fayetteville (5)
1880 Mortality	—	AR Hist. Commission (4)	U of AR, Fayetteville (5)
1850 Slave	M432, roll 32	—	NARA, Wash., DC (3)
1860 Slave	M653, rolls 53-54	—	NARA, Wash., DC (3)
California			
1850 Agricultural	—	U of CA, Berkeley (6)	CA State Library (7)
1860 Agricultural	—	U of CA, Berkeley (6)	CA State Library (7)
1870 Agricultural	—	U of CA, Berkeley (6)	CA State Library (7)
1880 Agricultural	—	U of CA, Berkeley (6)	CA State Library (7)
1880 Def/Dep/Del	—	U of CA, Berkeley (6)	CA State Library (7)
1850 Industry	—	U of CA, Berkeley (6)	CA State Library (7)
1860 Industry	—	U of CA, Berkeley (6)	CA State Library (7)
1870 Industry	—	U of CA, Berkeley (6)	CA State Library (7)
1880 Manufactures	—	U of CA, Berkeley (6)	CA State Library (7)
1850 Mortality	—	U of CA, Berkeley (6)	CA State Library (7)
1860 Mortality	—	U of CA, Berkeley (6)	CA State Library (7)
1870 Mortality	—	U of CA, Berkeley (6)	CA State Library (7)
1880 Mortality	—	U of CA, Berkeley (6)	CA State Library (7)
1850 Soc. Statistics	—	U of CA, Berkeley (6)	CA State Library (7)
1860 Soc. Statistics	—	U of CA, Berkeley (6)	CA State Library (7)
1870 Soc. Statistics	—	U of CA, Berkeley (6)	CA State Library (7)
Colorado			
1870 Agricultural	—	—	Duke University (8)
1880 Agricultural	—	—	Duke University (8)
1880 Def/Dep/Del	—	—	Duke University (8)
1870 Industry	—	—	Duke University (8)
1880 Manufactures	—	—	Duke University (8)
1885 Agricultural	M158, rolls 1-8	—	NARA, Wash., DC (3)
1885 Manufactures	M158, rolls 1-8	—	NARA, Wash., DC (3)

State /Year/ Schedules	Nat'l Archives and Heritage Quest Film Numbers	Other Microfilm at	Original Manuscripts Located at (No. in Address List)
1870 Mortality	—	—	Duke University (8)
1880 Mortality	—	—	Duke University (8)
1885 Mortality	—	—	Duke University (8)
1870 Soc. Statistics	—	—	Duke University (8)

Connecticut

1850 Agricultural	—	CT State Library (9)	CT State Library (9)
1860 Agricultural	—	CT State Library (9)	CT State Library (9)
1870 Agricultural	—	—	CT State Library (9)
1880 Agricultural	—	—	CT State Library (9)
1880 Def/Dep/Del	—	—	CT State Library (9)
1820 Manufactures	M279, roll 4	—	NARA, Wash., DC (3)
1850 Industry	—	CT State Library (9)	CT State Library (9)
1860 Industry	—	CT State Library (9)	CT State Library (9)
1870 Industry	—	CT State Library (9)	CT State Library (9)
1880 Manufactures	—	CT State Library (9)	CT State Library (9)
1850 Mortality	—	CT State Lib. (9) & FHL (10)	CT State Library (9)
1860 Mortality	—	CT State Lib. (9) & FHL (10)	CT State Library (9)
1870 Mortality	—	CT State Lib. (9) & FHL (10)	CT State Library (9)
1880 Mortality	—	CT State Lib. (9) & FHL (10)	CT State Library (9)

Dakota Territory

1880 Agricultural	—	—	SD State Hist. Soc. (11)
1885 Agricultural	—	—	SD State Hist. Soc. (11)
1880 Def/Dep/Del	—	—	SD State Hist. Soc. (11)
1880 Manufactures	—	—	SD State Hist. Soc. (11)
1885 Manufactures	GR27, roll 4	—	NARA, Wash., DC (3)
1860 Mortality	—	—	SD State Hist. Soc. (11)
1885 Union Soldiers	GR27, roll 5	—	SD State Hist. Soc. (11)
1880 Mortality	—	FHL (10)	Idaho Hist. Society (12)
1885 Mortality	GR27, rolls 3-4	—	SD State Hist. Soc. (11)
1870 Soc. Statistics	GR27, roll 5	—	SD State Hist. Soc. (11)
1885 Soc. Statistics	—	—	SD State Hist. Soc. (11)

Delaware

1820 Manufactures	M279, roll 17	—	NARA, Wash., DC (3)
1850 Agricultural	—	—	DE St. Arch., Dover (13)
1860 Agricultural	—	—	DE St. Arch., Dover (13)
1870 Agricultural	—	—	DE St. Arch., Dover (13)

State /Year/ Schedules	Nat'l Archives and Heritage Quest Film Numbers	Other Microfilm at	Original Manuscripts Located at (No. in Address List)
1880 Agricultural	—	—	DE St. Arch., Dover (13)
1850 Industry	—	—	DE St. Arch., Dover (13)
1860 Industry	—	—	DE St. Arch., Dover (13)
1870 Industry	—	—	DE St. Arch., Dover (13)
1880 Manufactures	—	—	DE St. Arch., Dover (13)
1850 Mortality	—	—	DE St. Arch., Dover (13)
1860 Mortality	—	—	DE St. Arch., Dover (13)
1870 Mortality	—	—	DE St. Arch., Dover (13)
1880 Mortality	—	—	DE St. Arch., Dover (13)
1850 Soc. Statistics	—	—	DE St. Arch., Dover (13)
1860 Soc. Statistics	—	—	DE St. Arch., Dover (13)
1850 Slave	M432, roll 55	—	NARA, Wash., DC (3)
1860 Slave	M653, roll 100	—	NARA, Wash., DC (3)
1870 Def/Dep/Del	—	—	DE St. Arch., Dover (13)

District of Columbia

State /Year/ Schedules	Nat'l Archives and Heritage Quest Film Numbers	Other Microfilm at	Original Manuscripts Located at (No. in Address List)
1820 Manufactures	M279, roll 17	—	NARA, Wash., DC (3)
1850 Agricultural	M1795	—	Duke University (8)
1860 Agricultural	M1795	—	Duke University (8)
1870 Agricultural	M1795	—	Duke University (8)
1880 Agricultural	M1795	—	Duke University (8)
1880 Def/Dep/Del	M1795	—	Duke University (8)
1850 Industry	M1795	—	Duke University (8)
1860 Industry	M1795	—	Duke University (8)
1870 Industry	M1795	—	Duke University (8)
1880 Manufactures	M1795	—	Duke University (8)
1850 Mortality	T655, roll 5	—	NARA, Wash., DC (3)
1860 Mortality	T655, roll 5	—	NARA, Wash., DC (3)
1870 Mortality	T655, roll 5	—	NARA, Wash., DC (3)
1880 Mortality	T655, roll 5	—	NARA, Wash., DC (3)
1850 Slave	M432, roll 57	—	NARA, Wash., DC (3)
1860 Slave	M653, roll 105	—	NARA, Wash., DC (3)
1850 Soc. Statistics	—	—	Duke University (8)
1860 Soc. Statistics	—	—	Duke University (8)
1870 Soc. Statistics	—	—	Duke University (8)

Florida

State /Year/ Schedules	Nat'l Archives and Heritage Quest Film Numbers	Other Microfilm at	Original Manuscripts Located at (No. in Address List)
1850 Agricultural	T1168, roll 1	—	FL State University (14)
1860 Agricultural	T1168, roll 3	—	FL State University (14)

State /Year/ Schedules	Nat'l Archives and Heritage Quest Film Numbers	Other Microfilm at	Original Manuscripts Located at (No. in Address List)
1870 Agricultural	T1168, roll 5	—	FL State University (14)
1880 Agricultural	T1168, rolls 7-8	—	FL State University (14)
1880 Def/Dep/Del	—	—	FL State University (14)
1885 Agricultural	M845, roll 1-13	—	NARA, Wash., DC (3)
1850 Industry	T1168, roll 2	—	NARA, Wash., DC (3)
1860 Industry	T1168, roll 4	—	NARA, Wash., DC (3)
1870 Industry	T1168, roll 6	—	NARA, Wash., DC (3)
1880 Manufactures	T1168, roll 9	—	NARA, Wash., DC (3)
1885 Manufactures	M845, rolls 1-13	—	NARA, Wash., DC (3)
1850 Mortality	—	—	FL State University (14)
1860 Mortality	—	—	FL State University (14)
1870 Mortality	—	—	FL State University (14)
1880 Mortality	—	—	FL State University (14)
1885 Mortality	M845, rolls 1-13	—	NARA, Wash., DC (3)
1850 Slave	M432. roll 60	—	NARA, Wash., DC (3)
1860 Slave	M653, roll 110	—	NARA, Wash., DC (3)
1850 Soc. Statistics	—	—	FL State University (14)
1860 Soc. Statistics	—	—	FL State University (14)
1870 Soc. Statistics	—	—	FL State University (14)

Georgia

State /Year/ Schedules	Nat'l Archives and Heritage Quest Film Numbers	Other Microfilm at	Original Manuscripts Located at (No. in Address List)
1850 Agricultural	T1137, rolls 1-3	—	Duke University (8)
1860 Agricultural	T1137, rolls 4-6	—	Duke University (8)
1870 Agricultural	T1137, rolls 7-9	—	Duke University (8)
1880 Agricultural	T1137, rolls 10-20	—	Duke University (8)
1880 Def/Dep/Del	T1137, rolls 26-27	—	Duke University (8)
1820 Manufactures	M279, roll 19	—	NARA, Wash., DC (3)
1880 Manufactures	T1137, rolls 21-22	—	NARA, Wash., DC (3)
1850 Mortality	T655, roll 7 (includes index)	—	NARA, Wash., DC (3)
1860 Mortality	T655, roll 8 (includes index)	—	NARA, Wash., DC (3)
1870 Mortality	T655, roll 9 (includes index)	—	NARA, Wash., DC (3)
1880 Mortality	T655, rolls 10-12	—	NARA, Wash., DC (3)
1850 Slave	M432, rolls 88-96	—	NARA, Wash., DC (3)
1860 Slave	M653, rolls 142-153	—	NARA, Wash., DC (3)
1850 Soc. Statistics	T655, roll 23	—	Duke University (8)
1860 Soc. Statistics	T655, roll 24	—	Duke University (8)
1870 Soc. Statistics	T655, roll 25	—	Duke University (8)

State /Year/ Schedules	Nat'l Archives and Heritage Quest Film Numbers	Other Microfilm at	Original Manuscripts Located at (No. in Address List)
Idaho			
1870 Agricultural	—	—	Idaho Hist. Society (12)
1880 Agricultural	—	—	Idaho Hist. Society (12)
1880 Def/Dep/Del	—	—	Idaho Hist. Society (12)
1870 Industry	—	—	Idaho Hist. Society (12)
1880 Manufactures	—	—	Idaho Hist. Society (12)
1870 Mortality	—	—	Idaho Hist. Society (12)
1880 Mortality	—	—	Idaho Hist. Society (12)
1870 Soc. Statistics	—	—	Idaho Hist. Society (12)
Illinois			
1850 Agricultural	T1133, rolls 1-4	—	Illinois St. Archives (15)
1860 Agricultural	T1133, rolls 5-11	—	Illinois St. Archives (15)
1865 Agricultural	T1133, rolls 12-13	—	Illinois St. Archives (15)
1870 Agricultural	T1133, rolls 13-23	—	Illinois St. Archives (15)
1880 Agricultural	T1133, rolls 32-56	—	Illinois St. Archives (15)
1820 Manufactures	M279, roll 27	—	NARA, Wash., DC (3)
1860 Industry	T1133, roll 30	—	Illinois St. Archives (15)
1870 Industry	T1133, rolls 30-31	—	Illinois St. Archives (15)
1880 Industry	T1133, rolls 24-29	—	Illinois St. Archives (15)
1850 Mortality	T1133, roll 58	—	Illinois St. Archives (15)
1860 Mortality	T1133, rolls 58-59	—	Illinois St. Archives (15)
1870 Mortality	T1133, rolls 59-60	—	Illinois St. Archives (15)
1880 Mortality	T1133, rolls 60-64	—	Illinois St. Archives (15)
1860 Soc. Statistics	T1133, roll 57	—	Illinois St. Archives (15)
Indiana			
1850 Agricultural	—	Indiana St. Library (16)	Indiana St. Library (16)
1860 Agricultural	—	Indiana St. Library (16)	Indiana St. Library (16)
1870 Agricultural	—	Indiana St. Library (16)	Indiana St. Library (16)
1880 Agricultural	—	Indiana St. Library (16)	Indiana St. Library (16)
1880 Def/Dep/Del	—	—	Indiana St. Library (16)
1820 Manufactures	M279, roll 20	—	NARA, Wash., DC (3)
1850 Industry	—	Indiana St. Library (16)	Indiana St. Library (16)
1860 Industry	—	Indiana St. Library (16)	Indiana St. Library (16)
1870 Industry	—	Indiana St. Library (16)	Indiana St. Library (16)
1880 Manufactures	—	Indiana St. Library (16)	Indiana St. Library (16)
1850 Mortality	—	Indiana St. Library (16)	Indiana St. Library (16)
1860 Mortality	—	Indiana St. Library (16)	Indiana St. Library (16)

State /Year/ Schedules	Nat'l Archives and Heritage Quest Film Numbers	Other Microfilm at	Original Manuscripts Located at (No. in Address List)
1870 Mortality	—	Indiana St. Library (16)	Indiana St. Library (16)
1880 Mortality	—	Indiana St. Library (16)	Indiana St. Library (16)
1850 Soc. Statistics	—	—	Indiana St. Library (16)
1860 Soc. Statistics	—	—	Indiana St. Library (16)
1870 Soc. Statistics	—	—	Indiana St. Library (16)

Iowa

1850 Agricultural	T1156, roll 1	—	State Hist. Soc. IA (17)
1860 Agricultural	T1156, rolls 2-5	—	State Hist. Soc. IA (17)
1870 Agricultural	T1156, rolls 6-14	—	State Hist. Soc. IA (17)
1880 Agricultural	T1156, rolls 15-36	—	State Hist. Soc. IA (17)
1880 Def/Dep/Del	T1156, roll __	—	State Hist. Soc. IA (17)
1850 Industry	T1156, roll 37	—	State Hist. Soc. IA (17)
1860 Industry	T1156, roll 38	—	State Hist. Soc. IA (17)
1870 Industry	T1156, rolls 39-41	—	State Hist. Soc. IA (17)
1880 Manufactures	T1156, rolls 42-45	—	State Hist. Soc. IA (17)
1850 Mortality	T1156, roll 54	—	State Hist. Soc. IA (17)
1860 Mortality	T1156, roll 55	—	State Hist. Soc. IA (17)
1870 Mortality	T1156, rolls 56-58	—	State Hist. Soc. IA (17)
1880 Mortality	T1156, rolls 59-62	—	State Hist. Soc. IA (17)

Kansas

1860 Agricultural	T1130, roll 1	—	KS St. Hist. Soc. Lib. (18)
1870 Agricultural	T1130, rolls 4, 8-12	—	KS St. Hist. Soc. Lib. (18)
1880 Agricultural	T1130, rolls 13-38	—	KS St. Hist. Soc. Lib. (18)
1880 Def/Dep/Del	T1130, rolls 45-48	—	KS St. Hist. Soc. Lib. (18)
1860 Industry	T1130, roll 1	—	KS St. Hist. Soc. Lib. (18)
1870 Industry	T1130, roll 4	—	KS St. Hist. Soc. Lib. (18)
1880 Manufactures	T1130, rolls 39-41	—	KS St. Hist. Soc. Lib. (18)
1860 Mortality	T1130, roll 1	—	KS St. Hist. Soc. Lib. (18)
1870 Mortality	T1130, rolls 3, 5	—	KS St. Hist. Soc. Lib. (18)
1880 Mortality	T1130, rolls 6-7, 42-44	—	KS St. Hist. Soc. Lib. (18)
1857 Shawnee Ind. Census	M1813, roll 2	—	KS St. Hist. Soc. Lib. (18)
1860 Soc. Statistics	T1130, roll 1	—	KS St. Hist. Soc. Lib. (18)
1870 Soc. Statistics	T1130, roll 2	—	KS St. Hist. Soc. Lib. (18)
1860 Soc. Statistics	T1130, roll 5	—	KS St. Hist. Soc. Lib. (18)

Kentucky

1850 Agricultural	M1528	—	Duke University (8)

State /Year/ Schedules	Nat'l Archives and Heritage Quest Film Numbers	Other Microfilm at	Original Manuscripts Located at (No. in Address List)
1860 Agricultural	M1528	—	Duke University (8)
1870 Agricultural	M1528	—	Duke University (8)
1880 Agricultural	M1528	—	Duke University (8)
1850 Def/Dep/Del	M1528	—	Duke University (8)
1820 Manufactures	M279, roll 20	—	NARA, Wash., DC (3)
1850 Industry	M1528	—	Duke University (8)
1860 Industry	M1528	—	Duke University (8)
1870 Industry	M1528	—	Duke University (8)
1880 Manufactures	M1528	—	Duke University (8)
1850 Mortality	T655, roll 13	—	NARA, Wash., DC (3)
1860 Mortality	M655, roll 14	—	NARA, Wash., DC (3)
1870 Mortality	M655, roll 15	—	NARA, Wash., DC (3)
1880 Mortality	M655, rolls 16-20 (includes index)	—	NARA, Wash., DC (3)
1850 Slave	M432, rolls 223-228	—	NARA, Wash., DC (3)
1860 Slave	M653, rolls 401-406	—	NARA, Wash., DC (3)
1850 Soc. Statistics	—	—	Duke University (8)
1860 Soc. Statistics	—	—	Duke University (8)
1870 Soc. Statistics	—	—	Duke University (8)

Louisiana

State /Year/ Schedules	Nat'l Archives and Heritage Quest Film Numbers	Other Microfilm at	Original Manuscripts Located at (No. in Address List)
1850 Agricultural	T1136, roll 5	—	Duke University (8)
1860 Agricultural	T1136, roll 6	—	Duke University (8)
1870 Agricultural	T1136, rolls 7-8,14	—	Duke University (8)
1880 Agricultural	T1136, rolls 9-13	—	Duke University (8)
1880 Def/Dep/Del	T1136, roll 4	—	Duke University (8)
1850 Mortality	T655, roll 21 (includes index)	—	NARA, Wash., DC (3)
1860 Mortality	T655, roll 22	—	NARA, Wash., DC (3)
1870 Mortality	T655, roll 21	—	NARA, Wash., DC (3)
1880 Mortality	T655, rolls 24-25 (includes index)	—	NARA, Wash., DC (3)
1850 Slave	M432, rolls 242-247	—	NARA, Wash., DC (3)
1860 Slave	M653, rolls 427-431	—	NARA, Wash., DC (3)
1850 Soc. Statistics	T1136, roll 1	—	Duke University (8)
1860 Soc. Statistics	T1136, rolls 1-2	—	Duke University (8)
1870 Soc. Statistics	T1136, rolls 1, 3	—	Duke University (8)

Maine

State /Year/ Schedules	Nat'l Archives and Heritage Quest Film Numbers	Other Microfilm at	Original Manuscripts Located at (No. in Address List)
1850 Agricultural	—	—	Maine St. Archives (19)
1860 Agricultural	—	—	Maine St. Archives (19)
1870 Agricultural	—	—	Maine St. Archives (19)

State /Year/ Schedules	Nat'l Archives and Heritage Quest Film Numbers	Other Microfilm at	Original Manuscripts Located at (No. in Address List)
1880 Agricultural	—	—	Maine St. Archives (19)
1880 Def/Dep/Del	—	—	Maine St. Archives (19)
1820 Manufactures	M279, roll 1	—	Maine St. Archives (19)
1850 Mortality	—	Maine St. Arch. (19) & FHL (10)	Maine St. Archives (19)
1860 Mortality	—	Maine St. Arch. (19) & FHL (10)	Maine St. Archives (19)
1870 Mortality	—	Maine St. Arch. (19) & FHL (10)	Maine St. Archives (19)
1880 Mortality	—	Maine St. Arch. (19) & FHL (10)	Maine St. Archives (19)
1850 Soc. Statistics	—	—	Maine St. Archives (19)
	—	—	Maine St. Archives (19)
	—	—	Maine St. Archives (19)
	—	—	Balt., MD, City Hall (21)
	—	—	Balt., MD, City Hall (21)
	—	MD St. Arch. (20) &U of NC (1)	MD State Archives (20)
1850 Agricultural (MD, except Balto.)	—	MD St. Arch. (20) &U of NC (1)	MD State Archives (20)
1860 Agricultural (MD, except Balto.)	—	MD St. Arch. (20) &U of NC (1)	MD State Archives (20)
1870 Agricultural (MD, except Balto.)	—	MD St. Arch. (20) &U of NC (1)	MD State Archives (20)
1880 Agricultural (MD, except Balto.)	—	MD St. Arch. (20) &U of NC (1)	MD State Archives (20)
1820 Manufactures	M279, roll 16	—	NARA, Wash., DC (3)
1850 Industry (Balto. city/county)	—	MD St. Arch. (20) &U of NC (1)	Balt., MD, City Hall (21)
1860 Industry (Balto. city/county)	—	MD St. Arch. (20) &U of NC (1)	Balt., MD, City Hall (21)
1880 Manufactures (Balto. city/county)	—	MD St. Arch. (20) &U of NC (1)	Balt., MD, City Hall (21)
1850 Mortality	—	—	MD State Archives (20)
1860 Mortality	—	—	MD State Archives (20)
1870 Mortality	—	—	MD State Archives (20)
1880 Mortality	—	—	MD State Archives (20)
1850 Slave	M432, rolls 300-302	—	NARA, Wash., DC (3)
1860 Slave	M653, rolls 484-485	—	NARA, Wash., DC (3)
1850 Soc. Statistics (Balto. city/county)	—	—	Balt., MD, City Hall (21)
1860 Soc. Statistics (Balto. city/county)	—	—	Balt., MD, City Hall (21)

State /Year/ Schedules	Nat'l Archives and Heritage Quest Film Numbers	Other Microfilm at	Original Manuscripts Located at (No. in Address List)
1850 Soc. Statistics (MD, except Balto.)	—	—	MD State Archives (20)
1860 Soc. Statistics (MD, except Balto.)	—	—	MD State Archives (20)

Massachusetts

State /Year/ Schedules	Nat'l Archives and Heritage Quest Film Numbers	Other Microfilm at	Original Manuscripts Located at (No. in Address List)
1820 Manufactures	M279, roll 2	—	NARA, Wash., DC (3)
1850 Agricultural	T1204, rolls 1-4	—	State Library of MA (22)
1860 Agricultural	T1204, rolls 11-14	—	State Library of MA (22)
1870 Agricultural	T1204, rolls 18-220	—	State Library of MA (22)
1880 Agricultural	T1204, rolls 24-29	—	State Library of MA (22)
1880 Def/Dep/Del	T1204, rolls 33-36	—	State Library of MA (22)
1850 Industry	T1204, rolls 5-6	—	State Library of MA (22)
1860 Industry	T1204, rolls 5-6	—	State Library of MA (22)
1870 Industry	T1204, rolls 5-6	—	State Library of MA (22)
1850 Mortality	T1204, rolls 9-10	—	State Library of MA (22)
1860 Mortality	T1204, roll 17	—	State Library of MA (22)
1870 Mortality	T1204, rolls 22-23	—	State Library of MA (22)
1880 Mortality	T1204, rolls 37-40	—	State Library of MA (22)
1850 Soc. Statistics	T1204, rolls 7-8	—	State Library of MA (22)
1860 Soc. Statistics	T1204, roll 16	—	State Library of MA (22)
1870 Soc. Statistics	T1204, roll 22	—	State Library of MA (22)

Michigan

State /Year/ Schedules	Nat'l Archives and Heritage Quest Film Numbers	Other Microfilm at	Original Manuscripts Located at (No. in Address List)
1850 Agricultural	T1164, rolls 1-4	—	MI State Archives (23)
1860 Agricultural	T1164, rolls 7-12	—	MI State Archives (23)
1870 Agricultural	T1164, rolls 16-24	—	MI State Archives (23)
1880 Agricultural	T1164, rolls 28-63	—	MI State Archives (23)
1850 Industry	T1164, roll __	—	MI State Archives (23)
1860 Industry	T1164, roll 13	—	MI State Archives (23)
1870 Industry	T1164, rolls 24-25	—	MI State Archives (23)
1880 Manufactures	T1164, rolls 64-68	—	MI State Archives (23)
1850 Mortality	T1163, roll 1	—	State Library of Ohio (34)
1860 Mortality	T1164, roll 15	—	MI State Archives (23)
1870 Mortality	T1164, rolls 26-27	—	MI State Archives (23)
1880 Mortality	T1164, rolls 74-77	—	MI State Archives (23)
1850 Soc. Statistics	T1164, roll 6	—	MI State Archives (23)
1860 Soc. Statistics	T1164, roll 14	—	MI State Archives (23)
1870 Soc. Statistics	T1164, roll 25	—	MI State Archives (23)
1880 Soc. Statistics	T1164, rolls 69-73	—	MI State Archives (23)

State /Year/ Schedules	Nat'l Archives and Heritage Quest Film Numbers	Other Microfilm at	Original Manuscripts Located at (No. in Address List)
Minnesota			
1850 Agricultural	M1802	—	MN St. Hist. Soc. (24)
1860 Agricultural	M1802	—	MN St. Hist. Soc. (24)
1870 Agricultural	M1802	—	MN St. Hist. Soc. (24)
1880 Agricultural	M1802	—	MN St. Hist. Soc. (24)
1880 Def/Dep/Del	—	—	MN St. Hist. Soc. (24)
1850 Industry	—	—	MN St. Hist. Soc. (24)
1860 Industry	—	—	MN St. Hist. Soc. (24)
1870 Industry	—	—	MN St. Hist. Soc. (24)
1880 Manufactures	—	—	MN St. Hist. Soc. (24)
1850 Mortality	—	—	MN St. Hist. Soc. (24)
1860 Mortality	—	—	MN St. Hist. Soc. (24)
1870 Mortality	—	—	MN St. Hist. Soc. (24)
1880 Mortality	—	—	MN St. Hist. Soc. (24)
1850 Soc. Statistics	—	—	MN St. Hist. Soc. (24)
1860 Soc. Statistics	—	—	MN St. Hist. Soc. (24)
1870 Soc. Statistics	—	—	MN St. Hist. Soc. (24)
Mississippi			
1850 Agricultural	—	U of NC, Chapel Hill (1)	MS Dept. Arch./Hist. (25)
1860 Agricultural	—	U of NC, Chapel Hill (1)	MS Dept. Arch./Hist. (25)
1870 Agricultural	—	U of NC, Chapel Hill (1)	MS Dept. Arch./Hist. (25)
1880 Agricultural	—	U of NC, Chapel Hill (1)	MS Dept. Arch./Hist. (25)
1850 Industry	—	U of NC, Chapel Hill (1)	MS Dept. Arch./Hist. (25)
1860 Industry	—	U of NC, Chapel Hill (1)	MS Dept. Arch./Hist. (25)
1870 Industry	—	U of NC, Chapel Hill (1)	MS Dept. Arch./Hist. (25)
1880 Manufactures	—	U of NC, Chapel Hill (1)	MS Dept. Arch./Hist. (25)
1850 Mortality	—	MS Dept. Arch./Hist. (25)	MS Dept. Arch./Hist. (25)
1860 Mortality	—	MS Dept. Arch./Hist. (25)	MS Dept. Arch./Hist. (25)
1870 Mortality	—	MS Dept. Arch./Hist. (25)	MS Dept. Arch./Hist. (25)
1880 Mortality	—	MS Dept. Arch./Hist. (25)	MS Dept. Arch./Hist. (25)
1850 Slave	M432, rolls 383-390	—	NARA, Wash., DC (3)
1860 Slave	M653, rolls 595-604	—	NARA, Wash., DC (3)
1850 Soc. Statistics	—	—	MS Dept. Arch./Hist. (25)
1860 Soc. Statistics	—	—	MS Dept. Arch./Hist. (25)
1870 Soc. Statistics	—	—	MS Dept. Arch./Hist. (25)
Missouri			
1850 Agricultural	—	—	MO State Archives (26)

State /Year/ Schedules	Nat'l Archives and Heritage Quest Film Numbers	Other Microfilm at	Original Manuscripts Located at (No. in Address List)
1860 Agricultural	—	—	MO State Archives (26)
1870 Agricultural	—	—	MO State Archives (26)
1880 Agricultural	—	—	MO State Archives (26)
1850 Def/Dep/Del	—	—	MO State Archives (26)
1850 Industry	—	—	MO State Archives (26)
1860 Industry	—	—	MO State Archives (26)
1870 Industry	—	—	MO State Archives (26)
1880 Manufactures	—	—	MO State Archives (26)
1850 Mortality	—	MO State Archives (26)	MO State Archives (26)
1860 Mortality	—	MO State Archives (26)	MO State Archives (26)
1870 Mortality	—	MO State Archives (26)	MO State Archives (26)
1880 Mortality	—	MO State Archives (26)	MO State Archives (26)
1850 Slave	M432, rolls 422-424	—	NARA, Wash., DC (3)
1860 Slave	M653, rolls 661-664	—	NARA, Wash., DC (3)
1850 Soc. Statistics	—	—	MO State Archives (26)
1860 Soc. Statistics	—	—	MO State Archives (26)
1870 Soc. Statistics	—	—	MO State Archives (26)

Montana

State /Year/ Schedules	Nat'l Archives and Heritage Quest Film Numbers	Other Microfilm at	Original Manuscripts Located at (No. in Address List)
1870 Agricultural	M1806	—	MT Hist. Soc. Lib. (27)
1880 Agricultural	M1806, M1795	—	MT Hist. Soc. Lib. (27)
1880 Def/Dep/Del	—	—	MT Hist. Soc. Lib. (27)
1870 Industry	M1806	—	MT Hist. Soc. Lib. (27)
1880 Manufactures	M1806	—	MT Hist. Soc. Lib. (27)
1870 Mortality	M1806	—	MT Hist. Soc. Lib. (27)
1880 Mortality	M1806	—	MT Hist. Soc. Lib. (27)
1870 Soc. Statistics	M1806	—	MT Hist. Soc. Lib. (27)

Nebraska

State /Year/ Schedules	Nat'l Archives and Heritage Quest Film Numbers	Other Microfilm at	Original Manuscripts Located at (No. in Address List)
1860 Agricultural	T1128, roll 2	—	NE St. Hist. Soc. Lib. (28)
1870 Agricultural	T1128, rolls 3-4	—	NE St. Hist. Soc. Lib. (28)
1880 Agricultural	T1128, rolls 5-12	—	NE St. Hist. Soc. Lib. (28)
1885 Agricultural	M352, rolls 1-56	—	NARA, Wash., DC (3)
1880 Def/Dep/Del	T1128, roll 16	—	NE St. Hist. Soc. Lib. (28)
1860 Industry	T1128, roll 2	—	NE St. Hist. Soc. Lib. (28)
1870 Industry	T1128, roll 4	—	NE St. Hist. Soc. Lib. (28)
1880 Manufactures	T1128, roll 13	—	NE St. Hist. Soc. Lib. (28)
1885 Manufactures	M352, rolls 1-56	—	NARA, Wash., DC (3)
1860 Mortality	T1128, roll 3	—	NE St. Hist. Soc. Lib. (28)

State /Year/ Schedules	Nat'l Archives and Heritage Quest Film Numbers	Other Microfilm at	Original Manuscripts Located at (No. in Address List)
1870 Mortality	T1128, rolls 3-4	—	NE St. Hist. Soc. Lib. (28)
1880 Mortality	T1128, rolls 14-15	—	NE St. Hist. Soc. Lib. (28)
1885 Mortality	M352, rolls 1-56	—	NARA, Wash., DC (3)
1860 Soc. Statistics	T1128, roll 2	—	NE St. Hist. Soc. Lib. (28)
1860 Soc. Statistics	T1128, roll 4	—	NE St. Hist. Soc. Lib. (28)

Nevada

State /Year/ Schedules	Nat'l Archives and Heritage Quest Film Numbers	Other Microfilm at	Original Manuscripts Located at (No. in Address List)
1880 Agricultural	M1794	—	Nevada Hist. Society (29)
1880 Def/Dep/Del	—	—	Nevada Hist. Society (29)
1880 Manufactures	—	—	Nevada Hist. Society (29)
1880 Mortality	—	—	Nevada Hist. Society (29)

New Hampshire

State /Year/ Schedules	Nat'l Archives and Heritage Quest Film Numbers	Other Microfilm at	Original Manuscripts Located at (No. in Address List)
1850 Agricultural	—	—	NH State Library (30)
1860 Agricultural	—	—	NH State Library (30)
1870 Agricultural	—	—	NH State Library (30)
1880 Agricultural	—	—	NH State Library (30)
1880 Def/Dep/Del	—	—	NH State Library (30)
1820 Manufactures	M279, roll 1	—	NARA, Wash., DC (3)
1850 Industry	—	—	NH State Library (30)
1860 Industry	—	—	NH State Library (30)
1870 Industry	—	—	NH State Library (30)
1880 Manufactures	—	—	NH State Library (30)
1850 Mortality	—	NH State Library (30)	NH State Library (30)
1860 Mortality	—	NH State Library (30)	NH State Library (30)
1870 Mortality	—	—	NH State Library (30)
1880 Mortality	—	NH State Library (30)	NH State Library (30)
1850 Soc. Statistics	—	—	NH State Library (30)
1860 Soc. Statistics	—	—	NH State Library (30)
1870 Soc. Statistics	—	—	NH State Library (30)

New Jersey

State /Year/ Schedules	Nat'l Archives and Heritage Quest Film Numbers	Other Microfilm at	Original Manuscripts Located at (No. in Address List)
1850 Agricultural	—	NJ State Library (31)	NJ State Library (31)
1860 Agricultural	—	NJ State Library (31)	NJ State Library (31)
1870 Agricultural	—	—	NJ State Library (31)
1880 Agricultural	—	—	NJ State Library (31)
1880 Def/Dep/Del	—	—	NJ State Library (31)
1820 Manufactures	M279, roll 17	—	NARA, Wash., DC (3)
1850 Industry	—	—	NJ State Library (31)

State /Year/ Schedules	Nat'l Archives and Heritage Quest Film Numbers	Other Microfilm at	Original Manuscripts Located at (No. in Address List)
1860 Industry	—	—	NJ State Library (31)
1870 Industry	—	—	NJ State Library (31)
1880 Manufactures	—	—	NJ State Library (31)
1850 Mortality	GR21, roll 1	—	NJ State Library (31)
1860 Mortality	GR21, roll 1	—	NJ State Library (31)
1870 Mortality	GR21, rolls 1-2	—	NJ State Library (31)
1880 Mortality	GR21, rolls 2-4	—	NJ State Library (31)
1850 Slave	M432, roll 466	—	NARA, Wash., DC (3)
1850 Soc. Statistics	—	—	NJ State Library (31)
1860 Soc. Statistics	—	—	NJ State Library (31)
1870 Soc. Statistics	—	—	NJ State Library (31)

New Mexico

State /Year/ Schedules	Nat'l Archives and Heritage Quest Film Numbers	Other Microfilm at	Original Manuscripts Located at (No. in Address List)
1885 Agricultural	M846, rolls 1-6	—	NARA, Wash., DC (3)
1885 Manufactures	M846, rolls 1-6	—	NARA, Wash., DC (3)
1885 Mortality	M846, rolls 1-6	—	NARA, Wash., DC (3)

New York

State /Year/ Schedules	Nat'l Archives and Heritage Quest Film Numbers	Other Microfilm at	Original Manuscripts Located at (No. in Address List)
1850 Agricultural	—	NY State Library (32)	NY State Library (32)
1860 Agricultural	—	NY State Library (32)	NY State Library (32)
1870 Agricultural	—	NY State Library (32)	NY State Library (32)
1880 Agricultural	—	NY State Library (32)	NY State Library (32)
1880 Def/Dep/Del	—	—	NY State Library (32)
1810 Manufactures	M1792, roll 1	—	NARA, Wash., DC (3)
1820 Manufactures	M279, rolls 5-11	—	NARA, Wash., DC (3)
1850 Industry	—	NY State Library (32)	NY State Library (32)
1860 Industry	—	NY State Library (32)	NY State Library (32)
1870 Industry	—	—	NY State Library (32)
1880 Manufactures	—	—	NY State Library (32)
1850 Mortality	—	—	NY State Library (32)
1860 Mortality	—	—	NY State Library (32)
1870 Mortality	—	—	NY State Library (32)
1880 Mortality	—	—	NY State Library (32)
1850 Soc. Statistics	—	—	NY State Library (32)
1860 Soc. Statistics	—	—	NY State Library (32)
1870 Soc. Statistics	—	—	NY State Library (32)

North Carolina

State /Year/ Schedules	Nat'l Archives and Heritage Quest Film Numbers	Other Microfilm at	Original Manuscripts Located at (No. in Address List)
1850 Agricultural	(no series #, rolls 1-2)	—	NC State Archives (33)

State /Year/ Schedules	Nat'l Archives and Heritage Quest Film Numbers	Other Microfilm at	Original Manuscripts Located at (No. in Address List)
1860 Agricultural	(no series #, rolls 3-4)	—	NC State Archives (33)
1870 Agricultural	(no series #, rolls 6-8)	—	NC State Archives (33)
1880 Agricultural	(no series #, rolls 9-22)	—	NC State Archives (33)
1880 Def/Dep/Del	GR2, roll 1 (certain counties only)	—	NC State Archives (33)
1820 Manufactures	M279, roll 19	—	NARA, Wash., DC (3)
1850 Industry	GR31, roll 25	—	NC State Archives (33)
1860 Industry	—	—	NC State Archives (33)
1870 Industry	GR25	NC State Archives (33)	NC State Archives (33)
1880 Manufactures	GR26	NC State Archives (33)	NC State Archives (33)
1850 Mortality	—	—	NC State Archives (33)
1860 Mortality	—	—	NC State Archives (33)
1870 Mortality	—	—	NC State Archives (33)
1880 Mortality	—	—	NC State Archives (33)
1850 Slave	M432, rolls 650-656	—	NARA, Wash., DC (3)
1860 Slave	M653, rolls 920-927	—	NARA, Wash., DC (3)
1850 Soc.Statistics	(no series #, roll 2)	—	NC State Archives (33)
1860 Soc.Statistics	(no series #, roll 5)	—	NC State Archives (33)
1870 Soc.Statistics	(no series #, roll 8)	—	NC State Archives (33)

North Dakota (See Dakota Territory)

Ohio

1850 Agricultural	T1159, rolls 1-11	—	State Library of OH (34)
1860 Agricultural	T1159, rolls 16-27	—	State Library of OH (34)
1870 Agricultural	T1159, rolls 31-43	—	State Library of OH (34)
1880 Agricultural	T1159, rolls 49-92	—	State Library of OH (34)
1880 Def/Dep/Del	T1159, rolls 99-101	—	State Library of OH (34)
1820 Manufactures	M279, rolls 21-25	—	State Library of OH (34)
1850 Industry	T1159, rolls 12-13	—	State Library of OH (34)
1860 Industry	T1159, roll 28	—	State Library of OH (34)
1870 Industry	T1159, rolls 44-48	—	State Library of OH (34)
1880 Manufactures	T1159, rolls 93-98	—	State Library of OH (34)
1850 Mortality	T1159, rolls 14-15	—	State Library of OH (34)
1860 Mortality	T1159, rolls 29-30	—	State Library of OH (34)
1870 Mortality	T1159, rolls 102-104	—	State Library of OH (34)

Oregon

1850 Agricultural	—	OR State Library (35)	OR State Library (35)
1860 Agricultural	—	OR State Library (35)	OR State Library (35)

State /Year/ Schedules	Nat'l Archives and Heritage Quest Film Numbers	Other Microfilm at	Original Manuscripts Located at (No. in Address List)
1870 Agricultural	—	OR State Library (35)	OR State Library (35)
1880 Def/Dep/Del	—	OR State Library (35)	OR State Library (35)
1850 Industry	—	OR State Library (35)	OR State Library (35)
1860 Industry	—	OR State Library (35)	OR State Library (35)
1870 Industry	—	OR State Library (35)	OR State Library (35)
1880 Manufactures	—	OR State Library (35)	OR State Library (35)
1850 Mortality	—	OR State Library (35)	OR State Library (35)
1860 Mortality	—	OR State Library (35)	OR State Library (35)
1870 Mortality	—	OR State Library (35)	OR State Library (35)
1880 Mortality	—	OR State Library (35)	OR State Library (35)
1850 Soc. Statistics	—	OR State Library (35)	OR State Library (35)
1860 Soc. Statistics	—	OR State Library (35)	OR State Library (35)
1870 Soc. Statistics	—	OR State Library (35)	OR State Library (35)

Pennsylvania

State /Year/ Schedules	Nat'l Archives and Heritage Quest Film Numbers	Other Microfilm at	Original Manuscripts Located at (No. in Address List)
1850 Agricultural	T1138, rolls 1-9	—	?
1860 Agricultural	T1138, rolls 10-19	—	?
1870 Agricultural	T1138, rolls 20-30a	—	?
1880 Agricultural	T1138, rolls 31-57	—	?
1880 Def/Dep/Del	M597, rolls 12-23	—	?
1820 Manufactures	M279, rolls 12-15	—	?
1850 Industry	T1157, rolls 1-5	—	?
1860 Industry	T1157, rolls 1-5	—	?
1870 Industry	M1796	—	?
1880 Manufactures	M1796	—	?
1850 Mortality	M1838	—	NARA, Wash., DC (3)
1870 Mortality	M1838	—	NARA, Wash., DC (3)
1880 Mortality	M1838	—	NARA, Wash., DC (3)
1850 Soc. Statistics	M597, rolls 1-5	—	?
1860 Soc. Statistics	M597, rolls 6-8	—	?
1870 Soc. Statistics	M597, roll 9	—	?

Rhode Island

State /Year/ Schedules	Nat'l Archives and Heritage Quest Film Numbers	Other Microfilm at	Original Manuscripts Located at (No. in Address List)
1870 Agricultural	—	—	RI State Archives (36)
1820 Manufactures	—	—	NARA, Wash., DC (3)
1870 Industry	—	—	RI State Archives (36)
1875 Manufactures	—	—	RI State Archives (36)
1885 Manufactures	—	—	RI State Archives (36)
1870 Mortality	—	—	RI State Archives (36)
1870 Soc. Statistics	—	—	RI State Archives (36)

State /Year/ Schedules	Nat'l Archives and Heritage Quest Film Numbers	Other Microfilm at	Original Manuscripts Located at (No. in Address List)
South Carolina			
1850 Agricultural	—	—	SC Dept. Arch/Hist (37)
1860 Agricultural	—	—	SC Dept. Arch/Hist (37)
1870 Agricultural	—	—	SC Dept. Arch/Hist (37)
1880 Agricultural	—	—	SC Dept. Arch/Hist (37)
1850 Def/Dep/Del	—	—	SC Dept. Arch/Hist (37)
1820 Manufactures	M279, roll 19	—	NARA, Wash., DC (3)
1850 Industry	—	—	SC Dept. Arch/Hist (37)
1860 Industry	—	—	SC Dept. Arch/Hist (37)
1870 Industry	—	—	SC Dept. Arch/Hist (37)
1880 Manufactures	—	—	SC Dept. Arch/Hist (37)
1850 Mortality	—	—	SC Dept. Arch/Hist (37)
1860 Mortality	—	—	SC Dept. Arch/Hist (37)
1870 Mortality	—	—	SC Dept. Arch/Hist (37)
1880 Mortality	—	—	SC Dept. Arch/Hist (37)
1850 Slave	M432, rolls 861-868	—	NARA, Wash., DC (3)
1860 Slave	M653, rolls 1229-1238	—	NARA, Wash., DC (3)
1850 Social Statistics	—	—	SC Dept. Arch/Hist (37)
1860 Social Statistics	—	—	SC Dept. Arch/Hist (37)
1870 Social Statistics	—	—	SC Dept. Arch/Hist (37)
South Dakota (See Dakota Territory)			
Tennessee			
1850 Agricultural	T1135, rolls 1-5	—	Duke University (8)
1860 Agricultural	T1135, rolls 6-10	—	Duke University (8)
1870 Agricultural	T1135, rolls 11-16	—	Duke University (8)
1880 Agricultural	T1135, rolls 17-29	—	Duke University (8)
1880 Def/Dep/Del	T1135, rolls 40-41	—	Duke University (8)
1820 Manufactures	M279, rolls 26-27	—	Duke University (8)
1850 Industry	T1135, rolls 30-32	—	Duke University (8)
1860 Industry	T1135, roll 32	—	Duke University (8)
1870 Industry	T1135, rolls 33-34	—	Duke University (8)
1880 Manufactures	T1135, rolls 35-36	—	Duke University (8)
1850 Mortality	M655, roll 26 (includes index)	—	NARA, Wash., DC (3)
1860 Mortality	M655, roll 27	—	NARA, Wash., DC (3)
1880 Mortality	M655, rolls 28-30	—	NARA, Wash., DC (3)
1850 Slave	M432, rolls 902-907	—	NARA, Wash., DC (3)
1860 Slave	M653, rolls 1281-1286	—	NARA, Wash., DC (3)
1850 Soc. Statistics	T1135, roll 37	—	Duke University (8)

State /Year/ Schedules	Nat'l Archives and Heritage Quest Film Numbers	Other Microfilm at	Original Manuscripts Located at (No. in Address List)
1860 Soc. Statistics	T1135, roll 38	—	Duke University (8)
1870 Soc. Statistics	T1135, roll 39	—	Duke University (8)

Texas

1850 Agricultural	T1134, rolls 2-3	—	Texas State Library (38)
1860 Agricultural	T1134, rolls 3-7	—	Texas State Library (38)
1870 Agricultural	T1134, rolls 7-13	—	Texas State Library (38)
1880 Agricultural	T1134, rolls 13-44	—	Texas State Library (38)
1880 Def/Dep/Del	T1134, rolls 49-53, GR2, roll 1	—	Texas State Library (38)
1850 Industry	T1134, roll 45	—	Texas State Library (38)
1860 Industry	T1134, rolls 45-46	—	Texas State Library (38)
1870 Industry	T1134, roll 47	—	Texas State Library (38)
1880 Manufactures	T1134, rolls 48-49	—	Texas State Library (38)
1850 Mortality	T1134, rolls 53-54, GR2, roll 2	—	Texas State Library (38)
1860 Mortality	T1134, rolls 54-55, GR2, rolls 2-3	—	Texas State Library (38)
1870 Mortality	T1134, rolls 55-56, GR2, rolls 3-4	—	Texas State Library (38)
1880 Mortality	T1134, rolls 56-60, GR2, rolls 4-8	—	Texas State Library (38)
1850 Slave	M432, rolls 917-918	—	NARA, Wash., DC (3)
1860 Slave	M653, rolls 1309-1312	—	NARA, Wash., DC (3)
1850 Soc. Statistics	T1134, roll 44	—	Texas State Library (38)
1860 Soc. Statistics	T1134, rolls 44-45	—	Texas State Library (38)
1870 Soc. Statistics	T1134, roll 45	—	Texas State Library (38)

Utah

1870 Mortality	T1134, roll 56	—	No longer at UT Archives. Current location unknown.

Vermont

1850 Agricultural	M1798, rolls 1-2	—	VT Dept. of Libraries (39)
1860 Agricultural	M1798, rolls 3-4	—	VT Dept. of Libraries (39)
1870 Agricultural	M1798, rolls 5-6	—	VT Dept. of Libraries (39)
1880 Agricultural	—	VT Pub. Recs. Div. (40)	VT Dept. of Libraries (39)
1880 Def/Dep/Del	—	—	VT Dept. of Libraries (39)
1820 Manufactures	M279, roll 3	—	NARA, Wash., DC (3)
1850 Industry	M1798, roll 7	—	VT Dept. of Libraries (39)
1860 Industry	M1798, roll 8	—	VT Dept. of Libraries (39)

State /Year/ Schedules	Nat'l Archives and Heritage Quest Film Numbers	Other Microfilm at	Original Manuscripts Located at (No. in Address List)
1870 Industry	M1798, roll 8	—	VT Dept. of Libraries (39)
1880 Manufactures	—	VT Pub. Recs. Div. (40)	VT Dept. of Libraries (39)
1850 Mortality	—	—	VT Dept. of Libraries (39)
1860 Mortality	—	—	VT Dept. of Libraries (39)
1870 Mortality	—	—	Texas State Library (38)
1880 Mortality	—	—	VT Dept. of Libraries (39)
1850 Soc. Statistics	—	—	VT Dept. of Libraries (39)
1860 Soc. Statistics	—	—	VT Dept. of Libraries (39)
1870 Soc. Statistics	—	—	VT Dept. of Libraries (39)

Virginia

State /Year/ Schedules	Nat'l Archives and Heritage Quest Film Numbers	Other Microfilm at	Original Manuscripts Located at (No. in Address List)
1850 Agricultural	T1132, rolls 1-3	—	VA State Lib./Arch. (41)
1860 Agricultural	T1132, rolls 1-3, M1808	—	VA State Lib./Arch. (41)
1870 Agricultural	T1132, rolls 11-14, 17	—	VA State Lib./Arch. (41)
1880 Agricultural	T1132, rolls 23-30	—	VA State Lib./Arch. (41)
1880 Def/Dep/Del	T1132, rolls 33-34	—	VA State Lib./Arch. (41)
1820 Manufactures	M279, roll 18	—	NARA, Wash., DC (3)
1850 Industry	T1132, roll 4	—	VA State Lib./Arch. (41)
1860 Industry	T1132, roll 8	—	VA State Lib./Arch. (41)
1860 Industry	M1808 (No.Halifax Co only)	—	Duke University (8)
1870 Industry	T1132, roll 15	—	VA State Lib./Arch. (41)
1880 Manufactures	T1132, rolls 31-32	—	VA State Lib./Arch. (41)
1850 Mortality	T1132, roll 1	—	VA State Lib./Arch. (41)
1860 Mortality	T1132, roll 5	—	VA State Lib./Arch. (41)
1860 Mortality	M1808 (No.Halifax Co only)	—	Duke University (8)
1870 Mortality	T1132, roll 10	—	VA State Lib./Arch. (41)
1880 Mortality	T1132, rolls 18-19	—	VA State Lib./Arch. (41)
1850 Slave	M432, rolls 983-993	—	NARA, Wash., DC (3)
1860 Slave	M653, rolls 1386-1397	—	NARA, Wash., DC (3)
1860 Slave	M1808 (No.Halifax Co only)	—	Duke University (8)
1860 Soc. Statistics	T1132, roll 9	—	VA State Lib./Arch. (41)
1870 Soc. Statistics	T1132, roll 16	—	VA State Lib./Arch. (41)

Washington

State /Year/ Schedules	Nat'l Archives and Heritage Quest Film Numbers	Other Microfilm at	Original Manuscripts Located at (No. in Address List)
1860 Agricultural	A1154, roll 1	—	WA State Library (42)
1870 Agricultural	A1154, roll 4	—	WA State Library (42)
1880 Agricultural	A1154, roll 6	—	WA State Library (42)
1860 Def/Dep/Del	A1154, roll 8	—	WA State Library (42)
1860 Industry	A1154, roll 2	—	WA State Library (42)
1870 Industry	A1154, roll 5	—	WA State Library (42)

State /Year/ Schedules	Nat'l Archives and Heritage Quest Film Numbers	Other Microfilm at	Original Manuscripts Located at (No. in Address List)
1880 Manufactures	A1154, roll 7	—	WA State Library (42)
1860 Mortality	A1154, roll 3	—	WA State Library (42)
1870 Mortality	A1154, roll 3	—	WA State Library (42)
1880 Mortality	A1154, roll 3	—	WA State Library (42)
1860 Soc. Statistics	A1154, roll 2	—	WA State Library (42)
1870 Soc. Statistics	A1154, roll 5	—	WA State Library (42)

West Virginia

State /Year/ Schedules	Nat'l Archives and Heritage Quest Film Numbers	Other Microfilm at	Original Manuscripts Located at (No. in Address List)
1850 Agricultural	—	WV Arch./Hist. (43) & U of NC (1)	WV Arch./Hist. Lib. (43)
1860 Agricultural	—	WV Arch./Hist. (43) & U of NC (1)	WV Arch./Hist. Lib. (43)
1870 Agricultural	—	WV Arch./Hist. (43) & U of NC (1)	WV Arch./Hist. Lib. (43)
1880 Agricultural	—	WV Arch./Hist. (43) & U of NC (1)	WV Arch./Hist. Lib. (43)
1880 Def/Dep/Del	—	—	WV Arch./Hist. Lib. (43)
1870 Industry	—	WV Arch./Hist. (43) & U of NC (1)	WV Arch./Hist. Lib. (43)
1880 Manufactures	—	—	WV Arch./Hist. Lib. (43)
1850 Mortality	—	—	WV Arch./Hist. Lib. (43)
1860 Mortality	—	—	WV Arch./Hist. Lib. (43)
1870 Mortality	—	—	WV Arch./Hist. Lib. (43)
1880 Mortality	—	—	WV Arch./Hist. Lib. (43)

Wisconsin

State /Year/ Schedules	Nat'l Archives and Heritage Quest Film Numbers	Other Microfilm at	Original Manuscripts Located at (No. in Address List)
1850 Agricultural	—	St. Hist. Soc. of WI (44)	St. Hist. Soc. of WI (44)
1860 Agricultural	—	St. Hist. Soc. of WI (44)	St. Hist. Soc. of WI (44)
1870 Agricultural	—	St. Hist. Soc. of WI (44)	St. Hist. Soc. of WI (44)
1880 Agricultural	—	—	St. Hist. Soc. of WI (44)
1880 Def/Dep/Del	—	—	St. Hist. Soc. of WI (44)
1850 Industry	—	St. Hist. Soc. of WI (44)	St. Hist. Soc. of WI (44)
1860 Industry	—	St. Hist. Soc. of WI (44)	St. Hist. Soc. of WI (44)
1870 Industry	—	St. Hist. Soc. of WI (44)	St. Hist. Soc. of WI (44)
1880 Manufactures	—	—	St. Hist. Soc. of WI (44)
1850 Mortality	—	St. Hist. Soc. of WI (44)	St. Hist. Soc. of WI (44)
1860 Mortality	—	St. Hist. Soc. of WI (44)	St. Hist. Soc. of WI (44)
1870 Mortality	—	St. Hist. Soc. of WI (44)	St. Hist. Soc. of WI (44)
1880 Mortality	—	—	St. Hist. Soc. of WI (44)
1850 Soc. Statistics	—	St. Hist. Soc. of WI (44)	St. Hist. Soc. of WI (44)
1860 Soc. Statistics	—	St. Hist. Soc. of WI (44)	St. Hist. Soc. of WI (44)
1870 Soc. Statistics	—	St. Hist. Soc. of WI (44)	St. Hist. Soc. of WI (44)

Wyoming

State /Year/ Schedules	Nat'l Archives and Heritage Quest Film Numbers	Other Microfilm at	Original Manuscripts Located at (No. in Address List)
1880 Agricultural	M1794	—	Duke University (8)

Repositories Holding Original or Microfilm Copies of Non-population Census Schedules

1. **University of North Carolina at Chapel Hill**
   Walter Royal Davis Library
   Special Collections
   Chapel Hill, NC 27599
   Interlibrary Loan Service: (919) 962-0077

2. **Alabama Department of Archives and History**
   624 Washington Avenue
   Montgomery, AL 36130-3601
   (205) 832-6510

3. **National Archives and Records Administration (NARA)**
   Eighth and Pennsylvania Avenue, N.W.
   Washington, DC 20408
   (202) 523-3218

4. **Arkansas Historical Commission**
   1 Capitol Mall
   Little Rock, AR 72201
   (501) 682-6900

5. **University of Arkansas, Fayetteville**
   Library, Special Collections
   Fayetteville, AR 72701
   Interlibrary Loan Service: (501) 575-5311

6. **University of California, Berkeley**
   The Library
   Special Collections
   Berkeley, CA 94270
   (415) 642-0704

7. **California State Library**
   914 Capitol Mall - PO Box 942837
   Sacramento, CA 94237-0001
   Interlibrary Loan Service: (916) 322-2620

8. **Duke University**
   William R. Perkins Library
   Durham, NC 27706
   Interlibrary Loan Librarian: (919) 684-3978

9. **Connecticut State Library**
   231 Capitol Avenue
   Hartford, CT 06106
   Interlibrary Loan Service: (203) 566-2300

10. **Family History Library**
    35 North West Temple
    Salt Lake City, UT 84150
    (801) 240-2331

11. **South Dakota State Historical Society**
    900 Governors Drive
    Pierre, SD 57501
    (605) 773-3804

12. **Idaho Historical Society**
    610 N. Julia Davis Drive
    Boise, ID 83706
    (208) 384-2120

13. **Delaware State Archives**
    Hall of Records
    Duke of York Street and Legislature Avenue
    PO Box 1401
    Dover, DE 19901
    (302) 736-5318

14. **Florida State University**
    Strozier Library
    Tallahassee, FL 32306-2047
    Interlibrary Loan Service: (904) 644-4466

15. **Illinois State Archives Division**
    Office of the Secretary of State
    Archives Building
    Capitol Complex
    Springfield, IL 62756
    (217) 782-4682

16. **Indiana State Library**
    140 North Senate Avenue
    Indianapolis, IN 46204
    (317) 232-3686

17. State Historical Society of Iowa
Library Archives Bureau
600 East Locust
Des Moines, IA 50319
(515) 281-5111

18. Kansas State Historical Society Library
6425 South West 6th Avenue
Topeka, KS 66615-1099
(785) 272-8681

19. Maine State Archives
State House Station #84
Augusta, ME 04333
(207) 289-5790

20. Maryland State Archives
Hall of Records Building
350 Rowe Boulevard
Annapolis, MD 21401
(301) 974-3914

21. Baltimore City Legislative Reference Library
626 City Hall
Baltimore, MD 21202-3468
(301) 396-4730

22. State Library of Massachusetts
341 State House
Boston, MA 02133-1099
(617) 727-2590

23. Michigan State Archives
Bureau of History
Department of State
717 West Allegan
Lansing, MI 48918
(517) 373-1408

24. Minnesota State Historical Society
690 Cedar Street
St. Paul, MN 55101
(612) 296-2143

25. Mississippi Department of Archives and History
Archives and History Building
100 South State Street, Capitol Green
PO Box 571
Jackson, MS 39205
(601) 359-6876

26. Missouri State Archives
600 West Main Street
PO Box 778
Jefferson City, MO 65102
(314) 751-3280

27. Montana Historical Society Library
Memorial Building
225 North Roberts Street
Helena, MT 59620
(406) 444-2681

28. Nebraska State Historical Society Library
Department of Reference Services
1500 R Street
PO Box 82554
Lincoln, NE 68501
(402) 471-3270

29. Nevada Historical Society
Museum-Research Library
1650 Virginia Street
Reno, NV 89701
(702) 789-0190

30. New Hampshire State Library
20 Park Street
Concord, NH 03301
(603) 271-2394

31. New Jersey State Library
State Library Building
185 West State Street - CN 520
Trenton, NJ 08625-0520
Interlibrary Loan Service: (609) 292-7894

32. New York State Library
State Education Department
Cultural Education Center
Empire State Plaza
Albany, NY 12230
(518) 474-5930

33. North Carolina State Archives
State Library Building
109 East Jones Street - PO Box 1881
Raleigh, NC 27611
(919) 733-3952

34. State Library of Ohio
65 South Front Street - Room 510
Columbus, OH 43266-0334
Interlibrary Loan Service: (614) 644-6956

35. Oregon State Library
State Library Building
Summer & Court Streets
Salem, OR 97310- 0640
Interlibrary Loan Service: (503) 378-4498

36. Rhode Island State Archives
State House, Room 43
82 Smith
Providence, RI 02903
(401) 277-2353, ext. 2353

37. South Carolina Department of Archives and History
Capitol Station
PO Box 11669
Columbia, SC 29211-1669
(803) 734-8577

38. Texas State Library
1201 Brazos, PO Box 12927
Austin, TX 78711
Interlibrary Loan Service: (512) 463-5455

39. Vermont Department of Libraries
Pavilion Office Building
Reference and Law Services
109 State Street
Montpelier, VT 05602
(802) 828-3261

40. Vermont Public Records Division
U.S. Route 2 - Middlesex
Montpelier, VT 05633-7601
(802) 828-3288

41. Virginia State Library and Archives
11th Street at Capitol Square
Richmond, VA 23219-3491
(804) 786-2332

42. Washington State Library
Capitol Campus
State Library Building, MS AJ-11
Olympia, WA 98504
Interlibrary Loan Service: (360) 753-3616

43. West Virginia Archives and History Division Library
Science and Cultural Center
Capitol Complex
Charleston, WV 25305
(304) 348-0225

44. State Historical Society of Wisconsin Library
816 State Street
Madison, WI 53706
(608) 262-3421

Section 5

Census Forms, 1790-1930

1790 Federal Census

Researcher: Date:

Heads of household extracted from the original text of the 1790 Population Schedules

NARA Microfilm Series M637 Roll no. Page no. STATE & COUNTY	Name of HEAD OF HOUSEHOLD	FREE WHITES			Slaves	Other free persons
		Males 16 & over	Males 0 - 15	Females		

First Census of the United States - 1790

General Information: In 1908, the Census Office in Washington, D.C., undertook a project to extract and index the 1790 census name lists, a publication now commonly known as the *1790 Heads of Families*. It includes the name lists for twelve of the sixteen federal court districts that were originally enumerated in the 1790 census. Vermont entered the Union as the 14th state in early 1791, its census taken as of 1 April 1791. Also, in 1790, Maine was still part of Massachusetts but had its own census because it was a separate federal court district. The same was true of Kentucky which was still part of Virginia but was a separate federal court district. The Census Office's 1790 volumes, therefore, are limited to the federal court districts of Connecticut, Maine, Maryland, Massachusetts, New Hampshire, New York, North Carolina, Pennsylvania, Rhode Island, South Carolina, Vermont, and Virginia.

Content: The 1790 census format included the name of a head of household, the number of free white males under 16, and 16 or older, the number of free white females of any age, the name of a slave owner, and number of slaves owned by that person.

Census losses: 1790 districtwide census losses include those for Kentucky, Delaware, Georgia, New Jersey, and Virginia. Since Virginia had extant tax lists covering all of its counties for the years immediately preceding 1790, the Census Office used these tax lists to reconstruct the 1790 name lists for the entire state of Virginia. A few 1790 counties of other states were also reconstructed from tax lists, including certain counties in North Carolina and Maryland.

Microfilm: The National Archives and Records Administration microfilm for the 1790 census is contained on 12 rolls of 35mm film, series M637. In addition, the 1908 printed volumes of the 1790 census were filmed on three rolls of 35mm film as series T498.

1800 Federal Census

Researcher: Date:

Heads of households extracted from the original text of the 1800 Population Schedules

NARA Microfilm Series M32   Roll no.:   State: County: Township:

Page	Name of HEAD OF HOUSEHOLD	FREE WHITE MALES					FREE WHITE FEMALES					Other free person	Slaves
		0 thru 9	10 thru 15	16 thru 25	26 thru 44	45 and over	0 thru 9	10 thru 15	16 thru 25	26 thru 44	45 and over		

Second Census of the United States - 1800

General Information: The 1800 federal census included two new states admitted to the Union since 1790: Kentucky, admitted in 1792; and Tennessee, previously the "Southwest Territory," admitted in 1796 for a total of 16 states in the Union. In addition, three territories were enumerated for the first time in 1800: Mississippi Territory, created in 1798 from lands obtained in a treaty with Spain; the Northwest Territory, created in 1787 (but not enumerated in 1790); and Indiana Territory, divided from the old Northwest Territory in early 1800. Maine was still a federal court district within the state of Massachusetts; and therefore, Maine had a separate census taken. The District of Columbia was created in 1791 from land ceded by Maryland and Virginia, but its first census of 1800 was taken with Maryland and Virginia.

Content: The 1800 census format included the name of a head of household, the number of free white males and free white females in specific age categories, the name of a slave owner, and number of slaves owned by that person.

Census losses: 1800 districtwide census losses include those for Georgia, Indiana Territory, Kentucky, Mississippi Territory, New Jersey, Northwest Territory, and Tennessee, which have no known substitutes except some isolated tax lists. The 1800 census for Washington County, Northwest Territory (later Ohio), was found among the papers of the New Ohio Company. The papers are now at the Special Collections Department, Marietta College Library, Marietta, Ohio, and microfilmed by the FHL in Salt Lake City. Washington County was about one-third of the population of the old Northwest Territory in 1800. The portion of the District of Columbia included with the Maryland side (Washington County, DC) survives and is part of the Maryland 1800 census. The portion for the Virginia side (Alexandria County, DC) is lost along with all of Virginia for 1800.

Microfilm: The National Archives and Records Administration microfilm for the 1800 census is contained on 52 rolls of 35mm film, series M32.

1810 Federal Census

Researcher: Date:

Heads of households extracted from the original text of the 1810 Population Schedules

NARA Microfilm Series M252   Roll no.:   State: County: Township:

Page	Name of HEAD OF HOUSEHOLD	FREE WHITE MALES					FREE WHITE FEMALES					Other free person	Slaves
		0 thru 9	10 thru 15	16 thru 25	26 thru 44	45 and over	0 thru 9	10 thru 15	16 thru 25	26 thru 44	45 and over		

Third Census of the United States - 1810

General Information: The 1810 federal census included the new state of Ohio, admitted in 1803, bringing the total to seventeen states in the Union. The 1810 census also included the District of Columbia, separated in the census schedules from Virginia and Maryland for the first time. In addition, six territories in the public domain were enumerated. Georgia ceded its western lands to the federal government in 1802. These were added to Mississippi Territory, doubling its size. In 1804, two new territories were created from the Louisiana Purchase: Louisiana Territory (renamed Missouri Territory in 1812); and Orleans Territory, which would become the state of Louisiana in 1812. The remainder of the old Northwest Territory left by the creation of the state of Ohio and a part of Indiana Territory were combined to become Michigan Territory in 1805. To complete the changes for the decade, Illinois Territory was created in 1809, reducing Indiana Territory to its present boundaries except it still included the northern peninsula of present-day Michigan.

Content: The 1810 census format included the name of a head of household, the number of free white males and free white females in specific age categories, the name of a slave owner, and number of slaves owned by that person.

Census losses: 1810 districtwide census losses include those for the District of Columbia, Georgia, Indiana Territory, Michigan Territory, Mississippi Territory, Louisiana (MO) Territory, New Jersey, and Tennessee. Partial losses included Illinois Territory which had only two counties (Randolph is extant, St. Clair is lost), and Ohio, all lost except Washington County.

Microfilm: The National Archives and Records Administration microfilm for the 1810 census is contained on 71 rolls of 35mm film, series M252

1820 Federal Census

Researcher: Date:

Heads of households extracted from the original text of the 1820 Population Schedules

NARA Microfilm Series M33   Roll no.:   State: County: Township:

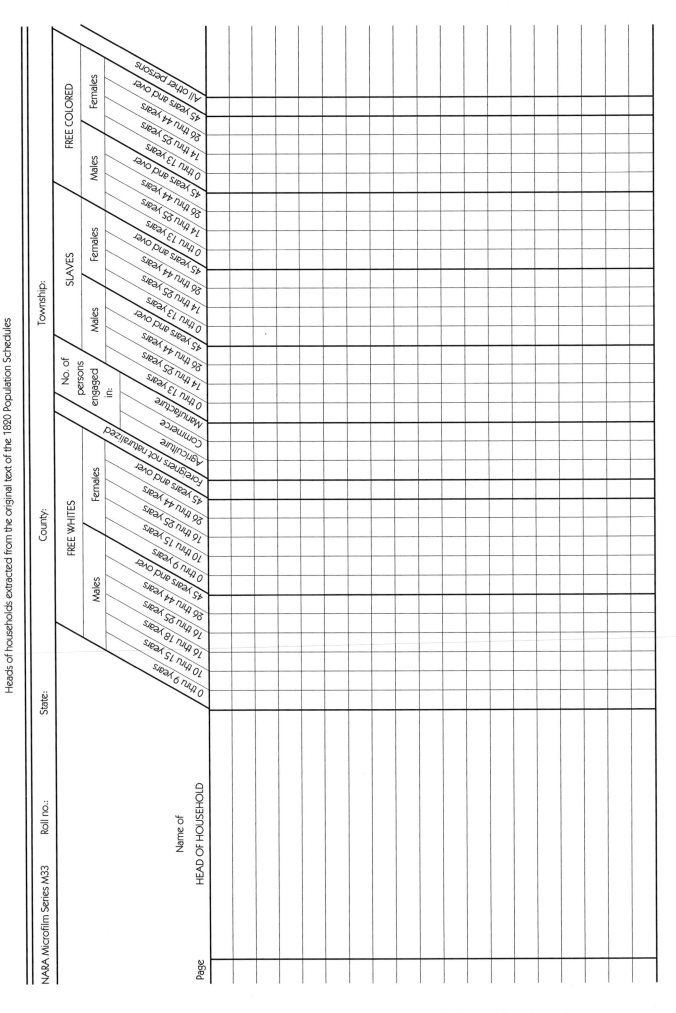

Fourth Census of the United States - 1820

General Information: By 1820 six new states had been formed bringing the total to twenty-three states in the Union. The six were: Louisiana, admitted in 1812; Indiana in 1816; Mississippi in 1817; Illinois in 1818; Alabama in 1819; and Maine in 1820. Orleans Territory became the state of Louisiana in 1812, and Louisiana Territory was renamed Missouri Territory the same year. Michigan Territory spanned the northern portion of the old Northwest Territory north of the states of Ohio, Indiana, and Illinois. A new Arkansas Territory was created from the southern area of Missouri Territory in 1819.

Content: The 1820 census format included the name of a head of household, the number of free white males and free white females in specific age categories, the name of a slave owner, the number of slaves owned by that person, the number of male and female slaves by age categories, and the number of foreigners (not naturalized) in a household.

Census losses: 1820 districtwide census losses include those for Arkansas Territory, Missouri Territory, and New Jersey. Partial losses were for over half the counties of Alabama. In 1820, Tennessee had two federal court districts, one with a U.S. Courthouse in Nashville, the other in Knoxville. The original censuses returned to Washington were from the Nashville district only, representing the western two-thirds of the state. The schedules for the twenty Eastern counties enumerated within the Knoxville 1820 district were not received in Washington and are presumed lost.

Microfilm: The National Archives and Records Administration microfilm for the 1820 census is contained on 142 rolls of 35mm film, series M33.

1830 Federal Census

NARA Microfilm Series M19   Roll no.:

Page:

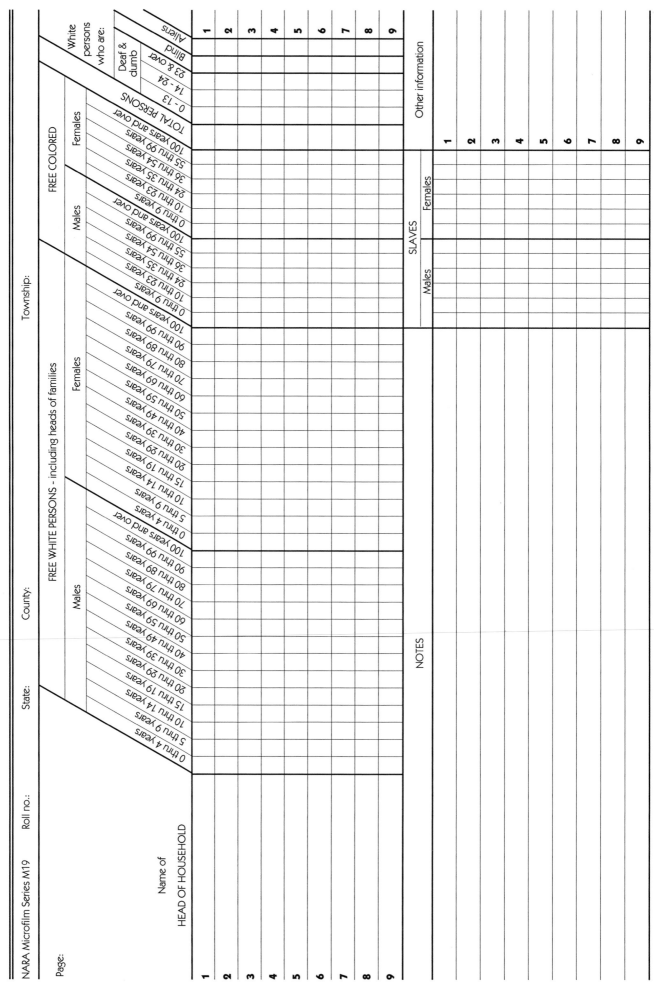

Extracted from the original text of the 1830 Census Schedules

Researcher: Date:

State: County: Township:

Name of HEAD OF HOUSEHOLD

FREE WHITE PERSONS - including heads of families

Males
0 thru 4 years
5 thru 9 years
10 thru 14 years
15 thru 19 years
20 thru 29 years
30 thru 39 years
40 thru 49 years
50 thru 59 years
60 thru 69 years
70 thru 79 years
80 thru 89 years
90 thru 99 years
100 years and over

Females
0 thru 4 years
5 thru 9 years
10 thru 14 years
15 thru 19 years
20 thru 29 years
30 thru 39 years
40 thru 49 years
50 thru 59 years
60 thru 69 years
70 thru 79 years
80 thru 89 years
90 thru 99 years
100 years and over

FREE COLORED

Males
0 thru 9 years
10 thru 23 years
24 thru 35 years
36 thru 54 years
55 thru 99 years
100 years and over

Females
0 thru 9 years
10 thru 23 years
24 thru 35 years
36 thru 54 years
55 thru 99 years
100 years and over

TOTAL PERSONS

White persons who are:
Deaf & dumb
0 - 13
14 - 24
25 & over
Blind
Aliens

SLAVES

Males
1
2
3
4
5
6
7
8
9

Females
1
2
3
4
5
6
7
8
9

Other information

NOTES

Fifth Census of the United States - 1830

General Information: Missouri became a state in 1821, bringing the total number of states in the 1830 census to twenty-four. Florida was purchased from Spain in 1819, but treaty ratification did not occur until 1821. Florida became a territory in 1822, and its first census taken was in 1830. No other new territories were added to the U.S. before this census year.

Content: The 1830 census format included the name of a head of household; the number of free white males and free white females in specific age categories; the name of a slave owner and number of slaves owned by that person; the number of male and female slaves by age categories; the number of foreigners (not naturalized) in a household; and the number of deaf, dumb, and blind persons within a household.

Census losses: None for 1830, except some countywide losses in Massachusetts, Maryland, and Mississippi.

Microfilm: The National Archives and Records Administration microfilm for the 1830 census is contained on 201 rolls of 35mm film, series M19.

1840 Federal Census

Date:

Researcher:

Extracted from the original text of the 1840 Census Schedules

NARA Microfilm Series M704   Roll no.:   State: County: Township:

Page:

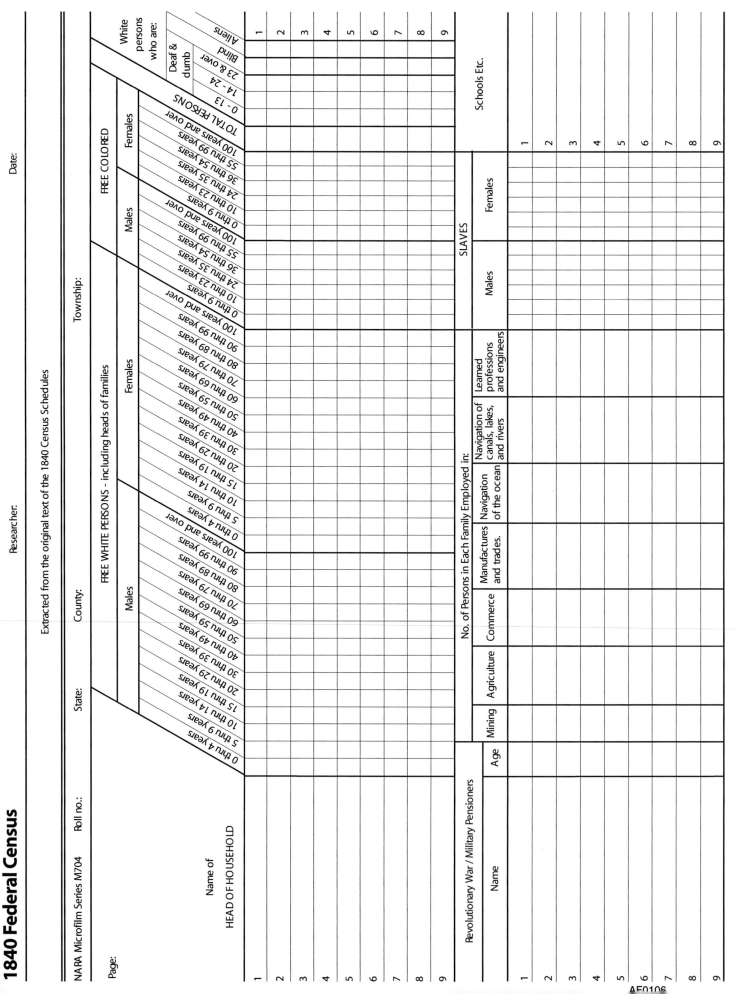

Sixth Census of the United States - 1840

General Information: Two new states were included in the 1840 federal census: Arkansas, admitted in 1836; and Michigan in 1837 bringing the total of states in the Union to twenty-six. Florida Territory was enumerated, as were two new territories: Wisconsin Territory, carved out of the bounds of Michigan Territory in 1836, including part of the area of present-day Minnesota; and Iowa Territory, created from the unorganized territory between the Mississippi and Missouri Rivers in 1838 and a northern area that later became Minnesota and Dakota Territories. The "Indian Territory" was created in 1828 from the western part of Arkansas Territory, but no federal census was taken in that area until 1860.

Content: The 1840 census format included the name of a head of household; the number of free white males and free white females in specific age categories; the name of a slave owner; the number of slaves owned by that person; the number of male and female slaves by age categories; the number of foreigners (not naturalized) in a household; the number of deaf, dumb, and blind persons within a household; the number and age of each person receiving a military pension; and the number of persons attending school.

Microfilm: The National Archives and Records Administration microfilm for the 1840 census is contained on 580 rolls of 35mm film, series M704.

1850 Federal Census

Researcher:

Date:

NARA Microfilm Series M432

Roll no.::

State:

County:

Township:

Page

Extracted from the original text of the 1850 Census Schedules

Dwelling-house no.	Family no.	Name of Person	Age	Sex	Color	Occupation	Value of real estate owned	Birthplace	Married within year	Attended school	Cannot read or write	Whether deaf and dumb, blind, insane, idiotic, pauper, or convict
1	2	3	4	5	6	7	8	9	10	11	12	13

Description (columns 4–6: Age, Sex, Color)

Seventh Census of the United States - 1850

General Information: Between 1840 and 1850, five new states were added to the Union: Florida and Texas, both admitted in 1845; Iowa in 1846; Wisconsin in 1848; and California in 1850 bringing the total to thirty-one states. In addition, four new territories were included: Oregon Territory, created in 1848; Minnesota Territory in 1849; and New Mexico Territory and Utah Territory, both created in 1850. No enumeration for the "Unorganized Territory" of the great plains was included in the 1850 census. This area later became all or part of the states of Nebraska, North Dakota, South Dakota, Montana, Wyoming, Colorado, Kansas, and Oklahoma.

Content: For the first time, the 1850 census schedules listed the name of every person in a household. The census was taken with a census day of 1 June 1850. The categories included the following for each person: name; age as of the census day; sex; color; birthplace; occupation; value of real estate; whether married within the previous year; whether deaf, dumb, blind, or insane; whether a pauper; whether able to read or speak English; and whether the person attended school within the previous year. No relationships were shown between members of a household.

Microfilm: The National Archives and Records Administration microfilm for the 1850 census is contained on 1,009 rolls of 35mm film, series M432, including free schedules and slave schedules.

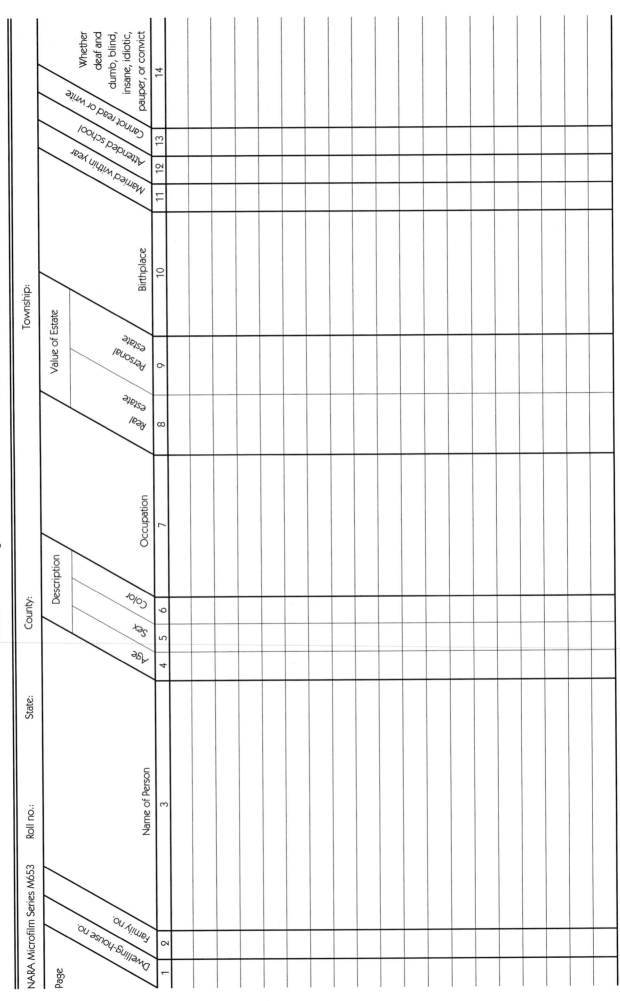

1860 Federal Census

Researcher:

Date:

Extracted from the original text of the 1860 Census Schedules

NARA Microfilm Series M653   Roll no.:   State: County: Township:

Page

Dwelling-house no.	Family no.	Name of Person	Age	Sex	Color	Occupation	Real estate	Personal estate	Birthplace	Married within year	Attended school	Cannot read or write	Whether deaf and dumb, blind, insane, idiotic, pauper, or convict
1	2	3	4	5	6	7	8	9	10	11	12	13	14

Description

Value of Estate

Eighth Census of the United States - 1860

General Information: Between 1850 and 1860, two new states were added to the Union for a total of thirty-three states: Minnesota was admitted in 1858, and Oregon in 1859. The existing territories of New Mexico and Utah were included in the 1860 census as were three new territories: Washington Territory, created in 1853 from Oregon Territory; and Nebraska and Kansas Territories, created from the "Unorganized Territory" in 1854. Washington Territory increased in size in 1859 when Oregon became a state, adding the area of present-day Idaho plus the portions of present-day Montana and Wyoming lying west of the continental divide. The region matching the present bounds of Oklahoma was unofficially called the "Indian Territory." In 1860, for the first time, a census was taken there, but only for non-Indians living in that region. The name lists for the non-Indians in the "Indian Territory" were added to the end of the Arkansas name lists. The remainder of the "Unorganized Territory" left by the creation of Nebraska Territory and the state of Minnesota was included in the 1860 census, enumerated as "Unorganized Dakota Territory."

Content: The 1860 census schedules listed the name of every person in a household with a census day of 1 June 1860. The categories included the following for each person: name; age as of the census day; sex; color; birthplace; occupation; value of real estate; value of personal estate; whether married within the previous year; whether deaf, dumb, blind, or insane; whether a pauper; whether able to read or speak English; and whether the person attended school within the previous year. No relationships between members of a household were given.

Microfilm: The National Archives and Records Administration microfilm for the 1860 census is contained on 1,438 rolls of 35mm film, series M653, including free schedules and slave schedules.

1870 Federal Census

Researcher:

Date:

Extracted from the original text of the 1870 Census Schedules

NARA Microfilm Series M593   Roll no.::   State: County: Township:

Page

1	2	3		4	5	6	7	8	9	10	11	12	13	14	15	16	17	18	19	20
Dwelling-house no.	Family no.	Name of Person		Age	Sex	Color	Occupation	Value of real estate	Value of personal estate	Birthplace	Father of foreign birth	Mother of foreign birth	If born within year	If married within year	Attended school	Cannot read	Cannot write	Whether deaf and dumb, blind, insane, or idiots	Male over 21	Denied vote

Description / Value of Estate

Ninth Census of the United States - 1870

General Information: Between 1860 and 1870—the decade of the Civil War—four new states were added to the Union for a total of thirty-seven states: Kansas became a state in 1861, West Virginia in 1863, Nevada in 1864, and Nebraska in 1867. In addition, six new territories were created: Dakota and Colorado Territories in 1861, Arizona and Idaho Territories in 1863, Montana Territory in 1864, and Wyoming Territory in 1868. New Mexico Territory was reduced to its present size with the creation of Arizona and Colorado Territories, as was Washington Territory with the creation of Idaho, Wyoming, and Montana Territories. Kansas was reduced to its present size with the creation of Colorado Territory, as was Nebraska with the creation of Dakota Territories, Montana and Wyoming. Utah Territory was reduced to its present size with the creation of the state of Nevada and Colorado Territory. The "Unorganized Territory," unofficially called the "Indian Territory" was not enumerated for non-Indians in 1870.

Content: The 1870 census schedules listed the name of every person in a household with a census day of 1 June 1870. The categories included the following for each person: name; age as of the census day; month of birth if born during the year; sex; color; birthplace; occupation; value of real estate; value of personal estate; whether married within the previous year; month of marriage if married within the previous year; whether deaf, dumb, blind, or insane; whether able to read or write; whether father or mother of foreign birth; and whether the person attended school within the previous year. No relationships between members of a household were shown.

Microfilm: The National Archives and Records Administration microfilm for the 1870 census is contained on 1,748 rolls of 35mm film, mostly in series M593. Some Minnesota schedules were filmed with series M593 on rolls 716-719. The entire Minnesota state copy is on series T132, rolls 1-13.

1880 Federal Census

Date:

Researcher:

Extracted from the original text of the 1880 Census Schedules

NARA Microfilm Series T9   Roll no.:   State: County: Township:

E.D.

Page

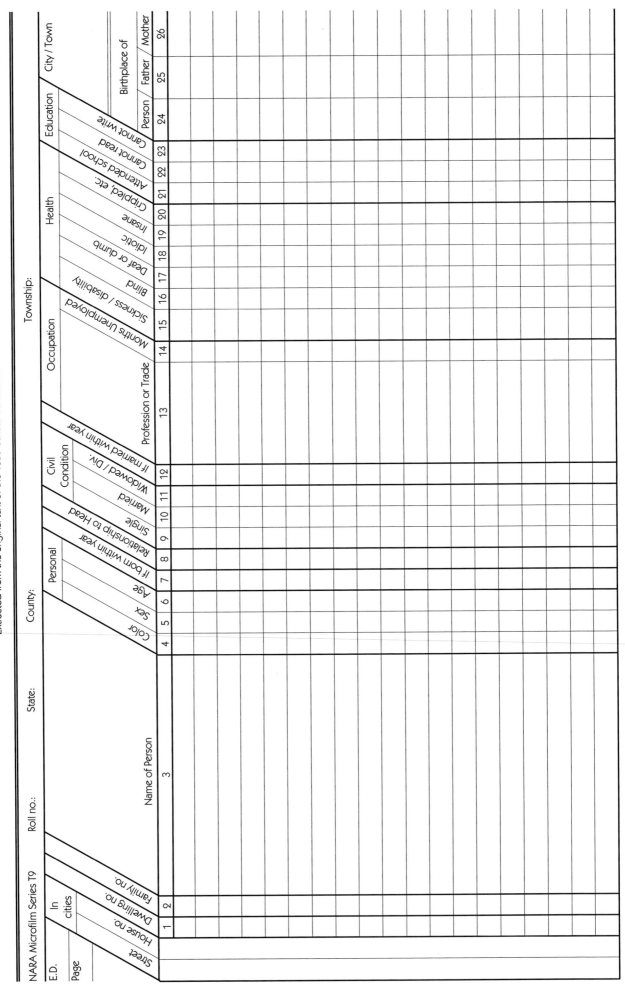

In cities				Name of Person	Personal				Relationship to Head	Civil Condition				Occupation		Health						Education			Birthplace of		
Street	House no.	Dwelling no.	Family no.		Color	Sex	Age	If born within year		Single	Married	Widowed / Div.	If married within year	Profession or Trade	Months Unemployed	Sickness / disability	Blind	Deaf or dumb	Idiotic	Insane	Crippled etc.	Attended school	Cannot read	Cannot write	Person	Father	Mother	City / Town
	1	2		3	4	5	6	7	8	9	10	11	12	13	14	15	16	17	18	19	20	21	22	23	24	25	26	

Tenth Census of the United States - 1880

General Information: Only one new state was admitted to the Union between 1870 and 1880 (Colorado in 1876) bringing the total to thirty-eight states. Eight territories were enumerated: Arizona, Dakota, Idaho, Montana, New Mexico, Utah, Washington, and Wyoming territories. Unorganized Alaska was enumerated, but the "Indian Territory" was not enumerated for non-Indians.

Content: The 1880 census schedules listed the name of every person in a household with a census day of 1 June 1880. The categories included the following for each person: name and age as of the census day; month of birth if born during the year; relationship to the head of house; name of street and number of house; sex; color; birthplace; occupation; marital status; whether married within the previous year; whether temporarily or permanently disabled; whether crippled, maimed, or deformed; time unemployed during the census year; whether deaf, dumb, blind, or insane; whether able to read or write; birthplace of father and mother; and whether the person attended school within the previous year.

Microfilm: The National Archives and Records Administration microfilm for the 1880 census is contained on 1,454 rolls of 35mm film, series T9.

1885 Census (taken with federal assistance)

Colorado, Dakota Territory, Florida, Nebraska, or New Mexico Territory

Researcher: _____

Date: _____

Extracted from the original text of the 1885 Census Schedules

NARA Microfilm Series _____ Roll no.: _____ State: _____ County: _____ Township: _____

E.D. _____ Page _____

House no.	Dwelling no.	Family no.	Name of Person	Color	Sex	Age	If born within year	Relationship to Head	Single	Married	Widowed / Div.	If married within year	Profession or Trade	Months Unemployed	Sickness / disability	Blind	Deaf or dumb	Idiotic	Insane	Crippled, etc.	Attended school	Cannot read	Cannot write	Person	Father	Mother
Street																										
1	2		3	4	5	6	7	8	9	10	11	12	13	14	15	16	17	18	19	20	21	22	23	24	25	26

In cities

Personal · Civil Condition · Occupation · Health · Education · Birthplace of · City / Town

1885 Censuses Taken with Federal Assistance

General Information: Congress allowed any state or territory to take a census in 1885 and have the federal government pay for part of the expense. Only five states or territories took up the government's offer: Colorado, Dakota Territory, Florida, Nebraska, and New Mexico Territory. The 1885 census followed the same format as the 1880 census schedules, except that the names usually give an initial letter instead of a first name for a person. Those federal copies of the 1885 census that have been microfilmed include Population Schedules (list of inhabitants), inter-filed with other schedules, such as Agricultural Schedules (lists of farmers and farm products), Manufactures Schedules (lists of companies, description of businesses, etc.), and Mortality Schedules (lists of persons who died within the previous twelve months).

Census Losses and Microfilm:

Colorado: The state copy of the Colorado 1885 census is located at the Colorado State Archives. The federal copy is at the National Archives and was microfilmed as series M158 (8 rolls). The federal copy is missing Fremont and Garfield counties, while the state copy has Fremont but is missing Garfield and eighteen other counties.

Dakota Territory: The 1885 census survives for just 37 of the 132 counties that existed in 1885, 17 in the present-day North Dakota portion and 20 in the present-day South Dakota portion. The surviving 1885 counties for present-day North Dakota are Allred, Bowman, Buford, Dunn, McIntosh, McKenzie, Mercer, Mountrail, Oliver, Renville, Stanton, Towner, Villard, Wallace, Ward, Wells, and Wynn. The surviving 1885 counties of present-day South Dakota are Beadle, Butte, Charles Mix, Edmunds, Fall River, Faulk, Hand, Hanson, Hutchinson, Hyde, Lake, Lincoln, Marshall, McPherson, Moody, Roberts, Sanborn, Spink, Stanley, and Turner. The South Dakota portion was microfilmed by the National Archives as series GR27 (3 rolls).

Florida: The Florida State Archives reported having no state manuscript of the 1885 census, just the microfilmed federal copy (microfilm series M845, 14 rolls). Missing are Alachua, Clay, Columbia, and Nassau counties.

Nebraska: 1885 federal copy was microfilmed by the National Archives as series M352 (56 rolls). Missing are Blaine and Chase counties.

New Mexico Territory: The federal copy of the New Mexico Territory 1885 census is complete for all counties and was microfilmed by the National Archives as series M846 (6 rolls). The state copy, microfilmed by the University of New Mexico - Albuquerque, is missing Bernalillo, Rio Arriba, Santa Fe, and San Miguel counties.

1890 Veterans Schedule

Researcher: _____ Date: _____

NARA Microfilm Series M123   Roll no.: _____   State: _____   County: _____   Subdistrict: _____

Extracted from the original text of the 1890 special schedules for surviving soldiers, sailors, marines, and widows

House no.	Family no.	Name of surviving soldiers, sailors, marines, or widows	Rank	Company	Name of Regiment or Vessel	Date of enlistment			Date of discharge			Length of service		
1	2	3	4	5	6	day	month 7	year	day	month 8	year	yrs	mos 9	days
1														
2														
3														
4														
5														
6														
7														
8														
9														
10														

	Post Office address 10	Disability incurred 11	Remarks 12
1			
2			
3			
4			
5			
6			
7			
8			
9			
10			

Eleventh Census of the United States - 1890
Union Veterans and Widows of Union Veterans

General Information: Over 99 percent of the 1890 census was destroyed as a result of a fire which took place in January 1921 in Washington, DC. A special census listing was extracted from the 1890 population schedules for surviving Union soldiers, sailors, and marines (or their widows), and a portion of that special census survives.

Content of 1890 Union Veterans Census: The schedules listed the name of each soldier, sailor, marine, or widow of a veteran in a household; the veteran's rank; company; regiment or vessel; dates of enlistment and discharge; length of service in years, months, and days; post office address; nature of disability, if any; and remarks.

Census losses: Of the forty-nine states and territories enumerated in 1890, sixteen of the states' Union Veterans' schedules (alphabetically from Alabama through Kansas) were apparently lost in the fire, as were about half of the names for Kentucky. State listings begin with the partial list for Kentucky and are complete from Louisiana through Wyoming.

Microfilm: The National Archives and Records Administration microfilm for the fragments of the 1890 census is contained on 3 rolls of 35mm film, series M407. An index to the surviving names of the 1890 census was compiled and microfilmed on 2 rolls of 16mm film, series M496.

The 1890 Special Schedules Enumerating Union Veterans and Widows of Union Veterans of the Civil War were microfilmed on 118 rolls of 35mm film, series M123.

1900 Federal Census

Date:

Researcher:

Extracted from the original text of the 1900 Census Schedules

NARA Microfilm Series T623   Roll no.:   State: County: Subdistrict:

City / Town: Ward:

Page   E.D.

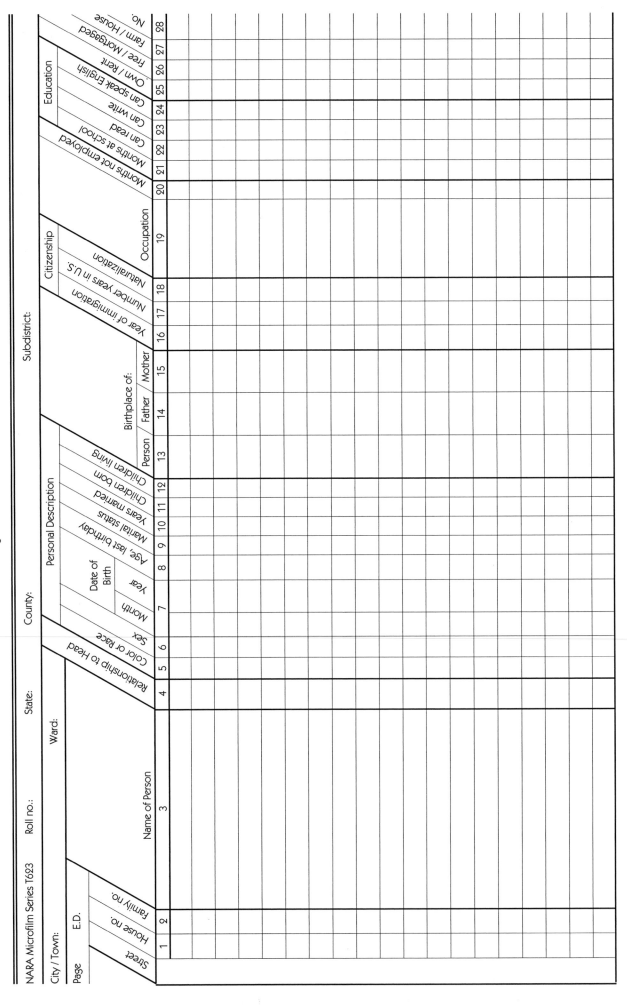

			Name of Person	Relationship to Head	Personal Description									Birthplace of:			Citizenship		Occupation	Education					
Street	House no.	Family no.			Color or Race	Sex	Date of Birth Month	Date of Birth Year	Age, last birthday	Marital status	Years married	Children born	Children living	Person	Father	Mother	Year of immigration	Number years in U.S. Naturalization	Months not employed / Months at school	Can read	Can write	Can speak English	Own / Rent	Free / Mortgaged	Farm / House No.
1	2		3	4	5	6	7	8	9	10	11	12	13	14	15	16	17	18	19	20 21 22	23	24	25	26	27	28

Twelfth Census of the United States - 1900

General Information: Utah was added to the Union in 1896 bringing the total number of states to forty-five. Oklahoma Territory, Arizona Territory, Hawaii Territory, "Unorganized (Indian) Territory," New Mexico Territory, and Alaska were also included. Hawaii was annexed to the U.S. in 1898 and became a territory in 1900. Unorganized Alaska was enumerated, but did not become a territory until 1912.

Content: The 1900 census schedules listed the name of every person in a household and included the name of each person; relationship to the head of house; name of street and number of house; sex; color; the person's age, plus the exact month and year of birth; birthplace; if female, number of children, and number of children still living in 1900; occupation; marital status, and if married, number of years; number of years in the U.S.; birthplace of father and mother; whether parents were of foreign birth; whether able to read or write; whether a person could speak English; and whether the person attended school within the previous year.

Microfilm: The National Archives and Records Administration microfilm for the 1900 census is contained on 1,854 rolls of 35mm film, series T623. The original census schedules, after microfilming in the early 1940s, were destroyed.

1910 Federal Census

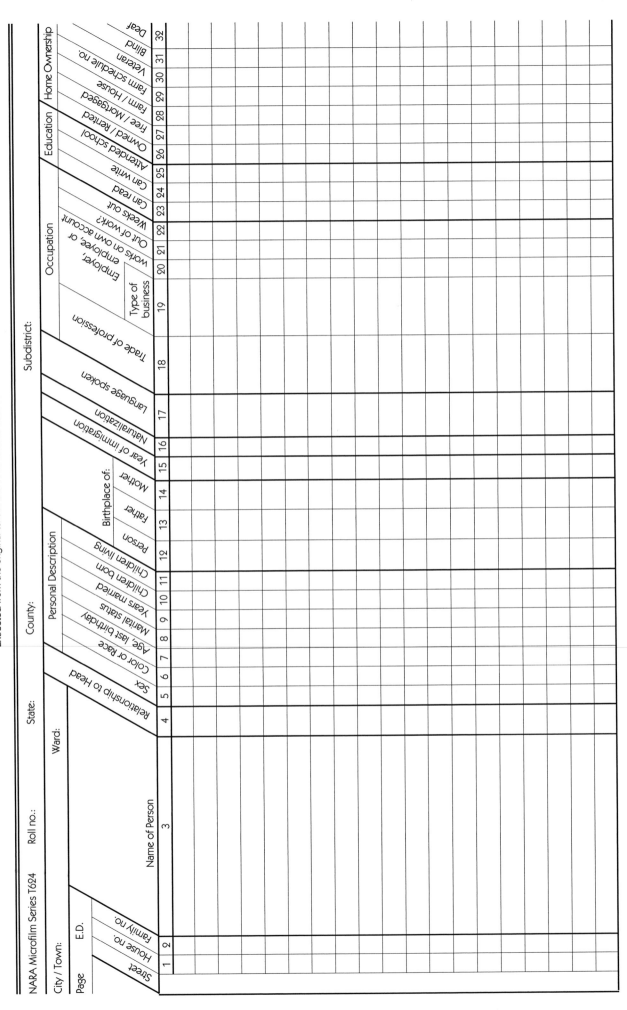

Researcher:

Date:

Extracted from the original text of the 1910 Census Schedules

NARA Microfilm Series T624   Roll no.:

State:

County:

Subdistrict:

City / Town:

Ward:

Page   E.D.

Street	House no.	Family no.	Name of Person	Relationship to Head	Sex	Color or Race	Age, last birthday	Marital status	Years married	Children born	Children living	Person	Father	Mother	Year of immigration	Naturalization	Language spoken	Trade of profession	Type of business	Employer, employee, or works on own account	Out of work?	Weeks out	Can read	Can write	Attended school	Owned / Rented	Free / Mortgaged	Farm / House	Farm schedule no.	Veteran	Blind	Deaf
1	2		3	4	5	6	7	8	9	10	11	12	13	14	15	16	17	18	19	20	21	22	23	24	25	26	27	28	29	30	31	32

Personal Description — Birthplace of: — Occupation — Education — Home Ownership

Thirteenth Census of the United States - 1910

General Information: Oklahoma was admitted to the Union in 1907 bringing the total number of states to forty-six. Arizona, Hawaii, and New Mexico Territories were also enumerated. Unorganized Alaska was enumerated, but did not become a territory until 1912. Also included in the census was the U.S. possession of Puerto Rico.

Content: The 1910 census schedules listed the name of every person in a household and included the name of a street and house number; the name and age of each person; relationship to the head of house; sex; color; if female, the number of children, and number of children still living in 1910; marital status, and if married, number of years; year of immigration to the U.S.; whether a naturalized citizen, alien, or papers pending; language spoken; trade or profession, type of business, and whether an employee, employer, or working on one's own account; whether out of work, and if so, the number weeks out; birthplace of father and mother; whether able to read or write; whether the person attended school within the previous year; whether a person own or rented a house; whether the house was mortgaged or mortgage free; whether a farm or a home; whether the person was a veteran; and whether the person was blind or deaf.

Microfilm: The National Archives and Records Administration microfilm for the 1910 census is contained on 1,784 rolls of 35mm film, series T624. The original census schedules, after microfilming in the early 1940s, were destroyed.

1920 Federal Census

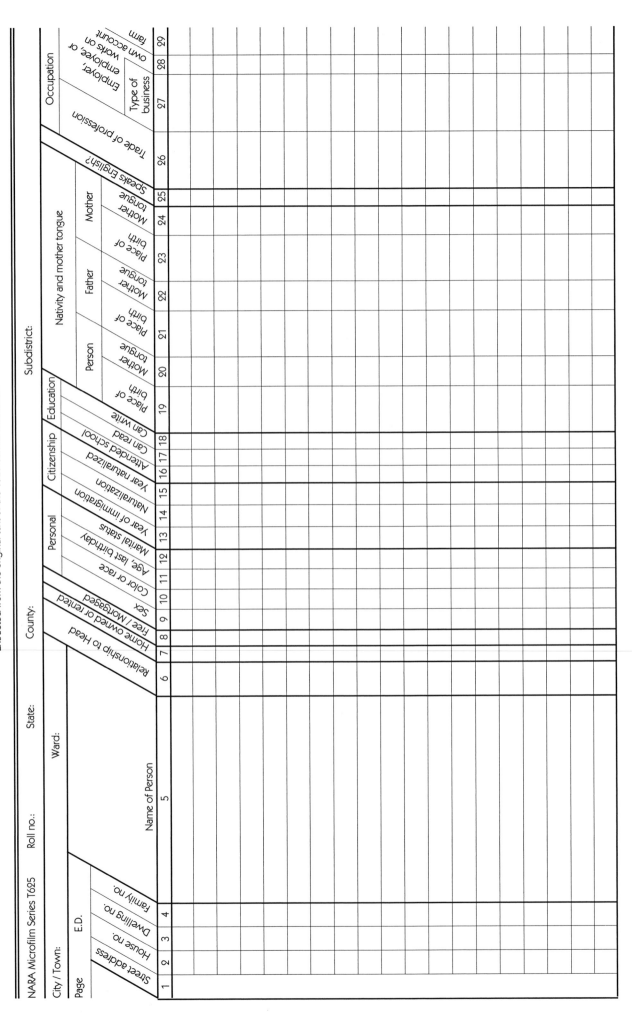

Researcher:

Date:

Extracted from the original text of the 1920 Census Schedules

NARA Microfilm Series T625   Roll no.:

State: County: Subdistrict:

City / Town: Ward:

E.D.

Page

				Name of Person	Relationship to Head	Home owned or rented	Free / Mortgaged	Sex	Color or race	Age, last birthday	Marital status	Year of immigration	Naturalization	Year naturalized	Attended school	Can read	Can write	Place of birth	Mother tongue	Place of birth	Mother tongue	Place of birth	Mother tongue	Speaks English?	Trade of profession	Type of business	Employee, or works on own account	farm
Street address	House no.	Dwelling no.	Family no.																									
1	2	3	4	5	6	7	8	9	10	11	12	13	14	15	16	17	18	19	20	21	22	23	24	25	26	27	28	29

Personal — Citizenship — Education

Nativity and mother tongue — Person / Father / Mother

Occupation

Fourteenth Census of the United States - 1920

General Information: Arizona and New Mexico both became states in 1912 bringing the total number of states to forty-eight. Hawaii Territory and Alaska Territory were enumerated along with the U.S. possessions of Guam, Midway, Canal Zone, Puerto Rico, American Samoa, the Virgin Islands, and Wake Island.

Content: The 1920 census schedules listed the name of every person in a household and included the name of a street and house number; the name, age, and birthplace of each person; relationship to the head of house; sex; color; if female, the number of children, and number of children still living in 1920; marital status, and if married, number of years; year of immigration to the U.S.; whether a naturalized citizen, alien, or papers pending; language spoken; trade or profession, type of business, and whether an employee, employer, or self employed; whether out of work, and if so, the number of weeks out; birthplace of father and mother; whether able to read or write; whether the person attended school during the previous year; whether a person own or rented a house; whether the house was mortgaged or mortgage free; whether a farm or a home; whether the person was a veteran; and whether the person was blind or deaf.

Microfilm: The National Archives and Records Administration microfilm for the 1920 census is contained on 2,076 rolls of 35mm film, series T625. The original census schedules, after microfilming in the early 1940s, were destroyed.

1930 Federal Census

Extracted from the original text of the 1930 Census Schedules

Researcher:

Date:

State:	NARA Microfilm Series:
County:	Roll no.:
Township, Town, Precinct, etc.:	Sheet no.:
Incorporated place:	Enumeration district no.:
Ward of city:	Supervisor's district no.:
Unincorporated place:	Enumeration date:
Block no.:	
Institution:	

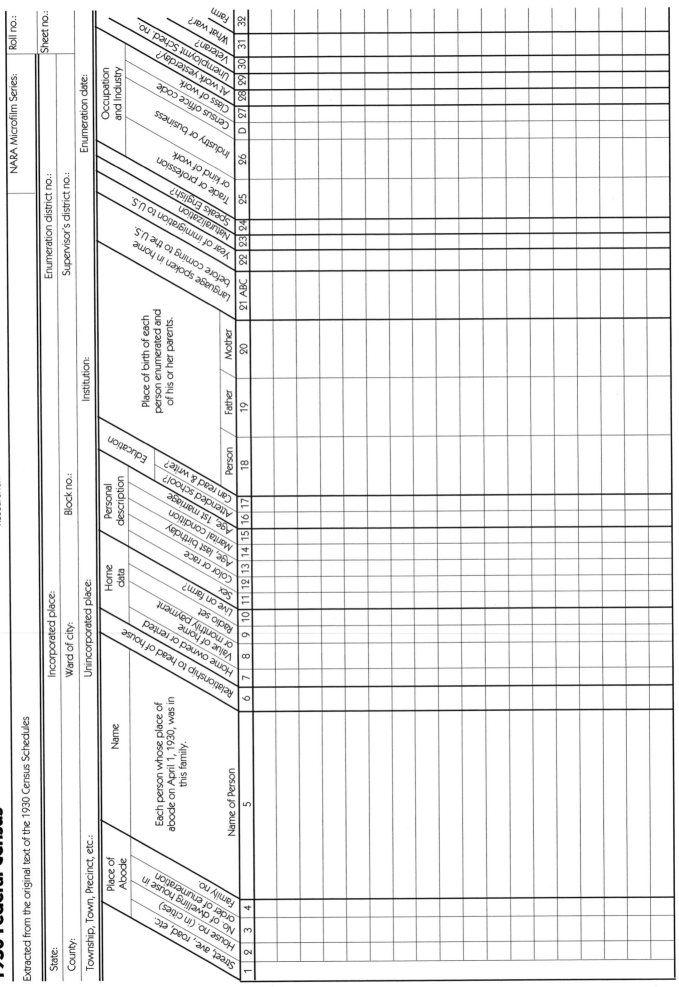

Place of Abode				Name	Relationship to head of house	Home data				Personal description					Education		Place of birth of each person enumerated and of his or her parents.			Language spoken in home before coming to the U.S.	Year of immigration to the U.S.	Naturalization	Speaks English?	Occupation and Industry					Veteran?	Farm
Street, ave., road, etc.	House no. (in cities)	No. of dwelling house in order of enumeration	Family no.	Name of Person — Each person whose place of abode on April 1, 1930, was in this family.		Home owned or rented	Value of home or monthly payment	Radio set	Live on farm?	Sex	Color or race	Age, last birthday	Marital condition	Age, 1st marriage	Attended school?	Can read & write?	Person	Father	Mother					Trade or profession or kind of work	Industry or business	Census office code	Class of work	At work yesterday?	Unemploymt Sched. no.	What war?	
1	2	3	4	5	6	7	8	9	10	11	12	13	14	15	16	17	18	19	20	21 ABC	22	23	24	25	26	D 27	28	29	30	31	32

Fifteenth Census of the United States - 1930

General Information: The National Archives and Records Administration is expected to release the population schedules of the 1930 census to the public in the year 2002. Forty-eight states were enumerated along with Hawaii Territory and Alaska Territory, plus the U.S. possessions of Guam, Midway, Canal Zone, Puerto Rico, American Samoa, the Virgin Islands, and Wake Island.

Content: The 1930 population census schedule has the categories of **Place of Abode:** listing the street number, avenue, or road, and family numbers in order of visitation; **Name:** listing the surname, first name and middle initial of each person as of 1 April 1930; **Relation:** listing the relationship of each person to the homemaker (indicated with "H"); **Home Data:** listing whether the home was owned or rented, the value of the home or monthly rental, whether the home had a radio set, and whether the family lived on a farm; **Personal Description:** listing the person's sex, color or race, coded to indicate White (W), Negro (Neg), Mexican (Mex), Indian (In), Chinese (Ch), or Japanese (Jp), age at last birthday, marital status, and the person's age at first marriage; **Education:** listing whether the person attended school or college any time since 1 September 1929; **Place of birth:** listing the place of birth (without abbreviating) of each person enumerated and of his or her parents, distinguishing Canada-French from Canada-English, and Irish Free State from Northern Ireland; **Mother Tongue (or Native Language) of Foreign Birth:** listing the language spoken in the person's home before coming to the United States and codes to indicate the mother tongue, country, and nativity; **Citizenship, Etc.:** listing the person's year of immigration to the U.S., indicating whether naturalized (Na), alien (Al), or first papers filed (Pa), and whether able to speak English; **Occupation and Industry:** listing the person's trade or profession or particular kind of work; industry or business, and whether an employer (E), wage or salary worker (W), working on own account (O), or an unpaid worker, as a member of the family (NP); **Employment:** listing whether the person was actually at work 31 March 1930, and if not, the line number on the unemployment schedule; **Veterans:** listing whether the person was a veteran of U.S. military or naval forces, and codes to indicate a war in which the person served: World War (WW), Spanish-American War (Sp), Civil War (Civ), Philippine Insurrection (Phil), Boxer Rebellion (Box), or Mexican Expedition (Mex); and finally, if the person lived on a farm, the number on the farm schedule.

Microfilm: Researchers are awaiting the 2002 release of the 1930 census on microfilm. Microfilmed in the early 1940s, the quantity and quality of the film is unknown to the public yet. The original census schedules, after microfilming, were destroyed.

1850 Slave Schedule

Researcher: Date:

Extracted from the original text of the 1850 census slave schedules

NARA Microfilm Pub. No. M432   Roll no.:   State: County:

Page City, Town, or Subdistrict	Names of Slave Owners	No. of Slaves	Age	Sex	Color	Fugitives from state	No. Manumitted	Deaf & dumb, blind, insane, or idiotic	
	1	2	3	4	5	6	7	8	

1850 U.S. Federal Census - Slave Schedule

General Information: Slave schedules were prepared for certain states as part of the 1850 census: Alabama, Arkansas, Delaware, District of Columbia, Florida, Georgia, Kentucky, Louisiana, Maryland, Mississippi, Missouri, New Jersey, North Carolina, South Carolina, Tennessee, Texas, and Virginia.

Content: The format listed the city, town, or subdistrict; name of slave owner; number of slaves; age, sex, and color; number of fugitives from state; number manumitted; and number deaf, dumb, blind, insane, or idiotic. Although the form did not provide for the names of the slaves, many enumerators added the slave's given name on the schedules.

Microfilm: The National Archives and Records Administration microfilm for the 1850 slave schedules is included in series M593. The slave schedules follow the free schedules for each of the 16 states and the District of Columbia.

1860 Slave Schedule

Researcher: Date:

Extracted from the original text of the 1860 census slave schedules

NARA Microfilm Pub. No. M653   Roll no.:   State: County:

Page City, Town, or Subdistrict	Names of Slave Owners	No. of Slaves	Age	Sex	Color	Fugitives from state	No. Manumitted	Deaf & dumb, blind, insane, or idiotic	No. of slave houses
	1	2	3	4	5	6	7	8	9

Description

1860 U.S. Federal Census - Slave Schedule

General Information: Slave schedules were prepared for certain states as part of the 1860 census: Alabama, Arkansas, Delaware, District of Columbia, Florida, Georgia, Kentucky, Louisiana, Maryland, Mississippi, Missouri, North Carolina, South Carolina, Tennessee, Texas, and Virginia.

Content: The format listed the city, town, or subdistrict; name of slave owner; number of slaves; age, sex, and color; number of fugitives from state; number manumitted; and number of deaf, dumb, blind, insane, or idiotic; and number of slave houses. Although the form did not provide for the names of the slaves, many enumerators added the slave's given name on the schedules.

Microfilm: The National Archives and Records Administration microfilm for the 1860 slave schedules is included in series M653. The slave schedules follow the free schedules for each of the 15 states and the District of Columbia.

1850 Mortality Schedule

Extracted from the original text of the 1850 census (Mortality) schedules

Researcher: _____   Date: _____

NARA Microfilm Pub. No.: _____   Roll no.: _____   State: _____   County: _____   Subdistrict: _____

Page _____

NAME OF DECEASED Name of each person who died during the year ending June 1, 1850	Age	Sex	Color	Free or Slave	Married or Widowed	Birthplace	Month of Death	Occupation	Disease or Cause of Death	No. of days ill
1	2	3	4	5	6	7	8	9	10	11

1850 U.S. Federal Census - Mortality Schedule

General Information: Mortality schedules were prepared for all states and territories in the U.S., taken from the 1850 population schedules. For all states, the name of any person who died within the previous year was given, along with information about the death. See the "Non-Population Census Schedules" section for a state-by-state listing showing the repositories holding original or microfilm copies of mortality schedules.

Content: The schedule listed the name of a deceased person who died during the year ending 1 June 1850, the person's age, sex, color, whether free or slave, whether married or widowed, birthplace, month of death, occupation, disease or cause of death, and the number of days the person was ill prior to the death.

1860 Mortality Schedule

Extracted from the original text of the 1860 census (Mortality) schedules

Researcher: _____   Date: _____

NARA Microfilm Pub. No.: _____ Roll no.: _____ State: _____ County: _____ Subdistrict: _____

Page _____

NAME OF DECEASED Name of each person who died during the year ending June 1, 1860	Age	Sex	Color	Free or Slave	Married or Widowed	Birthplace	Month of Death	Occupation	Disease or Cause of Death	No. of days ill
1	2	3	4	5	6	7	8	9	10	11

1860 U.S. Federal Census - Mortality Schedule

General Information: Mortality schedules were prepared for all states and territories in the U.S., taken from the 1860 population schedules. For all states, the name of any person who died within the previous year was given, along with information about the death. See the "Non-Population Census Schedules" section for a state-by-state listing showing the repositories holding original or microfilm copies of mortality schedules.

Content: The schedule listed the name of a deceased person who died during the year ending 1 June 1860, the person's age, sex, color, whether free or slave, whether married or widowed, birthplace, month of death, occupation, disease or cause of death, and the number of days the person was ill prior to the death.

1870 Mortality Schedule

Extracted from the original text of the 1870 census (Mortality) schedules

Researcher: _____ Date: _____

NARA Microfilm Pub. No.: _____ Roll no.: _____ State: _____ County: _____ Subdistrict: _____

Page _____

Family no. (from 1870 population schedule) 1	NAME OF DECEASED — Name of each person who died during the year ending June 1, 1870 2	Age, last birthday 3	Sex 4	Color 5	Married or widowed 6	Birthplace 7	Father foreign born 8	Mother foreign born 9	Month of Death 10	Occupation 11	Disease or Cause of Death 12

1870 U.S. Federal Census - Mortality Schedule

General Information: Mortality schedules were prepared for all states and territories in the U.S., taken from the 1870 population schedules. For all states, the name of any person who died within the previous year was given, along with information about the death. See the "Non-Population Census Schedules" section for a state-by-state listing showing the repositories holding original or microfilm copies of mortality schedules.

Content: The schedule listed the family number from the population schedules, the name of a deceased person who died during the year ending 1 June 1870, the person's age at last birthday, sex, color, whether married or widowed, birthplace, whether father was foreign born, whether mother was foreign born, month of death, occupation, and the disease or cause of death.

1880 Mortality Schedule

Extracted from the original text of the 1880 census (Mortality) schedules

Researcher: _____   Date: _____

NARA Microfilm Pub. No.: _____   Roll no.: _____

Page _____   State: _____   County: _____   Subdistrict: _____

E.D. _____

Family no. (from 1880 population schedules)	NAME OF DECEASED — Name of each person who died during the year ending May 31, 1880	Personal Description			Marital Status			Birthplace of:			Occupation	Month of death	Disease or cause of death	Months in county	Place disease contracted	Name of attending physician
		Age	Sex	Color	Single	Married	Widowed / divorced	Person	Father	Mother						
1	2	3	4	5	6	7	8	9	10	11	12	13	14	15	16	17

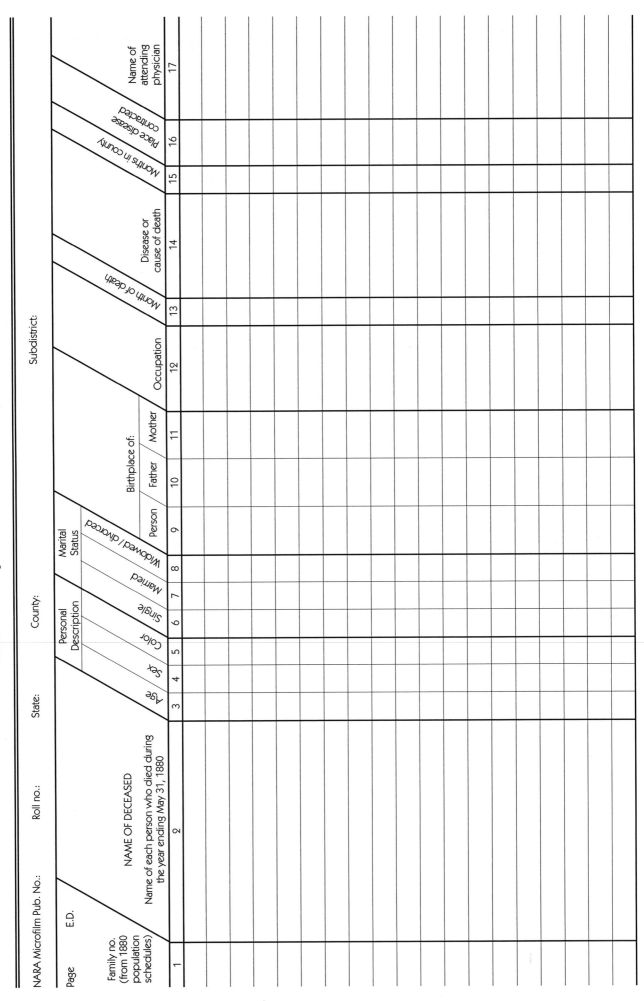

1880 U.S. Federal Census - Mortality Schedule

General Information: Mortality schedules were prepared for all states and territories in the U.S., taken from the 1880 population schedules. For all states, the name of any person who died within the previous year was given, along with information about the death. See the "Non-Population Census Schedules" section for a state-by-state listing showing the repositories holding original or microfilm copies of mortality schedules.

Content: The schedule listed the family number from the population schedules, the name of a deceased person who died during the year ending 1 June 1880, the person's age at last birthday, sex, color, whether married or widowed, birthplace, whether father was foreign born, whether mother was foreign born, month of death, occupation, and the disease or cause of death.

1880 Soundex

Researcher: _____

Date: _____

Extracted from the original text of the 1880 Soundex cards

Soundex Code				MEMBERS OF HOUSEHOLD						PLACE OF RESIDENCE					Reference to 1880 population schedule			
1 = b, p, f, v 2 = c, s, k, g, j, q, x, z 3 = d, t 4 = l 5 = m, n 6 = r	Microfilm pub. no. (T734 - T780)	Roll no.	State	Subdistrict	County	Name List name of Head of Family followed by each person included in the family	Relationship to Head	Age	Birthplace	Indicate house number, street, city, precinct, and township for Head of Family					Vol. no.	E.D. no.	Sheet	Line

1880 U.S. Federal Census - Soundex Index

General Information: Soon after the creation of the Social Security Administration in 1935, clerical workers from the Works Progress Administration (WPA) were called upon to create an index to the 1880 census. A special system of coding names was created, called "Soundex." 3" x 5" cards were prepared for each household which included children ten years old or younger. Families with children older than ten were not indexed, nor were persons living alone, or any household with no children. A person shown as 0-10 years old in the 1880 census would have been born after 31 May 1870 and before 1 June 1880. The same person in 1935 would have been 55 to 65 years old. The WPA Soundex index was prepared for confirming a person's age after he or she had applied for Social Security benefits, beginning in 1935. The information on the Soundex index cards was extracted from the full census schedules and included the full name, age, and birthplace for a head of household, and included any other person living in the household, regardless of their age. A citation to the original census schedules—which were bound into large books—indicated a state, county, volume, enumeration district, page, and line from which the family names were extracted. Each head of household's surname was given a Soundex code, and the cards were then arranged in alphabetical order by the Soundex code number and after that by the first name of the head of the household. After the 1880 census and 1880 Soundex cards were microfilmed in the 1940s, the need for knowing the volume was eliminated, since the census schedules were microfilmed in numerical order by Enumeration District. Therefore, the pertinent information one needs from the 1880 Soundex Index are the state, county, E.D. number, and page number to find a family in the census schedules.

Microfilm: The National Archives and Records Administration microfilm for the 1880 Soundex Index is contained on 2,367 rolls of 16mm film. Each state has a separate microfilm series, beginning with Alabama (T734) through Wyoming and Institutions (T780).

1900 Soundex

Researcher:

Date:

Extracted from the original text of the 1900 Soundex cards

Soundex Code
1 = b, p, f, v
2 = c, s, k, g, j, q, x, z
3 = d, t
4 = l
5 = m, n
6 = r

Microfilm pub. no. (T1030 – T1083)

Roll no.

PLACE OF RESIDENCE

Indicate house number, street, city, precinct, and township for Head of Family

State

Subdistrict

County

MEMBERS OF HOUSEHOLD

List name of Head of Family followed by each person included in the family

Name

Relationship to Head

Birth
Month
Year
Age

Birthplace

Citizenship

Reference to 1900 population schedules
Vol. no.
E.D. no.
Sheet
Line

1900 U.S. Federal Census - Soundex Index

Clerical workers from the Works Progress Administration (WPA) were called upon to create a comprehensive index to the 1900 census. Unlike the 1880 Soundex Index, the 1900 index was completed for every household in America. The information on the Soundex index cards was extracted from the full census schedules and included the full name, age, and birthplace for a head of household and included any other person living in the household with the person's relationship to the head of household. Persons in a household with a different surname than the head of household were given another separate card and included in Soundex code sequence. A citation to the original census schedules—which were bound into large books—indicated a state, county, volume, enumeration district, page, and line from which the family names were extracted. Each head of household's surname was given a Soundex code, and the cards were then arranged in alphabetical order by the Soundex code number and after that by the first name of the head of the household. After the 1900 census and 1900 Soundex cards were microfilmed in the 1940s, the need for knowing the volume was eliminated, since the census schedules were microfilmed in numerical order by Enumeration District. Therefore, the pertinent information one needs from the 1900 Soundex Index is the state, county, E.D. number, and page number to find a family in the census schedules.

Microfilm: The National Archives and Records Administration microfilm for the 1900 Soundex Index is contained on 7,846 rolls of 16mm film. Each state has a separate microfilm series, beginning with Alabama (T1030) through Wyoming (T1080), plus U.S. Military and Naval (T1081), Indian Territory (T1082), and U.S. Institutions and U.S. military and naval facilities worldwide (T1083).

1910 Soundex-Miracode

Researcher: Date:

Extracted from the original text of the 1910 Soundex or Miracode records

Soundex Code

1 = b, p, f, v
2 = c, s, k, g, j, q, x, z
3 = d, t
4 = l
5 = m, n
6 = r

PLACE OF RESIDENCE

Indicate house number, street, city, precinct, and township for Head of Family

State	County	Subdistrict

MEMBERS OF HOUSEHOLD

List name of Head of Family followed by each person included in the family

Name	Relationship to Head	Age	Birthplace

Reference to 1910 population schedules

Soundex only

Sheet no.	E.D. no.

Miracode only

Visitation (house) no.	E.D. no.	Vol. no.

Roll no.	Microfilm pub. no. (T1259 - T1279)

1910 U.S. Federal Census - Soundex/Miracode Index

The 1910 Soundex/Miracode Index was completed for twenty-one states only. This was the only census index prepared (in 1962) by the Age Search Group of the Bureau of the Census. For the fifteen states indexed using the Miracode system, it was the first census index in which electronic computers were employed. The original input data forms were entered on IBM punch cards and were not preserved. Only the computer printout data survives and was later microfilmed for public use. Each head of household and family members taken from the computer printouts were printed on a 1" x 4" strip of paper and later microfilmed in alphabetical order by Soundex code. Six more states were indexed using the Soundex system, on handwritten cards similar to other census indexes. The only difference between the two systems was in the citation to the page on the original census schedules. For each indexed head of household, the Soundex index cards cite the state, county, enumeration district, **page number** (within an E.D) and a line number; while the Miracode index cites the state, county, enumeration district, **visitation number** (within an E.D.), and line number. The visitation number indicates the order in which the families were visited by the census enumerator, numbered in the particular order the enumerator followed door-to-door. In both systems, each head of household's surname was given a Soundex code, and the cards were then arranged in alphabetical order by the Soundex code number, and after that by the first name of the head of the household.

1910 Soundex states: Alabama, Georgia, Louisiana (except Shreveport and New Orleans), Mississippi, South Carolina, Tennessee, and Texas.

1910 Miracode states: Arkansas, California, Florida, Illinois, Kansas, Kentucky, Louisiana (Shreveport and New Orleans only), Michigan, Missouri, North Carolina, Ohio, Oklahoma, Pennsylvania, Virginia, and West Virginia.

Microfilm: The National Archives and Records Administration microfilm for the 1910 Soundex/Miracode Index is contained on 7,846 rolls of 16mm film. Each state has a separate microfilm series, beginning with Alabama (T1030) through Wyoming (T1080), plus U.S. Military and Naval (T1081), Indian Territory (T1082), and U.S. Institutions, and military and naval facilities worldwide (T1083).

1920 Soundex

Researcher:

Date:

Extracted from the original text of the 1920 Soundex cards

Soundex Code 1 = b, p, f, v 2 = c, s, k, g, j, q, x, z 3 = d, t 4 = l 5 = m, n 6 = r	Microfilm pub. no. (M1548 - M1605)	Roll no.	PLACE OF RESIDENCE Indicate house number, street, city, precinct, and township for head of household				MEMBERS OF HOUSEHOLD List name of Head of Family followed by each person included in the family						Reference to 1920 population schedules				
			State	Subdistrict	County	Name	Relationship to Head	Age	Birthplace	Citizenship		Vol. no.	E.D. no.	Sheet	Line

1920 U.S. Federal Census - Soundex Index

The 1920 Soundex Index was completed for every household in America. The information on the Soundex index cards was extracted from the full census schedules and included the full name, age, and birthplace for a head of household and included any other person living in the household, with the person's relationship to the head of household. Persons in a household with a different surname than the head of household were given another separate card and included in Soundex code sequence. A citation to the original census schedules—which were bound into large books—indicated a state, county, volume, enumeration district, page, and line from which the family names were extracted. Each head of household's surname was given a Soundex code, and the cards were then arranged in alphabetical order by the Soundex code number and after that by the first name of the head of the household. After the 1920

census and 1920 Soundex cards were microfilmed in the 1940s, the need for knowing the volume was eliminated, since the census schedules were microfilmed in numerical order by enumeration district. Therefore, the pertinent information one needs from the 1920 Soundex Index is the state, county, E.D. number, and page number to find a family in the census schedules.

Microfilm: The National Archives and Records Administration microfilm for the 1920 Soundex Index is contained on 8,586 rolls of 16mm film. Each state has a separate microfilm series, beginning with Alabama (M1548) through Wyoming (M1596), plus Alaska (M1597), through Hawaii, Canal Zone, Military-Naval, Puerto Rico, Guam, American Samoa, Virgin Islands, and Institutions (M1605).

1930 Soundex

Researcher: Date:

Extracted from the original text of the 1930 Soundex cards

Soundex Code 1 = b, p, f, v 2 = c, s, k, g, j, q, x, z 3 = d, t 4 = l 5 = m, n 6 = r	Microfilm pub. no.	Roll no.	PLACE OF RESIDENCE Indicate house number, street, city, precinct, and township for head of household			MEMBERS OF HOUSEHOLD List name of Head of Family followed by each person included in the family					Reference to 1930 population schedules				
			State	Subdistrict	County	Name	Relationship to Head	Age	Birthplace	Citizenship	Vol. no.	E.D. no.	Sheet no.	Line

1930 U.S. Federal Census - Soundex Index

The 1930 Soundex index was completed for the states of Alabama, Arkansas, Florida, Georgia, Louisiana, Mississippi, North Carolina, South Carolina, Tennessee, and Virginia, plus seven counties in Kentucky and seven more in West Virginia. The information on the Soundex index cards was extracted from the full census schedules and included the full name, age, and birthplace for a head of household and included any other person living in the household, with the person's relationship to the head of household. Persons in a household with a different surname than the head of household were given another separate card and included in Soundex code sequence. A citation to the original census schedules—which were bound into large books—indicated a state, county, volume, enumeration district, page, and line from which the family names were extracted. Each head of household's surname was given a Soundex code, and the cards were then arranged in alphabetical order by the Soundex code number and after that by the first name of the head of the household.

Microfilm: The National Archives and Records Administration microfilm for the 1930 Soundex Index is scheduled for release to the public in the year 2002.

1790-1840
Census Worksheet

For each of the indicated years, show the number of males and females in the appropriate age brackets below. By comparing censuses, a more accurate span of years may be determined.

YEAR	HEAD OF HOUSEHOLD	STATE	COUNTY	REMARKS

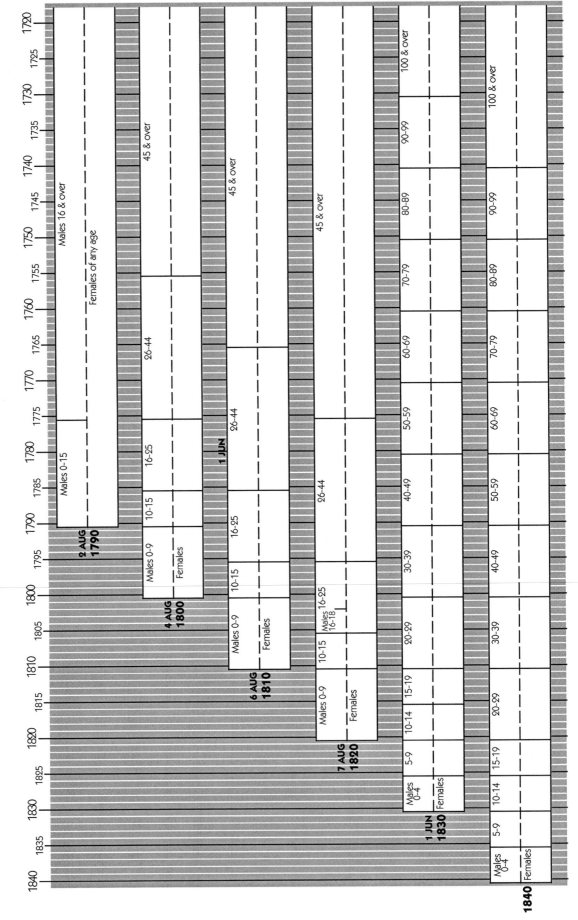

1790-1840 U.S. Census Worksheet

The heads of household censuses can be compared on this sheet. The top of the form has a place to identify the names of the heads of household for each of the years being compared. Within the boxes for the age categories for each census year, indicate the number of males and females. By lining up the census years on a background time-line, the age brackets overlap and a shorter range of years for a person's year of birth should be evident if two or more censuses are compared. A line drawn vertically on the form will indicate a particular age year for a person common to all of the census years, 1790-1840.

Note the difference in the census day for each census. The census day was the day for which all statistics were gathered, regardless of how long after that day it took the census enumerator to visit a particular house. From 1790 through 1820, the census day was the first Monday in August. Beginning in 1830, the census day was the first day of June. By comparing families appearing in 1830 and earlier censuses, this means that the reporting date has about a 60-day difference. For example, a child born between 7 June 1820 and 7 August 1820 will appear in the "0-9" age category in the 1820 census, and will appear in the "5-9" age category in the 1830 census, because, due to the later census day in the 1830 census, the child had not turned ten years old yet. This form allows this type of anomaly in censuses to be presented graphically.

Census Comparison Sheet

Researcher:

Year	State		County			Town or District		
	Series		Roll No.		Page	Dwelling No.		Family No.
	Name	**Age**	**Sex**	**Occupation**		**Birthplace**	**Other Information**	

Year	State		County			Town or District		
	Series		Roll No.		Page	Dwelling No.		Family No.
	Name	**Age**	**Sex**	**Occupation**		**Birthplace**	**Other Information**	

Year	State		County			Town or District		
	Series		Roll No.		Page	Dwelling No.		Family No.
	Name	**Age**	**Sex**	**Occupation**		**Birthplace**	**Other Information**	

1850-1930 U.S. Census Comparison Sheet

This form can be used to identify a family appearing in more than one census year. By placing them together on one sheet, it will be possible to see a better picture of the dates of birth, places of birth, and other facts. The census years compared do not have to be in sequence, and, up to three years, can be displayed.